THE NORTHERN SHORES OF LAKE CHAD, AS SEEN BY DENHAM IN 1822

Pioneers in West Africa

By SIR HARRY JOHNSTON
G.C.M.G., K.C.B.

NEGRO UNIVERSITIES PRESS
NEW YORK

Originally Published in 1912
by Blackie and Son Limited, London

Reprinted 1969 by
Negro Universities Press
A DIVISION OF GREENWOOD PUBLISHING CORP.
NEW YORK

Library of Congress Catalogue Card Number 69-18654

PRINTED IN UNITED STATES OF AMERICA

PREFACE

THE publishers of this book asked me to write a series of works for the reading of boys and girls which should deal with "real adventures", in parts of the world either wild and uncontrolled by any civilized government, or at any rate regions full of dangers, of wonderful discoveries; in which the daring and heroism of white men (and sometimes of white women) stood out clearly against backgrounds of unfamiliar landscapes, peopled with strange nations, savage tribes, dangerous beasts, or wonderful birds. These books would again and again illustrate the first coming of the white race into regions inhabited by people of a different type, with brown, black, or yellow skins; how the European was received, and how he treated these races of the soil which gradually came under his rule owing to his superior knowledge, weapons, wealth, or powers of persuasion. The books were to tell the plain truth, even if here and there they showed the white man to have behaved badly, or if they revealed the fact that the American Indian, the Negro, the Malay, the black Australian was sometimes cruel and treacherous.

A request thus framed was almost equivalent

to asking me to write stories of those pioneers who
founded the British Empire; in any case, the first
volumes of this series do relate the adventures of
those who created the greater part of the British
Dominions beyond the Seas, by their perilous explorations of unknown lands and waters. In many
instances the travellers were all unconscious of their
destinies, of the results which would arise from
their actions. In some cases they would have
bitterly railed at Fate had they known that the
result of their splendid efforts was to be the enlargement of an empire under the British flag.
Perhaps if they could know by now that we are
striving under that flag to be just and generous to
all types of men, and not to use our empire solely
for the benefit of English-speaking men and women,
the French who founded the Canadian nation, the
Germans and Dutch who helped to create British
Africa, Malaysia, and Australia, the Spaniards who
preceded us in the West Indies, and the Portuguese
in West, Central, and East Africa, in Newfoundland
and Ceylon, might—if they have any consciousness
or care for things in this world—be not so sorry
after all that we are reaping where they sowed.

It is (as you will see) impossible to tell the tale
of these early days in the British Dominions beyond
the Seas, without describing here and there the
adventures of men of enterprise and daring who
were not of our own nationality. The majority,
nevertheless, were of British stock; that is to say,
they were English, Welsh, Scots, Irish, perhaps
here and there a Channel Islander and a Manxman;

or Nova Scotians, Canadians, and New Englanders. The bulk of them were good fellows, a few were saints, a few were ruffians with redeeming features. Sometimes they were common men who blundered into great discoveries which will for ever preserve their names from perishing; occasionally they were men of Fate, predestined, one might say, to change the history of the world by their revelations of new peoples, new lands, new rivers, new lakes, snow mountains, and gold mines. Here and there is a martyr like Marquette, or Livingstone, or Gordon, dying for the cause of a race not his own. And others again are mere boys, whose adventures come to them because they are adventurous, and whose feats of arms, escapes, perils, and successes are quite as wonderful as those attributed to the juvenile heroes of Marryat, Stevenson, and the author of *The Swiss Family Robinson.*

I have tried, in describing these adventures, to give my readers some idea of the scenery, animals, and vegetation of the new lands through which these pioneers passed on their great and small purposes; as well as of the people, native to the soil, with whom they came in contact. And in treating of these subjects I have thought it best to give the scientific names of the plant or animal which was of importance in my story, so that any of my readers who were really interested in natural history could at once ascertain for themselves the exact type alluded to, and, if they wished, look it up in a museum, a garden, or a natural history book.

I hope this attempt to be accurate will not

frighten away young readers, who will find in between these zoological or botanical notes a variety of exciting incidents, and many a strange and fascinating glimpse of savage life; plenty of hair-breadth escapes, deeds of heroism or of bloodshed, and triumphs of courage and dogged perseverance. There will be no maudlin sentimentality about my stories; at the same time they will contain nothing that a healthy-minded boy or girl may not read unharmed. There are cannibals in *Robinson Crusoe*, and you will meet them—real ones—in these books; scalps are taken and the prisoners are tortured by Fenimore Cooper's Red Indians: well, I will show you the very originals of Fenimore's noble savages, as described by the first Europeans who met them. You shall see what the pirates of the Spanish Main and the seas of Borneo were really like; witness slave-raids in Central Africa, trials for witchcraft, deaths from thirst, and terrible episodes of almost complete starvation. Yet you shall also behold rare acts of kindness from savages towards white men and white men towards savages, attend feastings and frolics as well as deaths and scenes of torture. Your feelings shall not be unnecessarily harrowed, you will learn much of geography and natural history by the way; and, if you can have patience with the author and his desire to instruct you occasionally, you will, by reading this series of books on the great pioneers of British West Africa, Canada, Malaysia, West Indies, South Africa, and Australasia, get a clear idea of how the British Colonial Empire came to be founded.

You will find that I have often tried to tell the story in the words of the pioneers, but in these quotations I have adopted the modern spelling, not only in my transcript of the English original or translation, but also in the place and tribal names, so as not to puzzle or delay the reader. Otherwise, if you were to look out some of the geographical names of the old writers, you might not be able to recognize them on the modern atlas. The pronunciation of this modern geographical spelling is very simple and clear: the vowels are pronounced a = ah, e = eh, i = ee, o = o, $ó$ = oh, $ō$ = aw, $ö$ = u in 'hurt', and u = oo, as in German, Italian, or most other European languages; and the consonants as in English.

H. H. JOHNSTON.

CONTENTS

LIST OF ILLUSTRATIONS

COLOURED PLATES

BLACK-AND-WHITE ILLUSTRATIONS

A DETAILED DESCRIPTION OF THE
COLOURED ILLUSTRATIONS

Frontispiece. *The Northern Shores of Lake Chad, as seen by Denham in 1822*

We read in Denham's account of his journey of his first impressions of this great shallow lake, with the women driving in the fish to the shore, flocks of flamingoes put to flight by this invasion of the lake, and in the foreground the tame, crowned cranes and spurwinged geese, which in those days had no cause to fear man.

Page 42. *The Gambia River as seen and described by Captain Jobson*

This would be in some region above Kassa and the tidal influence. The banks would be bordered by wild date palms and tall acacia thorn trees, an occasional fan palm, clumps of magnificent *Albizzia, Khaya, Parinarium,* and fig trees of dense foliage. From the thorny branches of the acacia trees leaning over the water would hang the weaver-birds' nests, and on other accumulations of dry branches would be perched the beautiful, white egret herons. Hippopotami are basking on the sandbanks or idly floating in the warm, shallow water, the mothers carrying their little ones on their backs. In the foreground are crocodiles, also enjoying the warm sunshine, and quite unafraid of man; and in and out and about these grim reptiles walk and wade the black-and-white saddle-billed storks, and the tantalus storks with their yellow beaks and rosy-speckled backs.

Page 78. *The "Devil" visiting a Mandingo Town*

This is a picture of the scene which often takes place to-day, much as it was described by Jobson and Mungo Park. The "Devil" is a man dressed up.

13

Page 86. *Elephants destroying a Palm Grove*

The destruction wrought by elephants among the brushwood and small trees or palms is considerable. The trees are usually dragged down or uprooted, so that the elephant may eat the fruit or the rind of the fruit, the bark of the slender twigs, the fresh leaf shoots, &c. The spiky-leaved shrubs on the right-hand side are dracænas or tree-lilies. The palms are the borassus fan palm.

Page 136. *Mungo Park's first Sight of the Niger at Sego, in 1796*

The birds flying and wheeling in the air above the great river are small vultures (*percnopterus*) and big Marabou storks, attracted to the vicinity of these Niger towns to feed on the refuse. A caravan of slaves, with its Moorish driver, stops to look at the strange white man; and the slaves forget their own miseries (we are told) in laughing at the tattered, long-haired, long-bearded stranger.

Page 196. *In Bornu*

A great Baobab tree (*Kuka*) shades a native marketplace. It is springtime, and the tree is covered with large flowers with thick cream-white petals and golden stamens. A negro, off on a trading journey with tins of water and bales of cloth, is offering to sell one of his metal pots. A Kanuri man in a peaked straw hat and voluminous robe is driving a few sheep to market.

Page 250. *The Fulas*

Note the almost Egyptian features and yellow-brown skins of the man and woman; the sleek, long-horned cattle with a slight hump; the Egyptian-like architecture of the round buildings; and the stork perched on the roof. This is the white stork of Europe, which passes its winters in North Africa and northern Nigeria.

Page 266. *The Masked Mummers of Yoruba as seen by Clapperton and Lander*

These figures, though drawn to illustrate Clapperton's story, are mainly derived from quite modern examples. One dress is intended to imitate a crocodile, another a white man. The figure on the ground is an imitation of a python snake, made out of wooden hoops over which sacking has been stitched and painted. Inside the "snake" are two youths. The foremost opens and shuts his hands in the red mouth to imitate teeth. The local chief or king is watching the performance under the state umbrella, attended by his courtiers.

CHAPTER I

How and Why the White Man Came to West Africa

THE whole history of Africa seems to have been a continual advance from north to south, and from north-east to south-west, of invading tribes of animals and of mankind. Many, many thousands of years ago the mammals and birds native to North Africa were more like those we find in Central Africa at the present day. We know that the lion and the leopard, the hyena and certain gazelles and antelopes, and a few birds of real "African" type still exist in Morocco, Algeria, and Tunis. At the beginning of the Christian era the African elephant, rhinoceros, and giraffe inhabited western Morocco; and farther back, in the earliest days of human history, most of the great antelopes, hippopotami, and other beasts, now only found to the south of the Sahara, might have been met with on the coasts of the Mediterranean. In the same way the north of Africa was once inhabited partly or wholly by people of Negro race. They were driven southwards or killed out by the invading white races. Sometimes, however, the whites intermarried with the blacks, and that is why the complexion of most North African peoples at the present day is pale-yellow or brown. Even in True Africa, beyond the Sahara Desert, the different Negro tribes were always pushing to the south and west, towards the sea coasts. Occasionally the white races from the north would invade the region of the Niger, the countries round Lake Chad, or along the Upper Nile, and, although soon losing their pale skins by mingling with the black people, would penetrate far into Equatorial Africa.

In this way the Negroes (who were no doubt originally a very savage race, with but few arts or inventions of their own) received from the white races of Europe, North Africa, and Syria some of their languages, most of their religious ideas and simple manufactures, and all their domestic animals and cultivated plants. For perhaps ten thousand years some kind of commerce has been going on between the white peoples of Arabia, Egypt, and North Africa and the negroes of the well-watered regions beyond the Sahara and Nubian Deserts.

North Africa—Morocco, Algeria, Tunis, Tripoli, Cyrene, and Lower Egypt—is really part of Temperate Europe and Asia at the present day, so far as its plants, birds, beasts, insects, and fishes are concerned. Between North Africa and what is called the Sudan—the land of black people, great heat, heavy rains, and extraordinary wild beasts— there lies a vast stretch of desert, in places a thousand or even fourteen hundred miles in width. This desert is either covered in its lower parts with shifting sands, or in the more elevated regions there is sun-baked rock which crumbles into sand under the alternate effects of extreme heat and severe cold. But this desolate region—called Sahara in the west, the Libyan Desert in the centre, and the Nubian Desert in the east—was once partly under water, and at other times a land of forests permeated by great rivers. The sea retreated, or the lakes dried up, leaving extensive deposits of salt behind. Various causes drove away rain so that the forests died, and have left only their petrified remains here and there to show how different at one time was this region, now celebrated as being the most pitiless desert in the whole world.

Yet here and there man has been able to get access to the underground stores of water, either by digging in the beds of the ancient rivers or in depressions which were at one time fresh-water lakes; so that the Sahara as a whole is by no means uninhabitable, and even may, some day, by man's supreme energy, be restored to use as a fertile region producing many articles of food.

It is wonderful to think that in irrigating these deserts with water drawn up from wells, sometimes of great depth, we shall be employing the rain which the sun's heat evaporated from the ocean a million or so years ago, and which found its way to the regions beneath the sand and stones of the Sahara, whence it could not escape again into the atmosphere.

The drying up of the Sahara, so far as we are able to calculate (from the traditions of the natives, a few references in Egyptian, Greek, and Roman records, and the remains of plants and animals), has been a rapid and rather recent process; and

there is little doubt that a few thousand years ago
the Great Desert was better provided with water
and vegetation, and far more easily traversed by
men and beasts, than it has been since the close
of the Roman Empire. Two or three thousand
years ago the Libyans were able to cross it along
certain routes, by means of riding or draught oxen,
where now it is only passable by camels.

It is practically certain that the first white men
to visit the West Coast of Africa by sea were
Phœnicians, who sailed through the Straits of
Gibraltar, perhaps as early in history as 1000 B.C.
About the year 600 B.C. they are supposed to have
circumnavigated Africa at the suggestion of the
ruler of Egypt, Necho the son of Psammetik. On
this voyage they must have sailed down the Red
Sea and along the east coast of Africa till they
rounded the Cape of Good Hope, and thence
turned northwards and westwards past the Guinea
coast until they regained the Mediterranean.

A century afterwards the exploration of the West
African coast was continued by the Carthaginians,
themselves descendants of the Phœnician colonies
in North Africa. These Carthaginians, about six
hundred years before the time of Christ, had
founded small trading stations along the north-
west coast of Africa, as far south as the inlet known
as the River of Gold (Rio de Oro). Here there
was an island which they named Kerne, and which
is still called to the present day in the local dialect
Herne. It is evident that some race like the Fula
—white men tinged with negro blood—resorted to

this desert coast to trade with the Carthaginians, and brought to them gold from the regions of the Upper Senegal. When, in about 520 B.C., Hanno, a Carthaginian general, was dispatched by the Republic of Carthage to visit all these trading stations on the Atlantic Coast and to found others, he took with him (it is said) a concourse of 30,000 new colonists from Carthage, a statement which no doubt arises from an exaggeration or error in writing. But after he had reached the Island of Kerne at the River of Gold, he seems to have embarked several interpreters and guides of Fula race, and with the aid of these he sailed southwards along the West Coast of Africa till he reached and passed the Senegal River, and finally came to the Sherbro country, which now forms part of the British colony of Sierra Leone. Here his men seem to have captured some chimpanzees, the stuffed skins of which were brought back to Carthage.

No doubt the Carthaginians, by maritime and overland journeys, did much to bring negro West Africa into touch with the white nations of the Mediterranean, and thus encouraged a trade in gold.

Then, about the same time—several hundred years before the birth of Christ — there appears to have been a very marked extension of Egyptian influence from east to west across the Sudan. Traders, emigrants, slave-raiders, and persons in rebellion against the governments of Egypt seem to have passed through Darfur and Wadai to the region round Lake Chad, while others journeyed southwards up the Valley of the Nile till they reached Unyoro and Uganda. But the western migration of Egyptians and Egyptian influence went steadily on across the Sudan through Hausaland till it reached the Niger; and all along the Upper Niger, in the flat, alluvial country, something like a second Egypt was established, with domestic animals, cultivated plants, and house architecture of Egyptian types.

We may assume from various facts and traditions known to us, that the original Fula and negro population of the Upper Niger, stimulated by Egyptian influence, which reached Nigeria by way of Bornu, ·further developed the gold trade. Their adventurers would penetrate to the mountainous and forested region south of the Niger basin, and there they would find naked negroes who had already picked out small nuggets of gold from the river sands and from broken rocks, and were wearing them as ornaments. In this way, no doubt, there was first of all revealed indirectly to the world of the white man the gold of Bambūk and Ashanti.

The semi-white men of the Niger Valley kept up some fitful trade with Nubia and Egypt, and probably with Carthage. From these regions they obtained pretty beads of glass. These they were wont to exchange with the negroes against gold dust and nuggets; for the black man preferred a necklace of pierced glass beads like beautiful pebbles to fragments of a yellow metal, difficult for a people still in the Stone Age to fashion into portable ornaments. Thus the beads manufactured in Egypt and Italy three thousand to fifteen hundred years ago travelled to the naked, savage, probably cannibal negroes of the dense West African forests. After the death of the wearer the bead necklace was usually buried with him. In this and other ways these ancient glass beads from the far-distant Mediterranean became lodged into the soil of the West African coast lands, and are dug up from time to time or revealed by some flood or landslide. In Ashanti they are known as "agri" beads, and they bear silent testimony to the fact that West African gold was sent by roundabout ways to the civilized world long before the arrival from the north of the Hausa and Arab merchants, or the coming by sea of the Portuguese.

The crumbling of the Roman Empire, and the withdrawal of the Roman garrisons from the wells and oases of the mid-Sahara Desert, no doubt for a few hundred years checked the direct intercourse between negro Africa and the peoples of the Mediterranean. But this soon recommenced under the very agency which destroyed the Roman Empire over Africa—the Arabs. After the foundation of the Arab caliphate over Syria and Persia, the Arabs conquered Egypt and implanted their religion and rule over the whole of North Africa. They found in the Libyans or Berbers a kindred people, who made common cause with them in the invasion of negro Africa, of the "Sudan" or Land of Black People as it came to be called.

Although this Muhammadan invasion of North

Africa dealt a severe blow to the welfare of the
Mediterranean countries when it destroyed the
Christianity and civilization which the Romans and
Greeks had implanted there, nevertheless it carried
European knowledge about Inner Africa much
farther forward than the Greeks or Romans had
been able to do.   The Arabs brought with them
camels and good breeds of swift horses; they were
used to a desert existence, and were not frightened
by long journeys without water across shifting
sands, so that they passed to and fro from east to
west and from north to south, across the Sahara
Desert;   and other bands of them coasted along
the shores of North-west Africa in small ships (or
marched overland along the sea coast), and so
reached the mouth of the Senegal as early as
about 900 A.D.

The Senegal River has been a very remarkable
stream in the history of Africa.   It is the first flowing river of fresh water that the traveller by land
or sea encounters after he has left the River Draa
in the southern part of Morocco.   Between the
Draa and the Senegal there are about 840 miles
of coast, unbroken by any stream of water passing
into the sea.   This region is entirely blank desert
near the coast, though at some distance inland
there are hills, in the middle of which water may
be obtained by digging wells.   But all along this
dreary coast not a tree is visible between the more
fertile parts of Morocco on the north and the
vicinity of the Senegal River on the south.   The
sandy, treeless desert may even be said to come up

to the very banks of the Senegal itself, yet directly
that river is reached there are date palms and fan
palms, great baobab trees, with their enormously
thick trunks and gouty limbs, huge fig trees, and
other striking forms of vegetation. In the marshes
formed by shallow channels of the stream, or by
overflows of the river during the season of high
water, there are beds of tall reeds, with great
plumes of creamy-white blossom, and also vast
stretches of the intensely green and beautiful
papyrus rush.

In the eleventh century of the Christian era,
just before William the Norman was preparing to
invade Saxon England, civil war raged in Arabia
(as it often does), and whole tribes left that sun-
smitten peninsula and crossed the Red Sea into
Nubia. Hence some made their way—in hundreds
of thousands—to Tripoli, Tunis, Algeria, and
Morocco, while others stayed in the northern part
of the Egyptian Sudan or migrated to the countries
round Lake Chad. Some tribes even travelled
right across the Desert to the vicinity of the
Atlantic Ocean. In the north of Africa the Arabs
mingled much with the real natives of the country,
the Berbers or Libyans. These Libyans were white
men originally, with handsome features and clear
complexions — like good-looking French people
from Southern France, or Italians or Spaniards,
or the dark-haired type of Irish. They were a very
ancient people indeed in North Africa. Ages ago
they had dwelt in Palestine, they had helped to
colonize Egypt and Abyssinia, and branches of

this stock had populated much of southern and western Europe, even as far away as Ireland and south-west Scotland.   Other very remote extensions of this type had by mingling with the negro created the Fula race in Nigeria (of which you will presently read a good deal) and the Gala and Somali in East Africa.   When they mingled with the Arab invaders in the western Sahara they formed those tribes of "Moors" who have been such fierce enemies of the French in recent times, and who treated various British explorers so cruelly.   Of much purer Libyan race are the Tuareg of the central Sahara — the people who are said to have founded Timbuktu.[1]

Owing to their physical resemblance, their sharing the same Muhammadan religion, and constant use of the Arabic language, Berbers, Tuaregs, Moors, and Arabs appeared much the same people to the early European adventurers in West Africa.

The Arabs and Moors, when they began these great journeys across the Sahara a thousand years ago, soon got into touch with the gold trade about the sources of the Niger and in those countries, like Ashanti (called in a general way Wangara by Moorish geographers), which lay along the fringe

---

[1] It must not, however, be forgotten that the civilized negro kingdoms of the Songhai, of Bornu, Hausa, and of the Mandingos were existing in the Western Sudan several centuries before the Arabs and Tuaregs came on the scene.   They were probably relics of the Egyptian emigration into the Northern Sudan.   "Tuareg", it should be mentioned, is only an Arabic nickname *Tawariq*, which is the plural of *Tarqi*, an outlaw.   The *q* in these and similar Arabic names represents a hard *k*, often pronounced like a *g* in North Africa.   The Tuaregs are merely the Berber tribes dwelling in the Desert.   "Moors" usually means the mixed races, half Arab, half Berber.

A GROUP OF "MOORS" AND MUHAMMADAN NEGRO MERCHANTS IN ASHANTI

Photo. by Capt. T. C. Hincks

of the Great Forest to the south of the Niger basin. They also purchased or obtained the Kola nuts, the peppers, and spices that were yielded by the wonderful forest itself. The gold and the spices thus obtained reached the shores of the Mediterranean and were sold to the Christian nations.

So that it was first of all through the Arabs and Moors that the sea adventurers I am about to describe were led to understand that West Africa was the special country of pepper and gold. Wonderful stories were told to them by boasting Moors of a great city of learning and refinement— Tombutu or Timbuktu—which lay near the banks of a mighty river far across the desert, a river which some people thought was the same as the Nile, and yet which had a second outlet into the Atlantic Ocean (the Senegal).

Rumours of this river had even reached the Roman geographers, who had likewise heard that it lay far to the south of Morocco and contained sea-horses (hippopotami), crocodiles, and papyrus rushes.

During the thirteenth and fourteenth centuries a great increase of attention was given among the seafaring peoples of the Mediterranean and of Portugal to an improvement in the building and rigging of sailing ships, so that longer and swifter voyages might be made across the Mediterranean and along the Atlantic coasts of Western Europe. Before this period of the revival of science and enterprise in Southern Europe at the close of the Middle Ages, ships were as much moved by oars as by sails; in fact the sail of a simple lateen character was little more than an auxiliary to the force of men's arms in pulling the great sweeps or oars. The remembrance of the Roman galleys — *navis longa biremis*, *triremis*, &c. — the biremes and triremes, so named from their double or treble ranks of oars, is familiar to all of us who have made any studies in the classics. The use of propulsion by oars, or "sweeps", was carried to such an exaggerated extent in the Roman navy that there were even monster ships *sedecemremis*, or provided with *sixteen* banks of oars. The Saxons, the Northmen, and Danes who invaded England during the dark ages were mainly rowed across from one shore of the North Sea to another.

The Phœnicians about a thousand years before the time of Christ had brought their sailing vessels on the Persian Gulf and Indian Ocean to greater size and perfection of build. No doubt they were very like the present type of Arab *dau*, which is still to be found on the coasts of East Africa, Arabia, and India. The Chinese and Malays earlier still used sailing vessels with mat sails— the type that we know as "junks" — and, except for steering, it may be that all these Asiatic peoples had given up the use of the oar in order to rely altogether on their sails. But so far as the nations of Europe were concerned, the vessel which only progressed over the water by means of wind power was scarcely employed before the beginning of the thirteenth century after Christ, when the extended use of the mariner's compass made voyages into the open sea, out of sight of land, less terrifying.

As soon as distant voyages were undertaken men were obliged, by force of circumstances, to build bigger, taller ships and to resort to sails alone for their propulsion through the water. Thus the freeborn mariners and adventurers of the new nations of mediæval Europe, relieved from the heart-breaking fatigue of pulling oars,[1] began to undertake longer and longer journeys out into the Atlantic in search of new countries, where they might trade to advantage, and perhaps make wonderful discoveries of precious metals, or of realms of fairyland and earthly paradises on islands of the ocean. Sea-voyaging by means of well-constructed sails fitted to stout masts set in a broad ship with sides high above the water's edge, entailed far less danger and discomfort among the great billows and swells of the ocean than navigation in the long, narrow, low-built galleys, moved principally by the force of men's arms.

So that after these improved sailing vessels came into use in the thirteenth century, and the magnetic compass had made seafarers and landfarers independent of clear skies by day and night

---

[1] This fatigue was so terrible, and the life that accompanied it so short and full of misery, that the term "galley-slave" remains in our languages as an example of the worst type of toil and suffering. The men who rowed the Greek and Roman, and the mediæval French, Genoese, Pisan, Venetian, Byzantine, Turkish, and Moorish galleys were slaves chained to their oars. Later on in history—for sea navigation by oars did not die out till the beginning of the eighteenth century—the men who pulled the oars for hour after hour and day after day in the Mediterranean galleys were criminals or prisoners of war.

for directing their course, remarkable discoveries
began to be made by adventurous Genoese, Ma-
jorcans, Venetians, and Dutch, Normans, and Portuguese, and even Flemings from the Netherlands
coast.   The trade of the Mediterranean with the
coasts of England, Ireland, and Scotland was
greatly increased.   Mediterranean ships passed into
the North Sea and exchanged commerce with
Denmark and Norway.   Occasionally some vessels
reached as far as Iceland, where their captains or
navigators picked up hints of a great New World
lying far away to the west, a New World—North
America—which had really been discovered in the
tenth century of the Christian era by Norse ships
coming from Iceland and Greenland.

The Norman adventurers, however, from Dieppe
and other parts of the north coast of France were
at first more inclined to pursue their discoveries into
warmer seas, while the Genoese passed out through
the Straits of Gibraltar and got into friendly relations with the Portuguese, who were driving the
Moors out of Portugal and turning it once more
into a Christian kingdom.   The Genoese, Venetians, and other Italians, the Portuguese and the
Catalan people of eastern Spain and the Balearic
Islands, uniting their efforts, discovered, or redis-
covered, the Canary Islands, Madeira, and a
group of volcanic islands still farther to the west
—the Azores.   It is quite possible that all these
island groups—certainly the Canaries—were known
to the early Phœnician navigators and to their
relations the Carthaginians, but, except in regard

to the Canaries, all remembrance of these Atlantic Islands had been lost to Europe, except here and there in dim legends preserved by monkish poets.

The colonization of the Azores by the Portuguese and Flemings, together with the bringing of Iceland within the range of the civilized Christian world, were to lead to the conception in the minds of a few great thinkers of other lands lying far away to the west across the Atlantic, perhaps the eastermost prolongation of Asia, or some wonderful new country which certain men thought would prove to be Paradise, the Garden of Eden, removed from men's sight and encompassed by stormy seas.

But the thoughts of most of the adventurers of the fourteenth and fifteenth centuries were turned not so much to any wild venture across the wide Atlantic as to the reaching of those parts of West Africa from which the Moors of Morocco, Algeria, and Tripoli obtained pepper and other spices, and gold.

Much later on, European adventurers sailed to West Africa to obtain cargoes of slaves, which could be transported at a great profit to the islands and coasts of America; but so far as the British were concerned, the first great attraction about West Africa was its production of the scent bags of the civet-cat, and various grains, seeds, and nuts which could be made into pepper and spices. In the times of the Tudors and Stuarts the English people and the other European nations were inordinately fond of strong flavours and hot condiments in their cooking.   Queen Elizabeth, and even Charles II, ate food which was so stuffed with spice and pepper, and saturated with such strong essences, that we should turn nowadays with loathing from the dishes they ate of so greedily, and dislike the drinks which they swilled with such a relish.

Some people think that Norman ships from Dieppe were the first that sailed southwards of Morocco, and turned round the great western bend of Africa, till they came to that Gold Coast which the Moors were trading with overland on the north. But so far as accurate history is concerned, the first Europeans to achieve this wonderful feat of discovery were Portuguese seamen in Portuguese ships, who were helped a good deal, however, by mariners from Venice, Genoa, and Majorca.   They found the *spices* of which they were in search in the coast region between the Gambia and the delta of the Niger; and *gold* they readily obtained from the Gold Coast, though they also strove to search for it about the headwaters of the Senegal and Niger, being, however, prevented from doing so by the hostility of the Muhammadan negroes and the Moors, who no sooner saw the whites coming in ships to trade along the coast than they feared, what long subsequently took place, the conquest of all these regions by the white man.

Naturally the Portuguese strove to keep all these African discoveries to themselves and for the exclusive commerce of their own nation; just as the Spaniards forbade the ships of other nations

to visit Spanish America, and the British at different times also tried to reserve the commerce of
British North America entirely for the people of
England, or later on of Great Britain.   One in-
ducement to the Portuguese to find out what part
of Africa produced pepper and spices was that
hitherto the Republic of Venice entirely mono-
polized the European trade in these condiments.
From early days the Venetians had endeavoured
to keep up a friendly intercourse and a commerce
with the Saracens and Moors of the southern
Mediterranean coasts, so that they might thus
carry on an indirect trade with India and Central
Africa.   In their commercial greed they raised
the price of pepper and spice too high.   Then
the Portuguese, having learnt in their conquest
of Morocco that spices and pepper could be obtained from the West Coast of Africa, as well as
gold, and even that a way to India might be
found round the southern extremity of Africa, were
tempted to push their sea adventures in this direction; but certainly not with the idea of throwing
open their discoveries to the rest of the world.

During the time that we were fighting our
War of the Roses, our trade with Portugal was
steadily growing, and we were purchasing from
the Portuguese not only the wine of their own
country, but these wonderful new spices that they
brought from Africa.   Yet it began to occur to
the mariners of Bristol and Devonshire, Poole and
Southampton, London and Essex, that if Portuguese ships could obtain valuable trade commo-

dities by sailing south from Lisbon for a few weeks, British ships, already accustomed to trade with Portugal, Spain, France, and Ireland, might be able to venture in the same direction. And probably they made attempts as early as about 1480 to reach West Africa, because we find the King of Portugal writing to King Edward IV of England, asking him to restrain his subjects from poaching in these Portuguese preserves.

It is not recorded what the King of England said in reply, but during the succeeding reigns British mariners were more interested in the commerce of the North Sea and the Baltic; and the great adventures they made were more in the direction of North America. But the Land of Black People, of pepper, spices, and gold, was not forgotten. At first, English seamen shipped themselves as sailors or soldiers on Portuguese vessels, and in this way found out how to reach the "Guinea Coast" (Senegambia), where slaves, hides, cotton, and cotton cloths might be bought from the natives; the "Grain" coast (Liberia), where they traded for spice and pepper; or the "Gold Coast", where gold dust and elephants' tusks could be obtained by a very profitable barter of English, Irish, and Flemish manufactures. At last, in the reign of Edward VI, a British ship ventured to make the voyage to West Africa, and was followed by an increasing number of other vessels. Sometimes they managed to elude the Portuguese and to return with rich cargoes; sometimes their vessels were wrecked on this harbourless, surf-bound coast, and the mariners, unless actually killed by the Portuguese, were taken home as prisoners and held to ransom. The French were trying the same game. Occasionally the British and French united to beat off the Portuguese, and sometimes they fought between themselves.

Sir John Hawkins, in 1569, accompanied by his adopted son, Francis Drake, made apparently some contract with the Spanish Government for the obtaining of negro slaves from the West Coast of Africa to be landed at the Canary Islands, or taken direct by Hawkins to the West Indies. In these instances Hawkins either defied the Portuguese, or may possibly have come to an understanding with them through the good offices of Spain.

Soon afterwards — in 1580 — the Portuguese kingdom was swallowed up in the Spanish monarchy, and as henceforth England and Spain were at war, the British and Dutch ships boldly attacked the Portuguese on the West Coast of Africa, and afterwards did pretty much as they pleased in these waters.

In the early part of the seventeenth century Great Britain began to found colonies of her own on the coast of North America and in such small West India islands as had been abandoned by the Spaniards. When they had in this way begun the colonies of Virginia, Barbados, the Bermudas, and St. Christopher, and had occupied other small West India islands (besides trying to settle in what

is now British Guiana), they soon found that it was
not very agreeable or healthy for white men to
work under a tropical or a subtropical sun in
tilling the fields; so they copied the Spaniards
and Portuguese and began to acquire negro
slaves.   Until the latter part of the seventeenth
century, the British colonizers of America were
content to get their negro slaves through the
Dutch, for the Dutch had ousted the Portuguese
from the Gold Coast, and had also established
themselves on islands along the coast of Senegambia.   From these regions they supplied cargoes of negro slaves to all the nations who were
colonizing America.   But by the close of the reign
of Charles II the English had taken numerous
places from the Dutch on the Gold Coast and
had attempted to explore and to settle on the
Gambia River, first, with the idea of obtaining
gold, and, secondly, to get large supplies of slaves
for the cultivation of Jamaica and other British
possessions in the West Indies and on the Continent of North America.

Yet the exploration and conquest of West
Africa in connection with the slave trade scarcely
began till the commencement of the eighteenth
century; and meantime the English seamen and
gentlemen adventurers sought the West Coast of
Africa for pepper and spices, for ivory, for the
perfume of the civet-cat; and, above all, for gold.

CHAPTER II

Pioneers on the Gambia

THE first of the adventures I invite you to follow in detail was that of Richard Jobson, a native of London, who made a journey up the Gambia River in 1620. The Gambia is a river with a single wide and deep mouth which flows into the Atlantic about two hundred and fifty miles south of the Senegal. Of all the West African rivers it is perhaps the easiest to enter, as it has deep water over its "bar"—some twenty-six feet—and no dangerous shoals or breakers. It is, on the contrary, almost impossible for ships of any size or considerable draft to enter the Senegal from the sea across its dangerous and shallow bar, though, once launched on the Senegal, vessels of light draft can navigate that important river far into the interior.

The Gambia also marks the beginning of a distinct part of West Africa to observers coming from the north. The coast between the Senegal mouth and the vicinity of the Gambia is dry, rocky, and sterile, and possesses scanty vegetation. But when we reach the lower Gambia we enter the great West African forest belt, and thenceforth eastwards as far as Angola the coast regions will be densely covered with rich vegetation and luxuriant forest containing peculiar beasts and birds.

A certain Company of Adventurers, formed from amongst the merchants of London, had dispatched in 1618 a trader named George Thompson to explore the Gambia River in the hope that it might prove to be the sea outlet of the Niger, of the mysterious river of Timbuktu and the gold countries of Bambara. George Thompson had been a merchant trading on the coast of Morocco, and there had witnessed from time to time the arrival from across the desert of the great yearly caravans bringing slaves, gold, ivory, salt, and other products from the Niger regions. Queen Elizabeth, who was a very far-sighted woman, had taken advantage of the deep hostility between the power of Spain on the one hand, and the Turks of the Levant and the Moors of North Africa on the other, to open up diplomatic relations with the Muhammadan world. These countries were only too pleased to meet her advances halfway, so that their own trade products might reach the Western world. This action of Queen Elizabeth had the most far-reaching results, for it led by a series of events to the foundation of the British Empire in India and in Africa.

George Thompson had picked up some knowledge of Moorish Arabic, which it was thought would help him to get into communication with the natives of West Africa, many of whom had adopted the Muhammadan religion and could read the Koran or sacred book of the Muhammadans in Arabic.

But George Thompson's mission was a failure. He took out with him in his ship, the *Catherine* of London (which was only a vessel of 120 tons burden), a cargo worth £1860. His ship entered the Gambia River without any difficulty, and sailed up stream as far as a place called Kasson. Here, on account of the shallow water, Thompson decided to leave her in the charge of a few of his men whilst he continued his journey higher up the river in his ship's boats.

The arrival of this English ship was most unpleasing to the Portuguese settlers on the banks of the Gambia. We learn that in those days Portuguese seamen and soldiers often deserted from Portuguese vessels (or ran away because they were malefactors) and settled on the banks of the Gambia in order to make new homes for themselves or to engage in the slave trade. They married native wives, and their half-caste children, though called Portuguese, were equally related to the Africans amongst whom they dwelt. Kasson,[1] where the *Catherine* was anchored, was probably a trading town founded by the Portuguese; at any rate at that time it seems to have been ruled by a Portuguese trader. Some time after George Thompson's departure up country these Portuguese of Kasson induced the negroes to join with them in destroying the *Catherine* and murdering her crew. So that when Thompson had settled down amongst the friendly natives at Tenda, a place over two

[1] Kasson was situated at the head of the second bend of the Gambia, about 140 miles from its mouth.

hundred and forty miles from the mouth, he might have considered himself completely cut off from any further communication with his own country.

But the British are not easily daunted. Thompson sent off two or three of the English seamen with him to reach the coast by some means or other, and thus regain England. Possibly, to avoid the hostile Portuguese, they may have made a journey overland (which until recently would have been thought very wonderful) till they came to the vicinity of Goree Island (near Cape Verde). Here the Dutch had a settlement, and it may be that these travel-weary seamen found their way back to England in a Dutch ship. They delivered their message to the owners of the *Catherine*, and a small vessel of only 50 tons was sent out to the Gambia with more goods and men. Thompson accepted these reinforcements, but sent this little ship back again to England with letters urging that further efforts should be made to establish a great trading monopoly on the Gambia. For the English were no better in this respect than the Portuguese, and if George Thompson had had his way he would have built forts and have blocked the river to the ships of any other nation.

However, his great project came to nothing, for he was killed in a quarrel with one of his own men before the second relief vessel could arrive, in the year 1620.

When Thompson had settled down at this place —Tenda—he had found himself among a people which was chiefly Muhammadan, and which dressed in long flowing robes and turbans like Arabs. Not only could many of them speak the Arabic of Morocco, but there were actually Moors of that country visiting these regions of the Upper Gambia. They came in great caravans, with three hundred or more donkeys, bringing the trade goods of the Mediterranean to exchange for cubes and baskets of salt, for negro slaves, ivory, and gold. Like so many people of modern times who have first travelled in Muhammadan Africa or Asia, and have grown accustomed to splendid buildings, beautiful dresses, and the Eastern luxuries of life, Thompson had been disgusted with the squalor of the naked negroes along the Lower Gambia, with their paltry houses of grass, reeds, and sticks, and the coarse discomforts of a savage existence. He became so elated at meeting again the Moors of Barbary, and getting into touch with the commerce of the Mediterranean, that his manner towards the rough English seamen grew extravagant and insolent. According to the story of the natives, one of the sailors dealt him a blow in a quarrel which killed him.

Meantime, however, the merchants of London had sent to Thompson's assistance, in October, 1620, an expedition consisting of a ship called the *Syon*, of 200 tons, and a smaller ship or pinnace of 50 tons, that same *St. John* which had sailed out to the Gambia and back a year before. The man in charge of this expedition was evidently well chosen for his intelligence and pluck. He describes himself as "Richard Jobson, gentleman".

But he seems to have been selected by the Company of Adventurers from a different class to that which ordinarily furnished the mariners or supercargoes in the African trade, so that his appointment occasioned considerable jealousy, and the spiteful opposition and carelessness of some of the men associated with him made his remarkable expedition of little commercial profit. On his return, Captain Richard Jobson published a book called *The Golden Trade*, which is one of the most interesting works ever written about Africa before the days of Mungo Park, and singularly truthful in its observations.

His expedition left Dartmouth on 25 October, 1620, and, being favoured by the winds, reached and passed the Canary Islands early in November, and attained the River Gambia on 17 November, not having taken much more time over this journey than what you would do at the present day if you travelled from England by a slow steamer.

The sailing master of Jobson's vessel was unfortunately a drunkard. Jobson records that from the date of their departure from Dartmouth, in October, 1620, until the sailing master died in Africa in the following March, he was never twenty days sober. In these evil courses he was followed by the "chirurgion", or ship's surgeon, and one of the supercargoes or factors. They intoxicated themselves with "sacke", or, as we should say, sherry (a Spanish wine), and "aqua vitæ", which was probably French brandy.

In the England of Shakespeare and Queen

Elizabeth wine or beer were the customary alcoholic beverages. But from the beginning of the seventeenth century spirituous liquors became cheaper and cheaper (as the knowledge of chemistry and distillation spread), and seriously impaired the efficiency of British soldiers, sailors, and civilians in their enterprises abroad. Most of the Southern nations of Europe remained temperate in their habits and disliked these fiery forms of alcohol. But many a great expedition or battle ended in disaster or defeat to the Northern Europeans, because the English, the Danes, or even the Dutch were drunk at the time with brandy, rum, or gin. And although most of the Northern people conquered in the long run, their advance was much retarded by this addiction to strong waters.

Jobson complains that the principal factor or supercargo of his expedition, in organizing his branch of the trading expedition up the Gambia, would fill his boat with two large casks—one of sacke, or sherry, and the other of aqua vitæ, or brandy; and in making his selection from the crew, only chose those men who, like himself, were able to drink hard. The result was that most of the crew of this boat died from "dangerous sickness", and this branch of the expedition came to nothing. Jobson, on the other hand, succeeded with his party in travelling a distance of 420 miles farther than the other boat could reach, and returned without the loss of one man either on this or on his second journey. All the time he himself was never ill, nor was there ever much sickness amongst his crew. This good fortune he attributes to his great care in his men's diet, and to the prudence which all of them observed in regard to the drinking of spirits.

The first thing that impressed itself upon the minds of Captain Jobson and his men, as their two ships sailed up the Gambia, were the hippopotami, the crocodiles, and the storks (which they called "cranes"). The first-named, of course, they styled "sea-horses", for in those days the scientific name hippopotamus or river-horse had not been put together out of the Greek language. English students of the classics had, of course, read of the "river-horse" in the works of Herodotus and Aristotle, and some of them may have guessed that it was alluded to under various names in the Hebrew Scriptures; but it had become semimythical, like dragons, basilisks, unicorns, and phœnixes, in which people of Jobson's day believed just as much or as little.

Captain Jobson is not sure whether he is describing a fish or a beast when he deals with a hippopotamus! But, nevertheless, he was struck with its great resemblance to the horse in the shape of its body and head, which last seemed to him like that of a horse with short ears. Jobson describes its habits very accurately, how it lives all day in the river, yet every night repairs to the shore; where, besides feeding on grass and reeds, the hippo devours the rice and corn of the natives' plantations. In those reaches of the river which had the deepest water, yet lay nearest to suitable feeding-grounds, the hippos were found by Jobson

THE GAMBIA RIVER, AS DESCRIBED BY CAPTAIN JOBSON

in great numbers. From the place where they landed to where they fed might be the distance of a mile, but the path made by their broad feet would be beaten as hard " as London highway ".

Jobson and his men went through the same experiences when they travelled in boats, as has befallen many an African traveller of recent times: they found the hippopotami very bold and vicious, "snorting, neighing, and tossing the water, and making show of great displeasure", rushing at the boats and attempting to crush or overturn them with their teeth. Owing to the jealousy already mentioned regarding the selection of Jobson, the people in the trade who had fitted out the vessel had failed to supply sufficient gunpowder or muskets; therefore Jobson and his men were afraid to waste their powder in shooting at the "river-horses", or there were not enough guns to go round when the expedition was divided into several boatloads. At nighttime they would repel the attacks of the hippos on their camps by lighting candles or waving pieces of burning wood. The great beasts were always more dangerous when they had their young with them. "Being in the water, every female carries her young upon her back, so as when she puts up her head the young head likewise will look his share, and where they appear, many heads together, there is as much variety as from the great horse to the hunting nag." Jobson also notices how the hippos and the crocodiles seem to share the river without any enmity. "I have stood upon the bank and seen them swim, one by another, without offence."

As to the crocodile, Jobson mentions that its native name is *bumbo*, but as an alternative calls it "alegatha". This, of course, is a corruption of "alligator", a word apparently derived from the Spanish *el lagarto*, "the lizard". [When the Spaniards first discovered Florida and the mouth of the River Mississippi, and noticed the alligators in the swamps, they took them very naturally for huge lizards.] The word "crocodile" was first made use of by the Greeks in describing the huge, scaly monster of the River Nile. This was really the reptile seen by Captain Jobson in the Gambia, for there are *no* alligators seen anywhere in Africa or in the rest of the world, except only in North America and China. Nevertheless, careless travellers still continue to write and speak of "alligators" in African, Indian, or South American rivers.[1]

---

[1] There is a real crocodile in the West Indies and in Central America, and there are real crocodiles in Africa and Tropical Asia and Australia. In South America there is the Caiman, a creature which is allied to the alligator, but is still sufficiently separate not to be called by that name. In the great rivers of India there is a fish-eating reptile, the Gharial, with very slender jaws ending in a big knob round the snout. This is again quite different to crocodiles and alligators, though a reptile of the same order. If you were to visit the West African rivers you might think you had also found a Gharial there, for the kind of crocodile met with is not always the big, dangerous one which eats men and antelopes as well as fish, but a slightly smaller type with a very slender muzzle like the Gharial of India. This, however, is only a local species of true Crocodile, which has but an accidental resemblance to the Gharial of India, like which it lives wholly on fish. There is also a third kind of crocodile in West Africa which may perhaps extend as far west as the Gambia River. This is the Stumpy Crocodile, with a short, broad, turned-up snout, the bull dog of the Crocodile race, while the Slender-nosed form is the greyhound.

Of these dangerous Nile crocodiles Jobson writes: "The people of the country stand in such dread, that they dare not wash their hands in the great River, much less offer to swim or wade therein, reporting unto us many lamentable stories how their friends and acquaintances have been devoured by them: neither do they at any time bring any of their cattle to pass the river . . . but with great dread and ceremony. When they pass a beefe over, he is led into the water with a rope to his horns, whereby one holds him close to the boat, and another taking up his tail holds in the like manner; the priest, or maribucke,[1] standing over the middle of the beast, praying and spitting upon him according to their ceremonies, charming the crocodile; while another stands against him with his bow and arrows ready drawn to expect when the crocodile will seize. In this manner, if there be twenty oxen at a time, they pass them one after another, never thinking them safe until they be on the top of the river bank." However, Captain Jobson himself when he had to wade and drag his boat across shallow fords did not fear to go into water without his clothes, and was never once attacked. But this he ascribes quite rightly to the fact that the blacks who went with him kept up an incessant noise, clapping hands and shouting.

In the upper reaches of the Gambia Jobson found the great crocodiles far more abundant than lower down the river where the water was deep.

[1] Maribucke is a corruption of *Marabut*, a man learned in the Koran or sacred book of the Muhammadans.

He was much impressed with the musky odour of the crocodiles, which though he describes it as "smelling exceeding sweet", to our modern senses is one of the most repulsive of scents (to the African traveller). In some parts of the Upper Gambia, where the crocodiles were very numerous, the water was tainted with a "sweet, musky taste", so that Jobson and his men refused to drink of it or to have their food dressed with it. "Nay, more, those great fish which with our hooks we took in that place lost the savour they had below, and were in taste and relish as the crocodile smelt," so that Jobson and his men utterly refused to eat them, but bestowed them on the people of the country.

At night the bellowing cries of the male crocodiles resembled, to Jobson's thinking, the sound of a noise made in a deep well. Far away in the still night could be heard the distant challenges of crocodile calling to crocodile, so that Jobson felt the Gambia must continue far inland, and even issue from some great lake swarming with crocodiles.

Jobson and his men feasted frequently on the excellent fish to be obtained from the Gambia either by rod and line or, more conveniently, by the casting of nets. His men had a disagreeable surprise over the Electric Catfish, which, if incautiously handled, would make them for a time numb and powerless.[1] They also noticed whir-

[1] This was the *Malopterurus electricus* of Tropical Africa. It is about a foot long, and its scaleless skin is a dull greenish-grey spotted with black. But as a rule the body is covered by such a thick slime that the colour is concealed. This gelatinous coating is in some way connected with the

ring across the river the little "Running-fish",[1]
which he compared to an English roach with a
red tail. This fish skims along the surface of the
water to avoid his enemies below.

He notes the presence of the great Spur-wing
geese, black and white in colour, rather bigger
than our English tame goose, with a sharp spur
on the pinion of each wing.

In their progress up the Gambia these adventurers seem to have dealt fairly with the natives,
and consequently were everywhere greeted in the
friendliest manner, their only troubles arising occasionally from the Portuguese settlers; and even
amongst these there were exceptions, for it is related that at one place a Portuguese named
Consalves, "in friendly sort saluted us and carried
us up to his housing", where he gave the English
seamen an excellent breakfast in which roast fowls
figured. This kindly Portuguese host had heard
of the approach of Jobson's expedition from the
"singing men", or Mandingo musicians (*Juddis*
or *Jillis*), who wander about the country and collect and transmit information with almost tele-
graphic rapidity.

Jobson and his men in boats seem to have
ascended the Gambia as far as the Barakonda falls.
From here, with nine Englishmen and four blacks,

glands on the surface of the skin which generate the electric current. The
electric shocks proceed from a great cell near the base of the skull. This
catfish easily kills other fish by its electric shocks, and they are sometimes
sufficiently strong to paralyse temporarily human beings.

[1] The Running Fish of Jobson was probably the *Pantodon buchholzi* or
Fresh-water Flying Fish.

they took one boat and a native canoe to row up
the river above the falls. They had eleven days'
hard pulling against the full force of the stream.
Then they stopped at the mouth of a little tributary river and sent messengers to the large native
town of Tinda, at some distance inland, where
Jobson hoped to get in touch with a Mandingo
merchant, whom he styles Buckor Sano, and whose
first name was probably the Arabic *Bakr*, which
means "Blessing".

Whilst waiting for the return of the black
messengers, the nine English sailors, with Jobson,
became very restive and anxious, fearing, perhaps, that they had now placed themselves in the
power of the savages who would kill them, and
also that they might run short of food. But
Jobson dealt tactfully with them and assuaged
their fears. And noticing that there was much
game in the vicinity, he went out and shot a beast
"as big as a great stag, which had wreathed
horns", in all probability a large Sing-sing water
buck. Modern travellers would think this antelope not only dry of flesh, but coarse flavoured.
To Jobson's men, however, the meat was very
welcome.

Soon afterwards their fears were dispersed by
the arrival of one of their messengers, accompanied
by an envoy from the King of Tinda, and the
brother of the black merchant Buckor Sano. The
next day about noon came Buckor Sano himself,
with his "music" playing before him with great
solemnity, and his best clothes on, and about

forty attendants armed with their bows and arrows; altogether about two hundred men and women. This Mandingo trader brought with him an ox for a present, together with goats, and fowls, and corn, "so as there was no need to doubt any more about want of victual". He promptly accepted Jobson's invitation to visit him on the boat, and when he arrived on board he was saluted by the shooting of three guns, "at the noise whereof he seemed much to rejoice, calling the report of the powder by the name of the white man's thunder, and taking notice of the head and hide of the deer (antelope) which had been killed". When he learnt that this beast had been so easily slain by the discharge of a gun he told the people on shore, who sent from one place to another to say "that there was a people come, who with thunder killed the wild beasts in the wood and the fowls in the air". Apparently whilst waiting for these messengers, Jobson and his men (who do not seem to have been very squeamish in their tastes) had been shooting marabou storks and eating their flesh, besides preserving the graceful white marabou plumes which grow underneath the bird's tail.

The marabou stork is the greatest scavenger in Africa, and feeds entirely on putrid flesh and such small animals and reptiles as it can capture, so that its own flesh would be exceedingly rank and nasty; indeed there is probably no negro who would think of eating it. But this does not seem to have deterred the hungry sailors.

Unfortunately Jobson found that a new craving had arisen amongst these Mandingo negroes, who, if they were Muhammadans, were not very strict in their religion. They had acquired a knowledge of brandy and other distilled spirits from the Portuguese, and possibly the Dutch, but so far had little opportunity of indulging in distilled spirits. Jobson, who seems to have been a very temperate man himself, had brought with him a provision of good "rosa-solis", which was a strong, sweet cordial or liqueur, with, of course, a good deal of distilled alcohol as its basis. He offered a glass of this rosa‑solis to his friend Buckor Sano, who, after he had drunk, took off his sword and gave it to Jobson to put away, saying: "'Defend me here in your boat and I will keep you safe on shore.' He liked our drink so well he sucked it in," and, not knowing the strength of it, took so much that he soon fell asleep and did not awake till the morning, when he complained of a very bad head. This, fortunately, was a sufficient cure in his case, and he never again took more than a very small cup of rosa-solis before his meal, and one after; "and this ever gave him satisfaction".

Jobson thought that the Mandingos of the interior would be as ready and eager to purchase his supplies of what we should call "pig-iron", or his iron implements, as was the case with the absolutely savage negroes along the West African coast. But the Mandingos, with whom he was now trading, were very much higher in the scale

of civilization, and they told Jobson they had
people in the neighbourhood who fully understood
how to smelt iron from the stones.   Nevertheless,
the iron goods were well disposed of, and they
were offered hides in exchange.   But of all their
commodities, the thing which sold quickest was
salt, though this was of inferior quality.   It was
greatly appreciated by the negroes, who, after
they put a taste of it in their mouths, "would
look up and cry 'Allah', in token of the good
esteem they had of it".

When Buckor Sano returned on shore and had
got over his drinking bout, he proceeded to set
forth the merchandise of which he had to dispose,
and among these were a troop of young negresses,
their bodies crossed with white strings.   These
were offered for sale, but Jobson, living as he
did before the time when the English had taken
up the slave trade for the development of America,
told the Mandingo, "We were a people who did
not deal in any such commodities (as slaves),
neither did we buy or sell one another".   Buckor
Sano was greatly surprised, as he and his fellow
countrymen did a brisk trade in slaves with the
Dutch and Portuguese; but he and they were
soon to find out that the Englishman would become
for at least a hundred and fifty years more eager
to buy negro slaves than any other nation; so that
he might use them to cultivate tobacco, sugar,
coffee, and cotton in what are now the United
States and the British West Indies.

Asked as to his other produce for sale, he put

forward his hides, elephants' tusks, cotton yarn, and the handsome cotton robes woven, embroidered, and dyed in the Mandingo countries. Jobson was unable to buy the hides because his boat was too small to carry them down, but he seems to have invested in a quantity of ivory, Mandingo robes, and cotton yarn. In those days Europeans purchased cotton goods eagerly from the natives of West Africa, for their cultivation of the cotton plant by slave labour in America had not yet begun, and the manufacture of cotton yarn into calico had not as yet been started in the industrial towns of England. In those days of the early seventeenth century the only British manufactures of clothing material were linen from flax, and cloth, frieze, and flannel from wool; and cotton goods were *imported* from Asia and Africa, instead of being sent there in enormous quantities from Manchester, as they are at the present day.

All this time Jobson was really anxious to broach the question of gold, the principal object of his voyage. He and his companions were tantalized by seeing gold ornaments in the women's ears. But they were cautious about beginning their enquiries, lest the natives should fear they were bent on some conquest of the country if they found it rich enough in gold. Buckor Sano opened the question by admiring their "gilt" swords and gold trimmings. He remarked that apparently the English had much gold in their own country. Buckor Sano told them that if he had known they wanted gold he would have

brought down a supply to sell.   He averred that
far away in the interior was a wonderful country
where he had been four times, and had seen a
town of which the houses were actually roofed
with gold, and gold only.   It had taken him four
months' journey to reach this land of wonder
(possibly he had really been to Ashanti and had
seen gold plating on the beams of the fetish
houses).   The Mandingo trader described further
how they reached this land of gold.   They went
in large companies, with donkeys to carry their
burdens, occasionally resting for two or three
days in friendly towns, but they had sometimes
savage enemies to fight with on the way.

Jobson, examining the man's sword and the
bracelets of his wives, came to the conclusion that
there were amongst these Mandingos objects which
must have been manufactured in England.   He
asked, therefore, how such things reached them,
and was told—quite truly—that a people traded
with them on the north, whom they called Arabecks (Arabs and Moors). Jobson having questioned
them about these Arabecks, and being told that
they arrived in large caravans with many camels,
realized at once that Buckor Sano was telling him
truly of the great Moorish caravans plying between Morocco and these regions of Guinea across
the Sahara Desert.   He was further answered that
these Moorish caravans came as far south as a
place called Mumbare, about a week's journey
from the banks of the Gambia.   He told them
—enforcing his statement with an oath, the invo-

cation of God as a witness to his truth — that if
Jobson and his men liked to go with him, he,
Buckor Sano, would convey them to where they
might meet these Moors, and also satisfy themselves as to the reality of this trade in gold. The
reason why Jobson did not accept his invitation,
and perhaps thus forestall Mungo Park and many
later explorers in a discovery of the Niger and of
other West African secrets, is not very clear. He
puts it down to a misunderstanding with his chief
interpreter.

Friendly relations having thus been instituted
at this halting-place on the Upper Gambia, large
concourses of natives of different tribes came to
see the Englishmen and to run up booths of reeds
on the shore and so establish markets in which
they could exchange their produce for the trade
goods brought by Jobson. He soon noted, as the
people of the interior were brought to him, that
he had not only to deal with the relatively civilized, well-clothed Mandingos, who were in touch
with the great world beyond Africa by means of
their trade, but with simple savages who wore
little or nothing, that little being the dressed skins
of antelopes or monkeys, while the adornment of
the women consisted of deep cuts or prominent
blobs of skin, the whole of the back and much
of the front part of the body being, as it were,
carved by a knife at some time or another: exactly
what you may see nowadays amongst the savages
of the Congo Basin. Deep cuts are made into
the skin, and some irritating juice is introduced

which causes a larger scar to arise. Thus there are formed patterns of blobs, holes, slits, and pimples. Curiously enough, when elaborately finished, this work does actually produce an ornamental effect on the bronze skin. But the process is a most painful one.

Besides the strange people whom they saw, the adventurers were told by their Mandingo friends of others still more remarkable in the far interior: of those whose lower lips were so exaggerated that they partly hid the bosom, while the mucous surface exposed to the sun would putrefy if it were not constantly covered with salt. This, of course, was a ridiculous exaggeration; but no doubt at that period there were still in the interior of Western Africa, as there are at the present day in the forests of Equatorial Africa and between Lake Nyasa and the east coast, tribes whose women inserted wooden discs or plugs into the upper and lower lip, so that at last they produced a hideous deformity, making both eating and speaking very difficult.

Then they saw or heard of other tribes (such as are still found in the heart of West Africa) who slashed their cheeks with long cuts from a knife and rubbed in the juice of a plant, so that the scar might turn to a blue colour. This practice of slashing the cheeks prevails amongst many negro tribes between the Upper Gambia and the Egyptian Sudan.

Jobson also writes of the "silent trade" which takes place between the Moors of Barbary and the negroes of the gold-producing countries near the Upper Senegal River. The merchants coming from the north with their caravans of camels, chiefly loaded with salt, deposit what they have to sell in small heaps at the customary marketplaces. Then when they have returned to their camp, the negroes who wash or mine the gold come to the market-place and view the heaps of goods. Against what they decide to purchase they put the amount of gold dust which they think is the right price, and then depart. When the Moorish merchant returns, if he approves of the gold dust offered, he takes that away with him and leaves the goods. If not, he takes away a proportion of the gold, but leaves the rest as a token that a further payment must be made. When he has departed the negroes come back, and if they see some of their gold dust left, deposit yet a little more; and so this process of silent barter continues until both sides are satisfied. These silent bargainers were thought by Jobson to be the people with the great lips, so ashamed of their horrible deformity that they did not like to face a foreign merchant.

In all these stories there is more than a grain of truth. This silent bargaining seems to have been one of the earliest ways of doing trade in Africa. It is even to a certain extent carried on by the Pygmies in the heart of the Congo Forest, who will come at night and take what they require from the gardens and plantations of the taller negroes and deposit instead a haunch of venison, a well-dressed skin, or something of their own obtaining.

No doubt in ancient times, being utterly ignorant of each other's speech, the North African white men, the ancestors of the Fulas and Moors, would find their way across the deserts to the negro countries, deposit the salt or other goods which they had to sell, and the negroes, being far too timid to approach them, would wait till they had gone, and then place the gold or the ivory which they had to offer in exchange alongside the trade goods of the north. Both sides found in those primitive days that honesty was the best policy, that it did not pay to cheat each other.

Jobson was soon aware, after he had been trading on the banks of the Upper Gambia, that the population of these regions might be divided more or less into four classes. There were the savage negroes of the regions nearer the coast, of the forests and the mountains, who went naked or were sparsely covered with dressed skins, and whose bodies were ornamented with these patterns of raised scars; secondly, the courteous black Mandingos, more or less Muhammadan in religion, well clad in ample robes, and the women wearing gold ear-rings and ornaments; thirdly, a light-skinned, shepherd people whom he rightly calls the *Fulbe*; and, lastly, the Moors of Barbary, coming there as merchants, together with Arabs from the regions of the Upper Niger and the Sudan.

These last professed very strict Muhammadanism, and most of them affected to be saints, men of singular holiness of life. They viewed the drinking of fermented liquor with abhorrence.

They read the Koran, or sacred book of the Arabs, and they taught reading and writing in the Arabic language. These Moorish or Arab teachers he calls "marybuckes", but, as already stated, this word is probably a mishearing of *marabut*, a term of uncertain origin which prevails over North and West Africa and means a holy man learned in the Muhammadan religion.

Captain Jobson must have been a singularly acute and faithful observer for the period in which he lived and wrote, because so much of what he says of West Africa in his book is not only exactly true, but it has only been realized by most people quite recently. For instance, in referring to the gipsy-like Fulas, he calls them more or less by their proper name, *Fulbe*[1] (or, as he spells it, Fulbye). He describes them as tawny in colour, with a resemblance to the gipsies of England: the women are straight, upright, with very well-formed bodies and beautiful faces, their black hair being long and curly.

In Jobson's day these Fulbe were wont to wander about with their flocks and herds—cattle and goats—settling down where they found the

[1] The Fula language is one of those which change the meaning of words chiefly by altering the termination: thus pul*o* means a Fula man; Ful-*be* means the Fula people; Ful-*de*, the Fula language. For convenience we usually prefer to employ the conventional term "Fula" in referring to this most interesting race, though "Fulbe" may occasionally be used in quoting Jobson or Mungo Park. In the more eastern parts of Nigeria the Fulas are called *Fellani* by the Hausa and *Fellata* by the Arabs. We shall find the Fula connected with the recent history of all Nigeria from the source of the Niger to its Delta. Although the Fulas are so like Arabs in appearance, their language belongs to the Negro type, and is related to various Negro language families in West Africa.

ground and pasture most suited to their cattle. Here with the consent of the local negro chief they would establish themselves, building houses and towns. During the rains they retired with their cattle to the mountains and high ground. In the dry season they would return to the low plains and to the sides of the rivers. The cattle would be put into enclosures at night, which were surrounded with big fires to keep off the lions, leopards, and hyenas. They lived very frugally, subsisting chiefly on the milk, butter, and flesh of their cattle. Though obviously of a semi-white race they were humble in their demeanour towards the bullying black Mandingos. Jobson, however, notices not only that their language is quite distinct from that of the Mandingos, but that they are very refined and careful in the manner in which they treat their cows' milk, both fresh and sour, and their butter. These products of their cows would be brought for sale in great and small gourd-like dishes, "made up very handsomely, and", says Jobson, "you should have it so neat and clean that in your milk you should not perceive a mote, nor in the butter any uncleanliness".

Now since Jobson's visit to the Gambia the most surprising revolution took place amongst these meek, wandering Fulbe, these handsome, Egyptian-looking people of light complexion whose origin is so mysterious, and who formerly were confined to the countries watered by the Senegal, the Gambia, and the Upper Niger. They became converted five or six hundred years ago to Muham-

madanism, and all at once, at the close of the
seventeenth century, they got tired of living a life
of subjection to the black people around them.
They produced leaders, they organized for war, and
determined to convert all West Africa forcibly to
the faith of Muhammad. Their leaders by degrees
founded several powerful Fula kingdoms in Senegambia, and at the back of Sierra Leone; kingdoms
which were only reduced to something like subjection the other day by the French. But the
most important Fula States were created along
the Upper and Central Niger, in Borgu, and
Sokoto, and far away to the east of the Niger
between that river, the Benue, and Lake Chad.
The British Protectorate of Northern Nigeria was
once for the most part the great Fula Empire of
Sokoto, which joined on the west the powerful
Fula States of Gando and Masina. Thus these
half-white men displaced the Moors of Morocco,
and the various negro dynasties, and ruled over
the greater part of the countries between the
Senegal River in the west and Bornu in the east,
until the real white men came from France and
England, and conquered the country, so that it
might henceforth be controlled from Europe.

Jobson well describes the Mandingos, who were
mainly a negro race, of handsome features, semi-
civilized, and converted to Muhammadanism. They
were then the chief people of the Gambia and
Upper Niger. In the early part of the seventeenth
century, guns and gunpowder were almost unknown
among them, except as objects of wonder brought

Photo. by Capt. Foulkes

A FULA WARRIOR, NORTHERN NIGERIA

(He is wearing the Lisham or mouth-veil introduced as a fashion by the Tuaregs of the Sahara)

by Europeans. When the people went out to war they had a cavalry which rode small horses with peaked Spanish saddles, both horses and saddles of course originally introduced by the Moors from the north. On the left arm their cavalrymen carried a buckler, and in the right hand a lance. People going to war on foot carried a bow with a quiver of arrows slung to the back, the iron arrow tips being cleverly poisoned. They would also carry assagais or throwing-spears in their hands. The Mandingo men then went usually bareheaded, but round their necks or under the left arm were hung gri-gris or charms. These amulets were either stuffed into handsomely mounted rams' horns, or sewn up in hard leather cases.[1] The women had necklets of large blue beads. The garments of the men were loose, baggy breeches, just such as they wear now throughout the whole Sudan, and a very large upper garment or shirt, often called a *tobe*, with a hole in the middle through which the head was passed, and wide sleeve-openings.

The houses of the better sort were built of clay derived from the huge red anthills[2] of the country;

[1] Even at the present day many people, chiefly women, of the western-most part of Africa, may be seen wearing the horns of rams slung round them by chains or necklaces. The tip of the horn is frequently inlaid with silver or encased in a silver setting, and the broad end of the horn has a silver stopping. Inside these horns are rammed various nastinesses supposed to contain wonderful magic properties. In the days of Jobson and Mungo Park it is probable that the wearing of these horns was only confined to the Mandingo people of the interior, but now they are worn even amongst the savage tribes of the forests along the West African coast.

[2] These steeple-like eminences of twenty feet or more in height are really the homes of the termite, or "white ant", which is an insect quite different from the real ant.

the lesser people made their huts of reeds. Each town or settlement of any size was surrounded by a fortification of sticks and tree trunks, topped here and there by little turrets from which archers could shoot arrows at the enemy.

The Mandingos usually ate but one big meal a day, and that at sundown; and after this when night fell they would beat drums, shout, whoop, and sing. This, Jobson tells us, was not done entirely out of satisfaction at a good square meal, and because they were merry and not inclined to sleep, but for the reason that in those days when they had only bows and arrows and spears as weapons they went in terror of their lives from the attacks of lions, leopards, and large spotted hyenas.

Just as I myself have witnessed in Nyasaland years ago, so in this part of Senegambia lions were very bold. They would prowl round the fences of the towns or villages at night, attempting to find some weak place where they could either scramble over or force their way through. Then they would leap on to the thatched roof of some house, tear open the thatch, and come down with a plop into the middle of the sleeping people, perhaps a number of young persons using the same dwelling, or a husband and wife, or a mother with her child. They would kill right and left with their terrible paws and fangs, and then break out once more, dragging with them the body of a man, woman, or child, which they would scrunch up in the first open place they could reach. Leopards (whom Jobson calls ounces, though the ounce is really

the name for the large Snow Leopard of Central
Asia) were almost equally bloodthirsty, but they
made their attacks chiefly to obtain goats, sheep,
or dogs, and less with the idea of killing or eating
a human being. But the large hyenas were sometimes as much dreaded as the lions, and even at
the present day in the same countries are spoken
of by the natives with awe. They have tremendous
teeth, and more crushing power in their jaws even
than a lion. Of course they cannot leap like a
lion or a leopard, and are not nearly so brave, but
they can scratch with their fore legs and partly
burrow through the thin reed or thatch wall of a
house. They are not so easily seen as the other
beasts, their movements being very stealthy and
silent. Some travellers, indeed, have thought that
the Spotted Hyena of these West African countries
between the Gambia, the Niger, and the Senegal,
is larger in size and fiercer than the other hyenas
of Africa; more like the large Cave Hyena which
swarmed in distant prehistoric days in England,
France, and Spain, and was no doubt a dangerous
enemy to the naked savages of Europe many
thousand years ago.

So that the terrible din kept up by the men and
women through much of the night was partly made
to drive away the wild beasts, whom it certainly
did scare. In the same way they were obliged to
keep awake so as to maintain the watch fires, which
were also a deterrent to wild beasts. But for the
fires, the torches, and the clamour, not only would
lions, leopards, and hyenas break in and devour

the people or their domestic animals; but herds of elephants, after trampling through the plantations and perhaps destroying all the people's crops, were quite ready, from sheer wantonness, to smash the houses and trample the people.   The hippopotamus did likewise great damage to the crops unless he was driven off by fire, but of course would never think of venturing through any defences into a town.   Nevertheless, any native who might cross his path at night ran the risk of being bitten in half by the tremendous tusks and wide jaws of the angry beast, frightened that his retreat to the water was going to be cut off.

Then, too, it was not only wild beast enemies they sought to scare by clamour and fire: they were equally afraid of the unseen world, of devils and evil spirits, goblins, vampires, witches, and such-like horrors; not all imagination, as you might think, but founded on this element of fact: that amongst the black people themselves there were terrible cannibals, poisoners, and even mesmerists. Some of the men and women—I do not think this is mentioned by Jobson, but it is recorded by early Arab writers about this part of West Africa, and has been actually substantiated by many recent explorers of other parts of Africa, including the writer of this book—were possessed of horrible tastes.   They not only liked to eat human flesh, and would waylay (as they do in the south-eastern part of Sierra Leone at the present day) lonely men and women and children at night, kill them, cook them, and eat them, and pretend afterwards that they had been slain by leopards or lions; but they even preferred to eat those who were already dead, and would steal out at night to the burial places, dig up some corpse recently interred, divide it amongst their friends, eat a portion, and perhaps hide the rest away for future consumption. These were the people who are described as "ghouls" in the *Arabian Nights*, and this is one reason why there is such a horror of sorcery throughout Africa, because a sorcerer—even at the present day—as likely as not—is a corpse-eater, or a real vampire— that is to say, a person who will strive to suck blood from the veins of his or her victim.

All the stories of ogres, witches, vampires, and ghouls, with which you have been thrilled from the age at which it was safe to let you read about such dreadful things—safe because you knew these crea- tures no longer existed in England, or wherever your comfortable home was—were not all imagina- tion. They were based on real things which occurred within the experience of the prehistoric peoples of Europe (who recorded their legends, first from father to son and mother to child, and latterly by means of writing); and also on what used to occur, and even still occurs, in Africa, and which attracted the attention, firstly, of the early Arab travellers and writers, and latterly, of European explorers. It is probable that under the govern- ment of the French no such horrible things take place in the Senegambia to-day; and the towns which were visited by Jobson (some of which still exist) no longer need their defences to keep out wild beasts, nor their watchfulness at night to frustrate the evil purposes of wicked human beings.

As soon as the first crowing of the cocks showed that dawn was not far off, all this noise and hubbub in the towns and villages would cease, and the people would retire to their huts and fall into a profound sleep, not waking perhaps till the sun was actually above the horizon. Negroes are not ordinarily fond of getting up and going out before the sun has risen, because the dew falls very heavily in Africa. So heavy is it in many parts that you might think there had been a great downpour of rain. The herbage is weighed down with the pearly drops of water, and anyone passing through it would experience a cold shower bath. At this time the native feels uncommonly chilly, and prefers to wait until the sun has quickly dried up the moisture and dispersed the morning mists, which at some seasons of the year reproduce all the effects of a London fog without its element of yellow smoke. This heavy morning sleep, which so arrested Jobson's attention, has played a considerable part in African war tactics.

The great predatory tribes and warlike peoples which, unchecked by the white man, would keep all Africa in a state of unrest, make a special point of attacking their victims just at the dawn; when, after dancing, singing, and beating drums all night, they will be sunk into a profound slumber. Africans do not like fighting at night. They are timid of the darkness, which conceals pitfalls and barbed stakes. They prefer to wait till it is dawn and then take their foes completely by surprise. It is extraordinary how often these attacks succeed. It seems almost impossible for the negro, uninfluenced by the white man, to maintain enough discipline to keep sentries on guard after the small hours of the early morning. Though their life and that of their fellow countrymen depend on it, they must go to sleep as dawn approaches.

However, once up, in the pleasant, early-morning sunshine, the people would be brisk enough. They were not bothered with the elaborate toilettes which we have to perform in our civilization. But they were then in Jobson's day, and are now, far more particular about cleaning their teeth than is many a British boy or girl. They do this, indeed, after every meal, and all day long at intervals, and for this purpose carry about with them tooth-sticks, pieces of a fibrous wood which grows all over negro Africa, the ends of which fray out so that they become rather like a coarse toothbrush.

When they rise in the morning they will wash out their mouths, and perhaps splash a little water over their faces, cough and spit a good deal more than is pleasant or proper, stretch themselves, and then put on what simple clothes they wear—there is no bother about socks and shoes, and underlinen and stiff shirts, and collars and collar studs, and stays and ties; and no idea whatever of brushing the hair, in the early morning at any rate. If it was a Mandingo man who was rising, he would put on his loose trousers and slip his feet into the leather sandals, pass his head through the round hole in

the middle of his voluminous shirt or tobe, and
the arms through the sleeve holes, and there he
was, fully dressed.

The garments of the women in this region in
Jobson's day (and in our own) were scantier. They
usually wore nothing above the waist, unless they
were the wives of kings or chiefs, when their
shoulders might be swathed with a handsome
piece of cloth.

Except for munching a cob of roasted maize or
eating a banana or two, the men, women, or children had little of a breakfast. The men would go
out to hunt or fish, or conduct their commerce, or
visit their flocks and herds, or pursue whatever
avocation they had adopted. If they were slaves,
they attended to their master's cattle, or built
houses for him, or worked in the fields. The
women, if they were poor, or if they were slaves,
would also go to work in the fields, nearly all
the raising of the crops being done by them and
not by the men. The young women would go to
fetch water for their households, the older women
would grind corn and attend to their provision of
household food or to their young children. Other
women would make pots out of red clay, or proceed to bake the pots, if they were not contented
merely with having them dried in the sun. Everybody could find something to do between 6.30
and the middle of the day; for although the negro
is rather a fitful worker, he does not really like
being idle. When he is accused of idleness by
the white man, it generally means that either he

wants to work for himself, or that he does not care for the kind of work set for him by his white employer; but not that he likes all day long to sit still and do nothing.

During the heat of the day, from noon till about four in the afternoon, most of the men and women would certainly retire to their verandahs or the inside of their houses and go to sleep. The children, perhaps, might amuse themselves down by the river at various childish games. After four o'clock everybody would be up and doing. The women, above all, would be setting to work to prepare the great meal of the day, which would be eaten at sundown, the men eating first and the women and children afterwards. This meal, amongst the people described by Jobson, would consist in the main of boiled rice, with an appetizing relish something like curry; for the Arabs long ago had introduced rice into these regions from India. Nowadays they use Indian corn (maize) a great deal, but this excellent food is native to America, and was not introduced into Africa by the Portuguese until just before the time that Jobson was exploring the Upper Gambia.

If not boiled rice, then the substance of the meal would have been a thick porridge made of the flour of a large millet that is generally called *sorghum*. These sorghum grains are about the size of very large shot. They are ground between two stones, perhaps having been first softened in water. All over Africa, negroes are very fond of eating a thick stirabout made from the flour of sorghum grain or the smaller kinds of millet (*Pennisetum*). Where the meal consisted mainly of porridge, or of boiled rice, it would always be accompanied by little dishes of dainties—one dish would be a kind of boiled spinach, another would be boiled fish or fried fish; a well-to-do man might have stewed pigeons, or even occasionally stewed fowl; and from something or other might be made up a thick sauce or gravy. They would take up the rice or the porridge with their fingers, and make a large ball in this way, dip the balls into the relish or sauce, and swallow them, helping themselves alternately to little dishes of vegetables, fish, or fowl. The Fulbe and the Moors, or any wandering Arabs, would consume large quantities of rancid butter with this rice or porridge. Perhaps the Arabs or the Moors would bake rough dampers of flour, some sort of a cake, to eat with their butter and meat. They would drink large quantities of milk, but generally when it had purposely been made sour, for fresh milk is not thought wholesome by Africans. Every now and again a sheep or a goat or an ox would be killed, or the hunters would bring in the bodies of antelopes or wild pigs, and the people would have a thorough feast of meat, eating very often until they yelled with indigestion afterwards. Many an early explorer of Africa—and I myself—have seen negroes eating until they shrieked with indigestion. When this stage had been reached they would lie down on their backs and ask one of their friends to walk up and down on the suffering part of their body, and this extraordinary cure used actually to take away the pain and the indigestion!

But if they would at times, when meat was plentiful, gorge till they nearly burst, the same men and women could stand hunger better than a European; and though they might only have one big meal in the whole twenty-four hours, they generally were able to put by snacks for consumption at odd moments, whilst in most of the plantations there were banana groves yielding freely that delicious fruit which is so strongly praised by Jobson, who calls it "bonano".

The banana we are now so familiar with, and can buy in most British towns and villages for a penny or a halfpenny each, originally came from West Africa (as well as from Southern Asia). The name *banana* is a West African word. The plant was introduced by the Spaniards and Portuguese into the Canary Islands and the West Indies, where it soon grew so abundantly that many people think it is native to the West Indies, which is not the case.

With their meals these Africans, living as they did in Jobson's day, only drank water; but water was not their only beverage, even before the European introduced brandy, rum, or gin. They would brew a kind of beer from crushed grain, which had previously been soaked so as to induce germination. This in taste would be rather like a very thin, sour porridge, as much inclined—but no more—to go to one's head as a rather poor English ale. Of course, in a way, it was meat and drink in one. In some districts honey would be collected, mixed with water, and allowed to ferment, and the people would drink the same thing as the mead of our Saxon ancestors; or in other districts bananas would be pulped, and the liquid (tasting, when fresh, like melted pear-drops) kept till fermentation had made it sour and effervescent.

But their chief intoxicating drink was "palm wine". This is the sap derived from various kinds of palm—the oil palm, the wild date, and the fan palms. At first the taste (to a European) is perfectly delicious. It is like a sublime ginger beer, and fizzes and froths much in the same way. You feel, if you are thirsty and new to it, that you could drink and drink, and still drink again. Perhaps the nectar of Greek mythology was derived from some idea of palm wine. But a little of it goes a long way, and the European who takes too much gets a violent headache. The natives do not care for it when it is fresh and sweet, but put it aside to ferment, and then it is like the nastiest claret that you have ever tasted. But in this condition it is consumed in large quantities by men and women, and often makes them quarelsome or maudlin.

Curiously enough, Jobson, in his interesting narrative, says little or nothing about the oil palm. This important tree does not grow freely on the Upper Gambia, it is true, but it is abundant near the mouth of that river. Its nuts produce a thick, orange-coloured oil, which is very good to the taste, something like cocoanut, and as a flavouring for stews or soups it is one of the most appetizing things you could taste, though indulgence in it makes one rather bilious. Whenever I am very hungry, I wish before all things I could sit down to a West African palm-oil soup. To the oil a certain amount of water is added, and in this mixture fowls, pieces of mutton or goat, or other meat are slowly stewed, together with a quantity of yams, red peppers, okroes (a slimy but delicious bud of a large mallow), and the whole thing is served up in an immense bowl, or the largest pot that can be obtained. It is a beautiful golden colour, and frothy, as though eggs were put into it, and the taste of soup, meat, and vegetables is richer and better that anything you can obtain in our own land.

The oil palm also provides the best of all the palm wines, and its fronds are used to thatch roofs and houses. But where you get palm oil you very seldom get milk, because, as a rule, the cows will not live in the hot, damp countries where the oil palm likes to grow; and the sort of food in general that was eaten by Jobson's friends on the Upper Gambia is a little more like what one would get in North Africa than in West Africa. But even then you would not do at all badly if you trusted entirely to the food and cooking of the natives; and, of course, in Jobson's day they really ate and drank as well as he and his men did in England. For if you were asked to sit down to-day to the sort of meal that was eaten by Queen Elizabeth or James I, you would feel very disinclined to touch anything at all. The cooking would be coarse and greasy, and everything would be made disgusting with spice, pepper, garlic, and other strong flavours.

In Jobson's narrative no mention is made of the Moorish merchants drinking coffee. Nowadays in Senegambia these people attach as much importance to their black coffee, heavily sweetened with sugar, as they do elsewhere throughout the Muhammadan world. But although the Gambia regions that Jobson passed through abounded with wild coffee trees, he had probably never heard of such a beverage, and the natives of those countries only knew the coffee tree or shrub as a thing which produced sweet berries, of which they ate the pulp and threw away the stones. That these stones, if roasted and ground, would make a fragrant and stimulating drink was a fact apparently only discovered some centuries before by the Abyssinians, who introduced the plant and the custom of drinking its ground berries to the Arabs, from whom it spread, during the seventeenth century, throughout the civilized world. But coffee-drinking did not become common in West Africa until the nineteenth century, and even at the present day there are many tribes who have wild coffee growing in their forests who have not the least notion of how easily they might obtain a drink which is as stimulating and far more wholesome than their palm wine or the bad spirits they buy from Europeans.

Jobson not only tells us much about the eating

and drinking of the Mandingos, Fulas, and Moors, but he repeatedly refers to their love of music. He talks of the "juddies"[1] or fiddlers. I doubt very very much if he met with people who produced music by drawing a stick or bow across the strings of an instrument, but they certainly had in his day what they have now: several kinds of stringed instruments which they play with the fingers; also flutes, and an arrangement of wooden slabs fastened over cup-like gourds. These slabs are tapped with heavy sticks, and the wood gives out the most melodious sounds. Some of the Mandingo music is really pretty even to our ears, as there are very distinct tunes amongst the melodies that are played, tunes that are remembered and repeated by the players. In that country no man of any importance goes about without a band of music, and all the religious festivals and great occurrences are accompanied by the playing of instruments and the beating of drums. Except during the hours of great heat in the middle of the day, the whole country may be said to throb with music—I am referring, of course, to those regions of the Upper Gambia visited by Jobson, for in the districts of dense forest along the coast not nearly so much native music is heard, except the sullen or angry beating of drums. This musical character of Mandingo life makes much of West Africa a very cheerful country to live in, except for those of acute nerves who cannot sleep at night for the noise that is going on.

[1] This word farther to the east becomes *jilli* or *jelli*.

As to the religion of the people amongst whom
he travelled, they seem to have been mainly Muhammadans, but, like most African Muhammadans,
they had a great belief in magic and in the wearing
of charms or amulets.   These are called locally
"gri-gris", a word which Jobson corrupted into
"gregories".   These amulets or charms consisted
of little pieces of parchment or paper on which
some holy man has written in Arabic characters
a few words or a text in the Koran, but, as mentioned later on in the book, in the regions where
paganism is still powerful the gri-gris may be a
small bone of some animal or bird, dried leaves, a
peculiar stone, part of a human bone, or some nasti-
ness of hair and blood mixed with the glue-like sap
of a tree.   But whatever is the real contents of
the amulet, it is enclosed in an outer case of
leather, very neatly made, sometimes extremely
ornamental, and this leather packet, large or small,
is fastened to a wire ring or to a string, or a long
cord of plaited leather, and thus these charms are
hung all about the body: round the neck almost
in festoons, round the forehead, the arms, the
chest, or the stomach.   They even fasten amulets
round the necks of their horses, or on to their
bows, swords, or other weapons.

The religious practices introduced by the Muhammadans as recorded by Jobson—except the
superstition about the amulets—were of a reverent
and even beautiful character.   The marabut, or
Muhammadan holy man (whom Jobson calls the
marybucke), would attend all ceremonies and func-

tions of life, departures on journeys and returns, births, deaths, and marriages, and would distribute his blessings to those most concerned, blessings which were greeted reverently with the utterance "Amena, Amena"—a word which Jobson rightly identified with our "Amen", and this, as you know, is derived from the Hebrew. Jobson soon realized that these marabuts, like himself, were acquainted with Hebrew history. This knowledge they derived from the Koran, just as he obtained his from the Bible. And this community of knowledge made their relations much more friendly.

Yet he jumps to the conclusion that the God they worship cannot be the same as the God of the Christians, but must be a devil. Of course, he is referring more to the pagan ideas of God than to those which were entertained by the Muhammadans. Many of these people of the Gambia were more than half-pagan at heart. They called the Supreme Being, *Horé*, and, like so many pagans at the present day, thought that He delegated much of his power to subordinate spirits, who would condescend to be mere policemen, as it were, to keep society in order. The people of these countries, even at the present day, fashion hideous, black, wooden masks, attached to a covering of dried grass, or some other material in strips, like coarse hair. A man gets inside this mask and garment and enters a village, making, perhaps, hideous noises with his voice, or with a wooden instrument like what the Australians call a "bull-roarer". Most of the men of the place know who the supposed devil is, but the women and children really believe it is a god or a devil coming to administer rough justice to those who have done wrong.

Mungo Park, describing the customs of the Upper Gambian people a hundred and seventy-five years later, says, "The old men of the tribe instruct the young men in certain principles and practices which they think serve to keep the common people in order, and, above all, the women. It is pretended amongst them that there is a devil or demigod which at times will visit their town and punish all persons who have misbehaved or have commited a crime. All who have not been initiated really think that this awful-looking goblin, when he appears, is a real devil, instead of being a man dressed up something like our old custom of Jack-in-the-Green."

In some parts of West Central Africa the mask worn by the bogie is like the face of a gorilla, and the mantle, made of dried grass or palm fibre and dyed black, looks very like the coarse black hair of a great anthropoid ape, so that it is possible that this custom may have originated ages ago in a real scare caused by the invasion of the village by some huge male gorilla. But if this was really the origin of the device, it has long since been forgotten in native tradition. In the region visited by Mungo Park, he says that these policemen-devils are chiefly employed in punishing the women for misdemeanours, and that they were

THE "DEVIL" VISITING A MANDINGO TOWN

called "Mumbo-jumbo", words which have long
since entered the English language to describe
the procedure of some heathenish god. But this
dressed-up man or woman, posing as a bogie, is
called by many different names in each different
tribe of West Africa. Their visit (for sometimes
they are two or three in number) always takes
the village by surprise, though, of course, it is a
pre-arranged affair amongst the leaders. They
are fully aware beforehand of what they have to
do, the persons they must seize and punish, the
accusations they are to make of witchcraft or
theft, and so forth. Their approach is heralded
sometimes by the mysterious booming sound caused
by whirling the "bull-roarer" in the air. They
also utter loud and bloodcurdling screams in some
patch of forest near the town, if their visit is
timed for the approach of night. As soon as it
is dark the devil (or devils) enter the village and
proceed to the public meeting-place in the centre
of it—generally the great thatched roof without
sides, sheltering a space of hard, smooth clay.
Here the bogie instals himself, and then summons
to his presence by name the delinquents whom he
wishes to punish. By this time he is surrounded
by people wishing to display their own perfect
innocence in loud singing and obstreperous dancing. His victims, however, on being named, are
immediately seized, if they can be found, and
stripped naked, tied to a post, and then severely
flogged with rods, amidst the shouts and derision
of the whole assembly. It is usually the women

who are made to suffer, and instead of their being defended by the other women, the latter join eagerly with the male tormenters.

But sometimes in Mandingoland Horé did not appear in any bodily shape, but was consulted by means of divination. The "wise" men would kill fowls and look at the movements of the entrails, or throw down corn and see how many grains (and what grains) were picked up by the cocks, just as the Romans used to do. They would play with sand and make guesses of what was meant by the way in which the sand formed itself into shapes, or draw lots, or pass into a mesmeric trance. The people who made it a profession of consulting their god in this way were always very clever and quick at picking up information or making happy guesses, and no doubt they had spies all over the country who sent them information rapidly. Often the answers of these oracles were framed to suit the tastes of those who applied to them. But sometimes their prophecies were quite remarkable.

How the negro diviners could do this, I cannot say; but Jobson was astonished to find men at the court of the Mandingo kings whom he visited, telling him more or less precisely what had happened to his ship and his comrades farther down the river, and other matters in which he was deeply interested, though they were occurring at a distance of two or three hundred miles from where he was.

Jobson has much to say about the strange birds, beasts, and plants of this part of West Africa, though he does not always call them by the names

with which we are now familiar. As to the smaller
eagles, kites, and buzzards, he remarks that one of
them—probably the short-tailed Bateleur Eagle—
pounces sometimes with his claws on the face of
an antelope, or on the back of its head, and beats
his wings over the creature's eyes until it is dazed
and exhausted; whereupon the eagle is able to
attack the vital parts with his beak and claws.
He was much impressed by the vultures, though
he takes them to be some kind of kite or buzzard,
and says that they smell "wondrous sweet and
strong, after the savour of the crocodile"! He
notes the way in which the natives often find the
carcass of an elephant or some other large animal
lying dead in the forest by means of the concourse
of vultures flocking to the feast. He observed the
bee-eaters (though he does not remark on their
most beautiful plumage of crimson and azure blue)
who make holes "as artificially round, like auger
holes", for their nests in the steep high banks of
the river, each hole of an equal distance from the
others and a yard deep.

I have already mentioned that apparently he
and his men, together with the negroes of the
country, were willing to eat the nasty-smelling
flesh of the great marabou stork. But he also
mentions the Crowned crane, which he calls a
"Wake . . . in regard to the great noise which he
makes when he flieth". The crowned cranes of
West Africa are very beautiful birds, but not so
handsome perhaps as they are in Central and South
Africa. The kind which is seen on the Gambia is

smaller, the face has red wattles instead of white, the crown on the top of the head is like an aigrette of golden strings growing out of a mass of black velvet. Much of the plumage is dark slaty-black, but the wings are deep chestnut-red, and over the wings and back there hang long delicate feathers of creamy-white tipped with gold.

He notes the abundance of guinea fowl, of "partridges"—which are properly called francolins —and of wild pigeons; but in his day the people had no tame pigeons, as they have now. From his narrative, you would think that there were grey parrots with red tails to be found in this country; but here he has made a mistake. If he saw any, they were only tame birds brought from distant parts of West Africa farther to the east. But he saw the little green love-birds, with red foreheads and tails, and the ring-necked, long-tailed, green para- keets; perhaps also some small parrots that were dun colour, blue, and yellow. "One bird", he says, "has no legs, only two strings in his body, by means of which he hangs with his head downwards, thus resembling a dead leaf." It is very likely that this strange bird was nothing but a *bat*, which would be about that colour, and would hang from a branch by one or both of its hind legs! There is a fruit-eating bat of West Africa, which is a creature of awful hideousness; but the natives sometimes eat it after skinning the body carefully, for the skins of these goblin-headed fruit bats contain scent glands which exude a bad-smelling, oily substance.

Jobson thought that he had discovered another

wonder, "a strange bird . . . which flieth with
four wings; we see him not at all the day but an
hour before night. His two foremost wings are
largest, and the others are a pretty distance back-
ward, . . . a bird about the bigness of a turtle-
dove." This marvel, I should think, was probably
the remarkable pennant-winged goatsucker of West
Africa, in which one of the pinion feathers of the
wing is prolonged into a lengthy plume. As the
bird skims with an undulating flight through the
air at dusk, it really does strike the observer that
he has two pairs of wings, as these floating plumes
seem to proceed from the sides of the body. But
there is another goatsucker found to the north of
the Gambia region in which the tail feathers are
prolonged till they look like a second pair of wings.

As to the wild beasts, Jobson gives information
which is not only interesting, but remarkably accurate for the period in which he writes, when travellers were frequently unobservant and content to
invent stories of the strange animals they had met,
or to believe fables that were told them by the
natives. He deals first with the lion, which existed
then, and is occasionally found now along the
Upper Gambia, though it is totally absent from
all that part of West and Central Africa which is
heavily forested. He notes the apparent alliance
between the lion and the jackals; and the jackal
of which he writes may have been akin to the black,
grey, and orange-coloured jackals of South and
North-east Africa. This he calls "the small servant" of the lion, "which so soon as the evening

comes, hunts and bustles about for the prey, and coming on the foot, follows the scent with open cry, to which the lion being master huntsman gives diligent care". If it should so happen that the jackal is weary of waiting, or sets up his chase before the lion comes, he sends up doleful howls to urge the lion to hurry. "Then comes the haughty lion and seizeth on the weary prey." If, says Jobson, the lion fails to seize his prey after the third leap, he scorns to pursue or to fatigue himself by toiling after it; having succeeded in felling the object of his attack, he at once starts eating it, "making a kind of grumbling noise". Meantime "the small servant" stands barking and yelping by, waiting till the lion has satisfied his hunger. Then he too falls on the remainder. Thus a partnership seems to have grown up between the lion and the jackal, much the same, no doubt, as arose in early days between our wild human ancestors and the wild dogs or wolves which assisted the carnivorous human savages to run down the deer or bison, and then stood at a respectful distance till the men had satisfied their hunger or carried off large chunks of the meat for cooking.

The Gambia countries, according to Jobson, were full of "ounces" and leopards. He either gave two different names to the same animal, or quite possibly by the word ounce he meant what we now call a leopard, and by "leopard" that beautiful hunting cat known by its Indian name Chita (Cheetah). The chita, which is in reality very different from a real leopard and also from other cats, is about the same size as the leopard, only with much longer legs, with a very long, heavily-plumed tail, and a head which is short in the muzzle and more like the head of a lynx. The chita, which is found all over Northern and North-Central Africa, and also in Africa south of the Zambesi, runs down its prey in the open, just as dogs or wolves might do, and does not seek to catch it, like the leopard or the lion, by hiding and then springing. The leopards of the English king's coat-of-arms were really chitas or hunting leopards brought back from Syria by the Crusaders as a great curiosity.

It is possible also that by "leopard" Jobson may have meant not only the chita, but the large Serval cats, which are also long legged, spotted with single spots, and pursue their prey by running. The real leopard or panther is Jobson's " ounce". He remarks on its boldness and the fact that it is more dangerous in some districts than the lion; but we are led to infer from his story that it is rather more inclined to carry off children than grown-up men and women.

The great civet-cat is mentioned by Jobson as a creature that comes prowling around the houses to carry off the negroes' domestic fowls. This African civet produces, like the Indian civet, a substance found in a pouch in the skin which has a strong and—some people think—a very fragrant scent. This substance, indeed, enters into a great many perfumes more or less fashionable at the present day. In the Middle Ages, and down to the eighteenth century, well-to-do people in England and France liked the scent of the civet or the musk of the musk deer unadulterated, and dandies used to perfume themselves with civet till they must have smelt like wild animals. One of the earliest substances for which the Portuguese, French, and English traded with West Africa, including the Gambia, was these packets of dried civet obtained from the gland in this creature's skin. But Jobson also notices the porcupine, and accuses it likewise of carrying off fowls! This was a mistake on his part, for the innocent porcupine is a distant cousin of the squirrel and the rabbit, and only uses its gnawing and grinding teeth to eat up roots, nuts, and leaves.

Jobson was much impressed with the elephant, which in those days was abundant in the regions of the Upper Gambia (before the natives had guns). But he evidently did not get near enough to observe it very closely, or he would not have told us that his two great teeth are commonly set in his *lower* jaw. In all elephants which exist on the earth to-day —there are only two kinds, the Indian and the African—the great incisor tusks which furnish the ivory of commerce grow out of the upper jaw, and answer exactly to the outer pair of our upper incisor teeth. The way in which he describes the elephant bending down the top of a tree with his trunk, and using his tusks as a lever to break off the top or to root up the tree, is quite truthful; and he justly remarks that it is this use of the great tusks which so often results in their being cracked or broken.

ELEPHANTS DESTROYING A PALM GROVE

Most of the English people of his day thought the elephant shed its tusks periodically, as deer do their antlers.   But, of course, where the elephant is not killed on purpose, and the tusks removed from the skull, ivory can only be obtained by picking up fragments of broken tusks, or by chancing upon some place where elephants have died from an accident or extreme old age.   There are said to be places in Africa whither elephants resort when they are old and enfeebled, and where at last they lie down and die.   But elephants often meet with accidents; perhaps their very weight in wet weather may provoke a landslide on the side of a hill which may carry them over a precipitous cliff and dash them to pieces, or break their necks, spines, or limbs.   It is still a common incident in Africa for elephants to get bogged in the marshes, so completely stuck in the mud, that they are either drowned by a rise of the water, or starve where they stand, and gradually get buried in the mud or vegetation.   This is how those carcasses of mammoths have been preserved to us in Siberia, and most of the remains of extinct elephants which have taught us so much about the ancient history of this order are derived from animals which got stuck in a morass.

The negroes of the Upper Gambia in Jóbson's time, having no guns, were usually timid about pursuing the elephant, even when it came and ravaged their crops; but if there was a very brave hunter amongst them he would select a strong assagai or javelin—a throwing spear—and cover its iron, barbed head with a thick, poisonous substance derived probably from the seeds or sap of certain trees.   He would then creep and crawl through the grass till he got close enough to one of the elephants, where he could throw his spear with certainty of its penetrating the animal's body, probably one of its legs.   This poison would soon take effect, and a few hours afterwards the elephant would be found lying dead not far from the place where it had been struck.   Then the negroes would assemble, cut away the flesh where it was inflamed by the poison, and find the rest of the meat of this huge body quite fit for consumption. Afterwards would follow days of gorging on elephant's meat, till, as I have already told you, the people cried out with indigestion and had to get their friends to trample on their bodies.

Jobson mentions the buffaloes as being like wild bulls, which, of course, in a general way they are.   The buffaloes which he saw or heard of are of a dark blackish-brown colour, with not very long but rather sharp horns, which, besides being abruptly recurved, are rather flat along the greater part of their length, though they terminate in sharp points.   These black-brown buffaloes of the Gambia are quite different to the reddish-coloured buffaloes of the Gold Coast, Southern Nigeria, and the Congo Basin.   In these last, though the horns are very broad, flat, and wrinkled over the forehead, they are quite short, and are shaped almost like a long flattened pear.   The Gambia buffaloes are halfway between this type and the great black buffalo of South, Central, and East Africa, where the horns make a huge boss over the forehead, and the tips are sharply curved back. None of these buffaloes as they exist to-day are so grand as the extinct ones of North Africa and South Africa. These must have had broad horns that were 14 feet in length from base to tip!

Amongst the antelopes of the Upper Gambia, Jobson notices one, the hide of which was 14 feet in length, of a dun colour, and striped with white. This was evidently the great eland of West Africa, called the Derbian Eland, after that Earl of Derby who lived in the middle of the nineteenth century, and who, besides being famous as a statesman and prime minister, was also remarkable because he kept a magnificent zoological garden in his park at Knowsley in Lancashire. This Lord Derby used to send out men to collect wild animals for him all over the world, and especially to the regions of the Gambia, and that is why so many beasts and birds are called after him, either by his title or by his family name—Stanley.

The big eland of the Gambia, and its near relation, which is found in the western part of the Egyptian Sudan, is one of the most magnificent beasts that Africa produces, but it is so rare and shy (living only in dense thickets) that it is very seldom shot by European sportsmen, and no specimen has ever been exhibited alive in the Zoological Gardens. It is larger than the eland of South and East Africa (though that is a very big animal, as you can see in zoological gardens), and it has longer horns than the common eland. The Derbian Eland is not so much a dun colour as Jobson states, but the greater part of its body is a beautiful golden - brown with yellow stripes and a white edging to the limbs. There is a broad white stripe between the shoulders and the neck; and the neck and nose are brownish-black. There is a black patch on each fore limb.

Jobson might also have seen or heard of giraffes, for they inhabit the upper Gambia. Perhaps they were not in this country at the time of his visit — the winter season — but may have gone to other regions better supplied with vegetation. However, he noticed the wart hogs, which he describes as "Wild Boars, very huge and great, their colour being a dark blue . . . armed with great and large tusks, and carrying up their tufted tails of a great length, bolt upright, in a scornful manner". This is a very true description, though it has only been realized quite of late years that these fantastic-looking wart hogs do carry their tails in this eccentric fashion when they are excited or angry. In Jobson's day their thick hides, bare except for strong bristles along the back, were almost impenetrable to a native lance or arrow, and as the natives had no guns, the wart hogs did pretty much as they liked, and, if approached, merely walked away, did not run or attempt to bolt into the empty burrow of an ant-bear, as they would do nowadays.

Jobson pressed the Gambia people hard as to the existence of the unicorn in their country; for in those days the adventurers and explorers of Europe believed much more firmly in the existence of unicorns, dragons, and phœnixes than perhaps in a giraffe or a zebra. The story of the unicorn—a creature described as of the build and size of a horse, mainly white with blackish markings, a mane, a tufted tail like the cow's, and a single, twisted, annulated or spiral horn growing out of the forehead—was chiefly derived from some oryx-antelope of Arabia or North-east Africa, combined with a muddled account of the rhinoceros.

There are oryxes in the north of the Gambia region, but they are not of the unicorn type with the straight horns set close together. They are what is called the Leucoryx, in which the horns are gracefully curved. The natives of the Gambia seem to have described the leucoryx to Jobson, and at the same time to have mentioned the existence of the rhinoceros far away to the north-east, and therefore the description he gives of the supposed unicorn of the Gambia is a mixture between the two animals.

He and his men were perhaps more impressed with the baboons and the monkeys than with anything else they met with in the way of wild animals. He describes the trees of great bulk, which bear on a long stalk a large round fruit, yielding a kind of pleasant pith, on which the baboons and monkeys used to feed. These trees "are so big that six men, by extending their arms, cannot meet in encompassing one tree". In this he is referring to the immense baobabs of Tropical Africa. The pith of the large fruit is white or pinkish, and most agreeable to the taste after you can get over the first shudder, caused by its dryness. Chewed in the mouth, this pith not only provokes saliva and stays thirst, but tastes like concentrated lemonade. Frequently in the open country that borders the forests of West Africa, baboons and monkeys break open the rind of the baobab fruits and eat the acid pith.

There were many other fruits and nuts in the Gambia countries on which the monkeys fed. Some of the trees will have disappeared by now to give place to plantations of cotton and corn, and with their disappearance the baboons and monkeys will have gone too. In Jobson's day the huge baboons—the males having immense heads and lion‑like bodies — went in great herds and companies, as many as three or four hundred together. Jobson observed that they maintained a kind of commonwealth as in some human tribe, that they had leaders whose directions they obeyed. There might be amongst them one greater in size than all the others, like a lion in appearance, who would be styled by him and his men "the Commaunder" or "Maister Constable". The females of the herd carried their young on the under side of their bodies, the young one clinging to the mother's hair by his fists and feet. Some females apparently had, twins, and then one young one would cling to the back, whilst the other one held on below. The females generally

went with the few big males, in the fore part of
the caravan. The rearguard consisted of a great
company of young male baboons, "as a guard
against any pursuing enemy". They were very
bold, and if Jobson and his men were passing in
their boat on the river, the baboons would get
into trees to stare at them, and in a "kind of
choleric humour" the great ones would shake the
trees and clatter the branches in such a fashion
as could scarcely have been done by a strong man.
At the same time they would bark and make a
noise as if they were much offended. At nighttime they would assemble on the banks and set
up a great noise of many voices together until
"instantly one great voice exalts itself, and presently all are hushed and the noise is dashed, so
that we were wont to say, 'Maister Constable
speaks'".

If the party was travelling by land and met
these troops in the daytime, the bigger baboons
would come forward and grin in their faces, but
if a gun were aimed at them they would bolt.
Yet if one of their number was killed the others
would rush forward, pick it up, and carry it away.
Jobson relates that in the wilderness he has seen
places resorted to by these baboons in which the
branches of the trees and plants were wound together in an artificial manner and so thickly inter-
woven overhead as to keep away the sun, while
the ground of these shady places had been beaten
and smoothed. These places he declared were
used by the baboons for dancing and recreation,

and any man seeing such places would have at first believed they were made by man.

It is quite possible that the baboons of the Gambia, existing then in such large herds, may have done this; but it is also possible that Jobson is here mixing up an account of what he or others may have observed in connection with the chimpanzee; for that great anthropoid ape is still found in the region of the Gambia to the east and south of the river. Chimpanzees do seem to be able to construct some kind of an arbour or shade by arranging the branches of trees and boughs of leaves, and they are also fond of making smooth places where they can stamp and carry on a rude kind of dancing, which they accompany with great shouts and screams.

CHAPTER III
Pioneers on the Upper Niger

BUT although Jobson brought back such an in-
teresing and truthful account of the West African
interior, he had very little to show in the way of
successful commerce, and the great merchants who
sent him out appear to have been disappointed
with the results of their venture. He was evidently
conscious of this when writing his book, at the
close of which he proposes that he should now go
off on an expedition to Russia. The Gambia was
left alone after this until the last quarter of the
seventeenth century; then once more British traders
went there for the purpose of buying slaves to be
dispatched to Jamaica and North America. During
the eighteenth century which followed, British adventurers turned their attention much more to the
Gold Coast, from which the gold was exported to
make the English guineas (the name of which
shows the region from which the gold was obtained[1]). They also traded with Benin and the

[1] An account of the foundations of the modern Gold Coast Colony is
given in Chapter VII. British trading settlements on the Gambia increased
very much during the eighteenth century, and in 1783 the French Government recognized the Gambia river as a district under the exclusive control
of British merchants. In the early nineteenth century the Gambia was
taken under direct Government control by Great Britain, and it is now a
possession about 4000 square miles in extent (or more than half the size
of Wales). The upper waters of the Gambia now belong to France.

Niger Delta, without knowing that it was the outlet of the mighty Niger; and they had begun to take an interest in the wonderful harbour of Sierra Leone, partly because West Africa has very few safe harbours for ships, and partly because this region was a favourable one for the slave trade.

There were two causes which made the British Government and English people think about this westernmost part of Africa towards the close of the eighteenth century. People in England were beginning to get angry about the trade in slaves, and wished not only to put a stop to it but to find some part of West Africa to which could be sent back those negroes of America or the West Indies who had acquired their freedom, but whom the laws at that time would not permit to settle down as free citizens. Then, also, Great Britain did not know where she was to send her own criminals. Throughout much of the seventeenth and eighteenth centuries, whenever there were people who had done wrong, or who were thought to have done wrong, if they had not committed a crime worthy of death, or so small that it could be met by whipping, a fine, or being placed in the stocks, or kept for a few days in prison, they were sold as slaves (practically), and transported to North America or the West Indies. Here, after a certain number of years, they acquired their freedom, and could settle down as colonists. But when we lost the United States the question was: How were our criminals to be got rid of? It was not much use sending them to the West Indies, where it was too

hot for white men and women to work all day in
the sun as negroes are able to do. The solution
of this difficulty was for a time found in the discovery and occupation of Australia, and chiefly of
Tasmania. But expeditions were also sent out to
West Africa to see if a good place could be found
there to which English criminals could be deported,
as well as free black men who were out of place in
America.

The river and the mountainous peninsula of Sierra
Leone were finally selected for these purposes. The
name, which is a corruption of the Portuguese,
means "the lion-like chain of mountains". In all
this part of West Africa the coast is very flat and
marshy as a rule, but at this point called Sierra
Leone, a bold spur of mountains, nearly three
thousand feet in height at the highest point, comes
down to the very seashore, almost making a mountainous island surrounded by water or swamp.
These lofty peaks perpetually attract clouds which
dissolve in rain and discharges of electricity—
thunderstorms, in short. The noise of the thunder,
echoing, booming, and bellowing amongst these
forested peaks, sounds so like the roaring of terrible
lions, that the Portuguese seamen hit upon a very
appropriate name. But, of course, they saw no
lion here, because the lion carefully avoids the
forest regions of Africa.

No sooner were the British settled at Sierra
Leone[1] (and besides their slave trade with the

---

[1] Sierra Leone, from a peninsula about 322 square miles in area in
1800, had grown by 1900 to an important colony and protectorate of nearly
30,000 square miles, larger than Ireland.

Gambia they conquered and held for a time the French possessions on the Senegal) than they began to hear once more those stories of a wonderful river in the far interior flowing from west to east, and perhaps ending in some great lake in the heart of Africa, or joining the River Nile. These stories were not new. They originated in traditions brought from Carthage and Egypt to Rome, and picked up by the Romans themselves from the Berbers of Numidia and of the desert (for the Roman Empire had fortified posts right down into the heart of the Sahara, and sent expeditions to the vicinity of Lake Chad). These traditions led to Pliny writing of a North-west African river, called *Nigris*, and Ptolemy of Alexandria[1]—the great Egyptian geographer who wrote at the beginning of the second century after Christ—alluding to a River *Nigeir*, also in West Africa. Ptolemy's geography was the only standard work on the subject between 150 A.D. and the sixteenth century, and it was much studied by the early Portuguese navigators of the fifteenth century. They sought for the "Nigeir", or Nigris of classical geographers, and found some clue to the existence of the Niger; but, being misinformed by the Moors and Arabs, they thought the great West African river flowing from west to east was a branch of the Nile. It was probably in the seventeenth century that Dutch and French geographers gave the name of "Niger" to this river of the Western Sudan, identifying it with the Nigeir of Ptolemy (which, however, was

[1] His correct name was Claudius Ptolemæus.

more likely to have been the Senegal). The word Nigeir comes in all probability from one of the Berber (Tuareg) names for this or for any big river; and the Libyan ancestors of the Tuareg probably carried the name and the story of the great river of Negroland to Roman North Africa.

The Niger rises just beyond the north-east frontier of Sierra Leone at no great distance from the coast, and after flowing to the north and north-east and being joined by the great Bani affluent and passing through a region of many small lakes, takes a huge bend, and, coming southwards, meets with the mighty River Benue, which flows from the east to the west. Both unite some distance from the north of what is called the Niger Delta, and then their waters find their way through many spreading channels into that great corner or gulf of West Africa known as the Bights of Benin and Biafra. Far away to the east of the main Niger is Lake Chad, divided occasionally into two big lakes and some small lakelets, but at different times in history much larger and making one huge sheet of water. Into Lake Chad flows the River Shari, which in the height of the rainy season is sometimes connected by a tributary with the River Benue. Thus it may be said that the Lake Chad basin intermittently sends its waters towards the Niger. But in the rough-and-ready geography of the Arabs, and even the Romans and Greeks before them, Lake Chad was mixed up with the Niger and the Benue.

Somehow or other—partly, no doubt, owing

to the extremely dense forests, peopled in those
ancient days by the wildest, fiercest, nakedest
cannibals—neither Arab nor European, prior to
the end of the eighteenth century, thought of the
Niger as entering the Ocean in the Gulf of Guinea.
The Arabs confused its course with that of the
Benue and Shari, and believed that it flowed eastwards till it joined the Upper Nile. On the other
hand, the early Portuguese and British adventurers
imagined that this great river of North-west Africa
flowed westwards from the Nile across the continent
and entered the sea by two mouths, the Senegal
and the Gambia. One reason why Jobson was so
keen on the exploration of the Upper Gambia was
his conviction that if he followed it far enough up
stream he would enter the main Niger.

The Niger had a fascination for the European
imagination in the eighteenth and early nineteenth
centuries. The Nile of Egypt had its Pyramids and
Sphinxes, but where the land of Egypt changed
into the land of the Blacks, the great river flowed
through a pitiless, uninteresting desert, and beyond
that nothing was known of it except the vague
legend handed down from the days of the Romans
that the Upper Nile, after traversing a region of
immense marshes, had a twin origin in two great
African lakes, between which (and the legend was
perfectly true in fact) rose the snow-crowned Mountains of the Moon.

Our forefathers were essentially practical men,
and cared at that time but little either for snow
mountains or marshes. On the other hand, the

Niger, which they called the Nile of the Negroes, apparently flowed through a land of gold, and its whole imagined course, from Lake Chád to the vicinity of the Atlantic Ocean, lay through a fruitful country with immense negro towns, manufactures of cotton goods (which to our forefathers were as wonderful as the Manchester manufactures now seem to the primitive negroes), forests of enormous trees, and plains covered with elephants and other wild beasts, valuable for their tusks, horns, or splendid skins.

Slaves who were exported from West Africa to the British West Indies, and who had come from the regions of the Upper Niger, would describe and exaggerate the wonders of that river basin. So that it became in time an acute desire on the part of thoughtful people in England to reach the Niger from the west coast and trace it to its outlet, wherever that might be. No longer was it due to a wish to get more slaves for work in America. On the contrary, all the great explorations of Africa which began at the close of the eighteenth century were brought about by an association of persons who wanted to develop commerce with Africa, not in the bodies of men and women, but in the native products of the country: ivory, gold, ebony, dye-woods, hides for making leather, oils (for oil lamps were beginning to be used in English and French houses to read by), and wax for making candles. It was thought that a profitable trade thus commenced would gradually prepare people for the extinction of the slave trade, in which, a hundred and twenty years ago, so much English capital was embarked.

The scientific men of England at that time being so very uncertain as to whether the Niger ended in Lake Chad, or flowed on in the form of the Shari till it reached the sea under the name of Congo, were uncertain as to how it should be best approached. During the eighteenth century the British traders had become well established on the Gambia river as far as a place called Pisania, which is a little distance below the falls or rapids of Barakonda. But although from this point Englishmen had made their way as far as the Senegal river and its various tributaries, nobody had been able to reach the Niger. The natives were exceedingly jealous of this wonderful river, and not at all anxious that its waters should be discovered by the white man. They put all sorts of obstacles in the way of European travellers, besides the natural difficulties which were there already: floods and swamps in the rainy season, waterless wildernesses and steep mountains to cross in the dry season.

On this account, that so many explorers starting from the Guinea coast had failed, the African Association sent others to cross the Sahara and reach the Niger that way, and others again to travel through Egypt to Darfur and arrive at Lake Chad from the Nile basin. None of these expeditions were successful, so it was decided to try the Gambia route yet again, and the Association engaged Major Houghton to make the attempt. Houghton started from the little Island of Goree (near the modern Dakar), and journeyed directly inland to the large Muhammadan town of Medina, north of the middle course of the Gambia. Here, however, a large amount of his trade goods were burnt in a fire which broke out in his camp; but he passed through the mountainous country of Bambūk (where there are gold mines), and on the way was robbed of more of his goods by the son of a chief, Fenda Bakr. Nevertheless he crossed the Senegal and attempted a great overland march across the semi-desert country of Kaarta, which is overrun by fierce, nomad Moors from the southern part of the Sahara Desert. In the last message received from him he announced that he was well on his way to Timbuktu, but shortly afterwards the Moors robbed him of all his goods, and made slaves of his black followers, and left him to die in the desert, unless, indeed, they shortened his end by a spear thrust.

All that was known in England for some time afterwards was that Houghton had disappeared without leaving a trace; so, in 1793, the African Association engaged for a fresh expedition to the Niger a young Scottish surgeon named Mungo Park, who had already made himself remarked by his travels in Sumatra and India.

Mungo Park was born by the banks of the beautiful Yarrow River, not far from the town of Selkirk, and in the middle of some of the loveliest scenery of Scotland. He had thirteen brothers and sisters, and his father was a small farmer. Nevertheless he had received an excellent education at the Selkirk Grammar School. After going

through a University course in Edinburgh (where
he learnt a good deal of botany), he obtained a
post of surgeon on one of the great ships sailing
to India and the Malay Archipelago.

He was only twenty-four when he offered himself for service in Africa; tall, strong, and good-
looking.   Before setting out from Pisania, Park
describes the wretched slaves at the British factory
who were awaiting shipment, or sale to native
merchants.   They were kept constantly fettered
and chained together, and were given very little
food.   The negro slave merchants were known as
"slatis".   Many of them were African Arabs from
the Sudan; others were Fulas from Senegambia, or
Moors from Morocco.   Besides bringing slaves
from the interior to sell to these European traders
(mostly British on the Gambia), they also brought
with them gum from the acacia trees and frankin-
cense from the incense tree, and, above all, Shea
butter.   This vegetable butter or fat is still a valuable article of commerce in West Africa, but in
those days it really took the place of palm oil in
all those drier regions to the north of the great
West African forests.   They also brought with
them salt from the Sahara Desert.   In return they
purchased tobacco, robes woven of cotton, besides a quantity of cotton yarn; for in those days
Morocco and the other parts of the Mediterranean
were not flooded with cotton goods manufactured
in England or other parts of Europe.

Mungo Park took with him as a personal servant
a negro with the commonplace name of Johnson.

He had had quite a romantic history, having been born in these Mandingo countries of the Upper Gambia, but as a boy sold as a slave and sent to Jamaica. Here he was purchased by a kind English master, who, after some years of service, took him to England, and gave him his freedom. In England he lived for a number of years, and at last made his way back to Africa, and finally to the land of his origin. As he spoke English perfectly, as well as Mandingo, he was a useful interpreter.

Mungo Park bought a horse for the value of £7, 10s., and donkeys for his interpreter and servants. The countries through which he was going to travel had this great advantage over the regions farther south: they were for the most part open lands without areas of dense forest. Horses did not fall sick in these drier countries, it was therefore possible to ride almost everywhere; whereas farther to the south it is impossible to ride a horse or a donkey. In the first place the climate and the vegetation make them ill, or they are bitten by poisonous flies, but in the second, where the track lies through dense forest, the traveller would share the fate of Absalom if he attempted to travel on horseback. Therefore there is no alternative but to walk, unless he can get himself carried in a hammock slung upon a pole. But even this is difficult, as he may be knocked to pieces against stumps and stones, or have his eyes gouged out by spiky plants, long thorns, or sharp twigs.

The first place of importance which Park reached

on his way to the north-east was Medina, the
capital town of a large Mandingo kingdom called
Wuli.   Medina is the Arabic name for a city, and
is familiar to most of my readers as that of *the*
city of the Arabs, the birthplace of their prophet,
Muhammad.   It was supposed by Mungo Park
that the capital of this Mandingo kingdom must
have received an Arabic name, but it is more likely
that the word is simply an accidental coincidence,
and is derived from the Mandingo language.

In any case, at the close of the eighteenth century it was a very important centre of trade in
West Africa.   To Medina came Moors and Arabs
from the north and north-east, Fulas from the
north-west and south-east, and the representatives
of many pagan and savage tribes from the forested
countries nearer to the sea.   The King of Wuli
bore the title of Mansa, which means chief or
sovereign, and was formerly a very common term
in the Arabic history of these regions, hundreds of
years before they were visited by the British.   The
boy or girl who reads this book, and who takes an
interest in the British Empire, should pay particular
attention to the Mandingos,[1] as they have figured
largely in the history of West Africa, and may have
a great deal to say in the future, whether they live
under the British or the French.

Where the Mandingos came from is uncertain,
but they probably reached westernmost Africa from
the east, perhaps following the course of the Niger

[1] A description of Mandingo life in the early seventeenth century by
Jobson is given on pages 61–64.

upstream. They are a tall, handsome race of dark-skinned negroes, but are much mixed with Arab and Moorish blood in some districts. They founded a great empire (usually known as Malé or Melle) many centuries ago between the Upper Niger, the Gambia, and the Senegal; and, coming into contact with the first Arabs or Muhammadan Moors who reached these regions by way of the Atlantic coast from Morocco, they were amongst the earliest converts to Muhammadanism in the history of West Africa.

This conversion from a pagan, and no doubt barbarous, condition made them a very strong, warlike, and adventurous people; so much so, that under their Mansas, or great chiefs, they brought beneath their sway much of the western Sahara Desert, and carried their conquests as far to the east along the Niger as the Hausa countries. From the twelfth century onwards, one or other of their kings would proceed by way of the Sahara Desert to Egypt or Nubia, and thence across the Red Sea to the holy cities of Arabia. On their return journey they would bring much Asiatic civilization back with them to the very heart of West Africa. But after a time their power was broken by the Moors in the north and by the Songhai people in the east.

Then again, much later on, a hundred years or more after the visit of Jobson to the Upper Gambia, the Fula herdsmen and nomads[1] in Mandingoland rose against living in subjection to the

[1] See pages 59-60.

rule of a black people, and not only became the dominant power in the very heart of Mandingoland, but effected still more wonderful conquests on their own part, as is related elsewhere. Yet a hundred years ago, and more, there were still small Mandingo kingdoms like Wuli, which remained more or less independent of the Fulas in the regions of the Upper Gambia.

In those days the Mandingos were almost invariably friendly to the European, especially the British; it was the Fulas who were hostile, and still more the Moors of the Sahara Desert. In after years the Mandingos united under a great leader, Samori, and attacked both the French and British, but they were subdued by French armies, and there is now complete peace in the regions traversed with so much difficulty by Mungo Park and the earlier explorers. An ordinary tourist can go through all these lands with no more danger than if he were crossing Central Europe.

In Mungo Park's day the Mandingos were divided into two sects, those called Bushrin, who were Muhammadans and teetotallers, and those called Sonanki, or Kafir, who were still pagans, and were addicted to drinking any kind of alcohol they could get hold of, either native beer or wine or European distilled spirits. The mass of the people were either freemen (often called the Horia or Slati) or slaves (Jong). The slaves took the place of what we should call peasantry, and under the rule of a good chief they were not disturbed unless they committed a crime; in which case they were sold by their master or owner, and sent to the coast to be carried by Europeans to America.

Mungo Park, like previous travellers, found the aged King of Wuli a kind old man. In the case of Mungo Park, the King told him he would offer up prayers for his safety on the journey he was about to undertake; and it is pleasant to record that on Mungo Park's return to Medina eighteen months afterwards he was able to send word to the aged king that his prayers had been answered.

When introduced to the King in December, 1795, Mungo Park was advised by his courtiers that he must not presume to shake hands with their monarch, as it was not usual to allow this liberty to strangers. He found him on this and on other occasions seated on the hide of a bullock and warming himself before a fire of sticks, for the morning was a cold one at the beginning of the African winter, though it seemed warm enough to Mungo Park fresh from Europe. On either side of the King were a number of men and women singing and clapping their hands. The King's reception of the Scottish explorer was so cordial that one of Mungo Park's attendants felt moved to roar out an Arabic song of praise and thanksgiving, to which the King at intervals responded "Amen! amen!", for, although not a confessed Muhammadan, he was really a good man and respected all forms of genuine religion. He tried hard to dissuade the young Scotchman from his quest of the Niger, telling him that Major

Houghton had already been killed in the Desert by the pitiless Moors, and that all the peoples to the eastward of his country were very badly disposed towards Europeans; but finding his warnings of no use he merely sighed, and gave orders that everything should be done by his people to make the white man's journey easy.

CHAPTER IV

Mungo Park in Senegambia

DURING Mungo Park's stay in this pleasant country of Wuli, he witnessed from time to time the wrestling matches which are still popular amongst many negro tribes between the Gambia and the Upper Congo. (You will read presently accounts of the wrestlers of Hausaland and Bornu, in following the travels of Denham and Clapperton.) In Mandingoland these matches took place at the *bentang* or central meeting-hall of a town or village. The spectators arranged themselves in a circle, leaving the intermediate space for the wrestlers, who were strong, active young men. These having been stripped of their clothing, except a short pair of drawers, and having their skin anointed with oil or shea butter, would approach each other generally on all-fours. They would fence and parry with their hands until they saw a good opening, and then rush in and catch the rival wrestler by the knee. After this would follow a desperate struggle, decided in the long run more by sheer strength than by skill.

The wrestling (which was accompanied by the incessant rhythmical beating of drums) would be succeeded by a dance, in which all the performers

had little bells fastened to their legs and arms,
so that a very pretty tinkling sound accompanied
the drum playing.   Mungo Park found that the
drummers were remarkably skilful in varying their
tones, and even — as we now know is done over
much else of Negro Africa — could in some way
make the drums speak, give out sounds that were
very like Mandingo words.   Thus they were able
to tap out a sentence that sounded much like the
Mandingo words for "All sit down"; whereupon
the audience would squat on the ground, or they
would give the signal to the wrestlers by imitat-
ing the words, "Amuta, Amuta!" meaning "Take
hold!"

During these entertainments beer was handed
round, which Mungo Park not only found very
good, but extremely like the beer of his native
land.   It was made in the same way from corn
which had been malted—that is to say, the grains
allowed to germinate and sprout till they were
sweet and sugary, and then pounded in water and
left to ferment.   The liquid was flavoured with a
grateful bitter very like hops, and the corn with
which the beer was made was that which I have
already described—the sorghum.

The next kingdom reached by Mungo Park
was that of Bondu, situated along the Faleme, an
important affluent of the Senegal.   This was the
kingdom where the Fulas already ruled, not the
Mandingo.   Here his treatment was of a varied
character.   As a rule the Fula men or the Moors
were hospitable and well conducted; but the women

most unruly. They were dressed in a fine gauze, which seemed to Mungo Park very picturesque. But they were bold beggars, and when they did not get all the beads or pieces of amber they desired, they would assault him and his servants, cut the brass buttons from their clothes, and make themselves very objectionable, often following his caravan, yelling and cursing for half a mile or so.[1] In entering Bondu, Mungo Park found himself in a much more civilized country than anything farther south. It was a land more suggestive of the East, or of North Africa. There was no more rich forest, but woods or groves of tall acacia trees, and a good deal of the land was under careful cultivation. There were few or no human porters carrying burdens, but great troops of asses instead, which conveyed merchandise from one part to another. Many of these were loaded with tusks of ivory, for in those days elephants, now quite extinct, still swarmed amongst the mountains and less-frequented parts, and the Fula young men were bold hunters. The ivory, together with ample supplies of corn, fish, and other food products, was sold to the Moors of the desert, or to the advance posts of the French merchants on the Upper Senegal. The rivers contained quantities of fish, and these, after being caught, would be pounded up with a little salt in a wooden mortar and then exposed to dry in the sun in great lumps like long loaves of bread. The smell they gave out was very nasty, but these black loaves of

1 Very different to the gentle Fula women of Borgu. See p. 318.

slightly putrid fish were much esteemed by the
Moors of the desert, who would break off pieces,
put them in boiling water, and mix them with their
kūskūs. (Kūskūs, which is the principal food of all
the Muhammadan peoples between the Senegal
and the Mediterranean coast of North Africa, is
a preparation of boiled and pounded wheat, a
little like very stiff oaten porridge. As served
in North Africa, it is a delicious food, for it is
flavoured and mixed with meat, gravy, raisins, and
almonds.)

The great chief of the Bondu country was a
Fula, but it is doubtful whether at that period he
was a Muhammadan, though most of his people
belonged to that faith. He was called—and similar
Fula chieftains are called to this day — Al Mami,
which is possibly a corruption of the Arabic words,
Al Imam, the high priest; for in these countries
it was difficult sometimes to distinguish between
the chief medicine - man or high priest and the
civil ruler; very often they were one and the same,
and when the ruler of a negro state became a
Muhammadan he generally took the leading part
in directing the prayers. The houses belonging
to this Fula king and his family were surrounded
by a lofty mud wall, and the interior was subdivided into different courts. As in Uganda and
other negro countries where a certain degree of
civilization has arisen, it was customary to pass
from one court to another before you reached the
real dwelling-place of the great chief, and at the
entrance to each court there would be a guard

standing at the time of Mungo Park's visit, already armed with muskets, though Jobson, 170 years before, would probably have found nothing but spears or bows and arrows. When at last the entrance of the king's dwellings was reached, all the attendants on Mungo Park took off their sandals and called out the king's name loudly, not daring to go on till they were answered.

This Fula monarch was much surprised and very suspicious that anyone like Mungo Park should wish to travel except for purposes of trade. Many explorers between the days of Mungo Park and the end of the nineteenth century have suffered from a like suspicion. The negro could understand a journey being made for a slave raid or a conquest, or for hunting, or for purposes of commerce; but that anybody should risk his life and leave his own land merely in order to see things, to survey, to make maps, and to write books, seemed to them very strange and sinister, and therefore many an explorer or missionary has been obstructed and kept back where anybody coming merely for purposes of trade would have received all possible assistance. This same chief had done much to place difficulties in the way of Major Houghton. In the case of Mungo Park, he was conciliated by the gift of the explorer's blue coat with brass buttons. Poor Park surrendered the coat most reluctantly, for he was not well supplied with clothes, though he does not seem to have realized what a very silly garment it was (together with his tight breeches and black tall-crowned

hat[1]) for an African traveller.   However, he quietly
gave it up.

The chief then hearing that he was a doctor
by profession wished to try what scientific blood-
letting was like.   But when Park displayed his
lancets the chief's courage failed.   Afterwards he
was requested to visit the wives of the Al Mami,
whom he found to be handsome Fula women,
wearing on their heads ornaments of gold and
beads of amber.   They chaffed him much about
the whiteness of his skin, saying that it had been
produced by his mother having dipped him in
milk when he was a child; and the prominence of
his nose, which had been produced artificially by
its being pinched up in childhood.   It was curious
that they should have been so surprised at the
prominent nose of a European, because one of the
characteristics of the Fula men (if not the women)
is the big well-formed nose like that of a European.

Mungo Park was much interested in these
Fula people, and gives a very good description
of them.   The farther he goes north the lighter
he finds them in colour.   They count themselves
as a white people, and look down upon the negroes
around them as quite an inferior race, though only
a hundred years before they themselves were little
else than the serfs of these negroes.   The Fula
hair was long and wavy, or worn in corkscrew
ringlets.   As a rule, the features of the face were

---

[1] Though the tall crown of his beaver hat was to become famous, for in
it he stored the most precious of his documents, and managed to keep this
hat when everything else was taken from him.

small and delicately shaped, though, as already mentioned, some of the men had big noses. The Fulas are a tall and slender people, with bodies much more like those of Europeans, though, of course, the skin colour is still very dark, a reddish-brown or yellow.

One of the leading traits about the Fulas, or, more correctly, the Fulbe, is their love of cattle. Originally they seem to have been just simple tribes of herdsmen and shepherds who wandered with their flocks from one pasturage to another. But in the hundred and seventy-five years that had elapsed between the visits of Jobson and Mungo Park they had become settled agriculturists, and were now remarkable for the corn and vegetables which they grew.

The cattle of Senegambia, though a smaller breed than that of the Sudan and of Equatorial East Africa and Galaland, are very handsome, tall beasts with well-shaped limbs, a straight back, a dewlap, and· rather a long graceful head, surmounted with very big horns growing upwards and outwards and turning backwards, differing from the horns of our European cattle, which tend to grow horizontally and forward. The Fulas, according to Mungo Park, displayed great skill in the management of their cattle, making them extremely gentle by kindness and familiarity. On the approach of night they would be collected from the woods where they had been feeding and put into folds —*korri*—which were constructed in the neighbourhood of each village. In the middle of every large

cattle fold (which would be surrounded by thick
hedges of thorns and logs) a small hut was erected
for one or two watchmen, who would keep a fire
burning all night to scare away the lions and
leopards. The cattle were milked every morning
and evening, and the milk was afterwards made
into thick, sour curds and whey, or into butter.
This butter they would use not only for cooking,
and keep it in small earthen pots, but would also
anoint their heads and bodies with it, so that sometimes, though a clean people, they would smell
rather rancid.

The Fula, when first heard of through their own
traditions, seem to have been migrating from the
north or north-east to the River Niger, and to have
conquered from a race of red pygmies some of the
land which lay to the south of the Niger. Gradually, from one direction or another, they concentrated most of their numbers in the elevated,
healthy, and fertile regions between the Upper
Gambia and the Upper Senegal. It was here
that the first Fula kingdoms arose and became
powerful. The remainder settled in the countries
south of the Niger bend.

Although the Fulas of West Africa had become
very contemptuous of Europeans since they adopted
the Muhammadan religion, and were a very proud,
exacting people, still, Mungo Park felt much more
at home with them than he did with the next tribe
he was to visit—the Serawule people on the north
side of the Senegal River. These were a tall race,
of jet-black skin, whose language shows that they

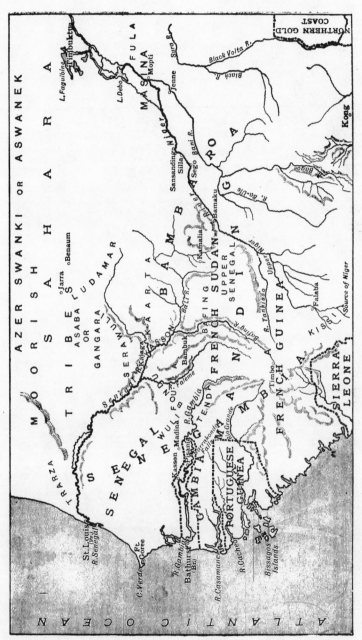

MAP OF THE SENEGAMBIA REGION

are allied in origin to the Mandingo. At the town
of Joag, near the banks of the Senegal, Mungo
Park was robbed, under the plea of customs duties,
of quite half his small provision of trade goods
and baggage, including the present of gold dust
which had been made to him by the Fula King
of Bondu. He was feeling most despondent at
his position, wondering whether he dared proceed
any farther without a sufficiency of means to pay
his way, and knowing that in any case he would
have to pass the night without any food, when
a kindly old woman slave, who was passing by,
enquired into his condition, and, finding that he
was hungry, gave him her basket of groundnuts.
These groundnuts, with which one feeds the monkeys in Zoological Gardens, and which, therefore,
are often called monkey-nuts, are the seeds of a
little bean-like plant, which actually ripen under
the ground. Those of the Niger have an agreeable taste, and are full of an oil like olive oil, which
is very nourishing. Therefore, when Mungo Park
had to make his dinner off them he was thank-
ful, and did not grumble. Moreover, the next
morning he had a delightful surprise. The nephew
of the Mandingo king of the neighbouring country
of Kasson paid him a visit and offered to escort
him a farther distance on his road towards the
Niger. With great thankfulness he started at
once, and was much amused on the way at his
interpreter Johnson—the Mandingo slave who had
spent seven years in England—attempting to con-
ciliate the spirits of the wilderness by offering them

the sacrifice of a white chicken. This he did by tying the unfortunate bird by one leg to the branch of a tree, telling Mungo Park at the same time that the spirits of the woods were a powerful race of beings of a white colour, with long, flowing hair.

This is a prevalent belief amongst many negro races, especially to the north of the Equator, and it really seems to be founded on the fact that when, ages ago, their forests were first invaded by some race of white adventurers from the north, no doubt coming by way of the Nile valley and answering very much to the ancestors of the Fula, they really took these wonderful strangers for gods or spirits of the dead, amazed at their light skins and their flowing hair. To this day the Bahima of Equatorial Africa are often called by the negro tribes "demigods", or spirits of the deceased, even though, in the course of many centuries of residence and mixture with the surrounding peoples, their hair has become as short and woolly as that of the negro. The black Australians, as we know, think that after death they turn into white people, and because so many negro tribes believe that spirits are white in colour, they cover their own bodies with white paint at the times of great religious ceremonies.

Upon reaching the main Senegal river, Mungo Park met with further difficulties in being plundered of half his goods by Demba Sego, the nephew of the Mandingo King of Kasson, who had befriended him a few days previously in Kajaga. However, the uncle of his plunderer—

the King of Kasson—treated the white man very kindly, and in his country Mungo Park managed to add to his small means by applying to a negro trader named Salim Daukari, who was in the debt of Dr. Laidley, the agent in charge of the English factory at Pisania. This instances the peculiar code of honesty prevalent in so many parts of Africa. Mungo Park had arrived at the court of the King of Kasson quite powerless to resist ill-treatment and poor in trade goods. It would have been easy for Salim Daukari to have evaded any payment of his debts to Dr. Laidley. Nevertheless he paid up in gold dust all that he could spare. Negroes living out of touch with European civilization are usually very honest in commercial transactions until they find themselves deceived by the white man. On the other hand, if they are not traders by profession, they think nothing of stealing from the stranger or robbing him by force of all his goods.

CHAPTER V

Mungo Park among the Moors

From Kasson Mungo Park made his way to the country of Kaarta, which lies between the Upper Senegal and the main Niger to the south of the Sahara Desert. Soon after entering this country of the tall Bambara negroes (who are related to the Mandingos), he one day rode in advance of his caravan, and thus met suddenly two negro horsemen armed with muskets, who had heard nothing of the coming of a white man and were quite unprepared to see such a strange object; not only unfamiliar to them with his absolutely white skin, grey eyes, and brown hair, but clad in the extraordinary costume in which Mungo Park travelled — a white waistcoat with brass buttons,[1] a high-crowned, stiff, black hat, and tight white breeches. To show how easily myths and legends can be started, it is related by Mungo Park that after these horsemen had gazed on him for a few minutes with looks of horror, they had covered their eyes with their hands and had ridden away, muttering prayers to be saved from this unknown monster. At a little distance they encountered Park's caravan, to whom

[1] He had given away his high-shouldered, blue, long-tailed coat.

they related how they had just seen an awful spirit, clad in flowing robes, who had suddenly made his appearance as though coming from the sky, bringing with him a cold blast of wind.

As the kingdoms of Kaarta and Bambara were at war, and this blocked the direct route to the Niger, Mungo Park decided unwisely to make an excursion northwards into the Moorish state of Ludamar (on the borders of which Major Houghton had perished) in the hope of travelling round the northern side of Bambara and reaching the Niger beyond the region of the disturbances.

He arrived at the frontier town of Jarra, on his way noticing the use which was made by the negroes of the lotus plant, a species of *Rhamnus*. This was a thorny shrub with oval-shaped leaves and small flowers growing at the juncture of the leaf and the stalk, flowers which were succeeded in time by small, yellow berries of delicious taste, very sweet and floury. The way in which these berries were made into food was by exposing them for some days in the sun and then pounding them gently in a wooden mortar, until the farinaceous or outer covering was separated from the little stone or kernel. The pounded berries were mixed with water and made into cakes, and these, after being dried in the sun, resembled the sweetest gingerbread in colour and flavour. The stones of the berries were put into vessels of water and shaken about to separate the mealy substance which still adhered to them. So sweet was this, and so strong in flavour, that it turned the water into a very pleasant-tasting drink. This lotus-sweetened water was thickened by a little flour till it became a thin gruel or porridge, and it then formed the substance of the first meal of the day during the winter and early spring in this country of Ludamar. According to Mungo Park, these lotus bushes grow not only to the north of the Senegal and Niger, but are also found in Southern Tunis and along the northern limits of the Sahara Desert. He believed that they were identical with the "lotus" mentioned by Pliny and other classical writers as being the food of the Libyans. It is, in fact, true, that Pliny described in his writings the way in which these berries were made into sweet-tasting cakes. Other people have thought that the "lotus" of Greek legends may have been the date. Perhaps their descriptions of a sweet and delicious berry which could be made into cakes and was a sufficient food for men, were derived from accounts both of the date palm and the rhamnus.

As Park approached nearer to the desert he saw once or twice troops of wild asses, perhaps the same as the wild ass of Nubia, which is the parent of our domestic donkey. He also witnessed the making of gunpowder by a negro, to whom the art no doubt had been taught by Moors from the north. On the borders of the desert the water of the dried-up pools would leave behind it crystals of nitre, found as a white efflorescence on the mud. To this the negro added sulphur brought by the Moors from the Mediterranean, and charcoal; and made a gunpowder which was of a less explosive character than that produced in Europe, but which enabled the Moors, at any rate, to use guns without being dependent on European trade.

So long as Mungo Park travelled amongst negroes he was kindly treated, but his hopes regarding the Moors were soon dispelled. A party of Moors unexpectedly entered his hut at Jarra and told him they had been sent by the Moorish sultan Ali to convey him, by force if necessary, to the great camp at Benaum. The impatience of the Moorish chief arose from the curiosity of his wife Fatima, who had heard so much about white Christians that she was very anxious to see one. On the way Park met one of the sons of Ali, who immediately handed him a double-barrelled gun and told him to dye the stock of the gun a blue colour and to repair one of the locks. Park told him that he knew nothing whatever about gunsmith's work. "Then," said the Moor, "you must give me some knives and scissors immediately." When Park's interpreter explained that he had no such articles with him, the young Moor attempted to shoot the inter-preter, and was only prevented by his companions interfering.

Continuing through a country which was more and more sandy and arid, and sometimes chewing acacia gum to allay their thirst, they came at last in sight of the great camp capital of the Moorish chief Ali. It consisted of a number of dirty-looking tents scattered without order over a large space of ground, and among the tents appeared large herds of camels, cattle, and goats. Mungo Park was at once surrounded by noisy Moors, who examined his clothes with much roughness, and insisted on his repeating the Muhammadan expression of faith: There is no God but God, and Muhammad is the Prophet of God. Park was taken before the Moorish sultan, who received him in a sullen and disagreeable way. Asking for food, he was presented with a wild hog—probably what is known as a warthog. The Moors thought that if this animal was released it would at once make for Mungo Park and tear him with its tusks; but, on the contrary, it ran at his oppressors instead. He was grudgingly allowed a little boiled corn and salt, all his property was taken from him except his compass, and at a council of nobles it was proposed to put out his eyes because they were like those of a cat, and then turn him loose in the desert to starve. But he was preserved from this fate by the desire of the Sultan to keep him as a curiosity until his wife Fatima arrived from the desert. Park, after being shown to various Moorish ladies in the vicinity of Benaum, was carried north into the desert to make the acquaintance of Fatima, the principal wife of Ali; but she treated him with a certain amount of kindness, and occasionally supplied him with milk and food. At times, however, he came near to dying of both thirst and hunger, for the slaves of the Moorish chief would forget for two or three days to send him any food, and no Moor would allow him to drink out of vessels used by Muhammadans. Sometimes he only got a drink by putting his head into the trough that was being filled for the cattle. But he fortunately had his horse restored to him—the horse on which he had ridden the whole way from the Upper Gambia —and he was allowed to accompany Ali on a journey to the south, towards the very town of Jarra where he had first been seized by the Moors.

These Moors of Kaarta were not precisely like the Moors of North Africa, the people one sees in Morocco, Algeria, and Tunis. These last very often have a complexion no darker than that of a Spaniard or an Italian, and their hair is straight and sometimes brown instead of black, while there are even Moors with grey eyes and reddish hair. But the Moors of the South-Western Sahara are really an ancient cross between the Moor of the North, the Arab of the East, and the negroes who once inhabited the oases of the Sahara Desert. Their hair is curly, and their complexions are yellow, or even brown. But the nose is straight, and the features are finely cut.

Like the peoples of North Africa, they think that a beautiful woman should be very fat, and before a girl is married she is usually confined to the house and obliged to consume enormous quantities of milk and boiled corn till she becomes in time almost like a fat woman at a fair. But this corpulence is generally confined to the wives of the well-to-do, the common women becoming lean and scraggy with the hard lives they lead and occasional scarcity of food.

The kūskūs, so often alluded to by Mungo

Park, is usually made of wheat which is soaked in water, then pounded in a mortar and cooked by steaming, so that it comes out like a mass of rice. It is very good when served with pieces of fowl, mutton, raisins, and almonds, or rich gravy; but it is doubtful whether Mungo Park got more than just the boiled corn flavoured with a little salt, and perhaps a few strips of raw beef dried in the sun.

The Moors had brought with them across the Sahara, in the course of centuries, not only camels, oxen, goats, and donkeys, but also horses of the Barb or North African breed, a race which is not unlike the fine-limbed Arab horses, though it is rather sturdier. Park describes these Senegal Moors as being very good horsemen; but their saddles being high-peaked both in front and behind, make it difficult for the rider to fall off (and not very easy to get on!). They were fond of milk-white horses, and would usually dye the tails of these white horses a bright-red colour. All the men rode, and, of course, it was by means of these horses that they were so often able in those days to plunder the negro countries and escape from reprisals. They took the greatest care of their horses, feeding them three or four times a day, and in the evening giving them large quantities of sweet milk from their herds of cows.

Mungo Park noticed the ostriches, the antelopes, and wild pigs, the lions, hyenas, and jackals (he miscalls the last-named "wolves", though there are no wolves in any part of Africa) to be found in the country between the Senegal and the Niger.

No doubt he also saw giraffes, chitas, and leopards, and perhaps buffalo, near the water-holes. The antelopes that were killed by the Moors for food were probably the Leucoryx and the Addax. The Addax is found in all parts of the Sahara Desert between the Nile and the Atlantic Ocean where there is sufficient vegetation. Its hoofs are broadened, so that it may cross the sand without sinking in. It has a considerable mane of hair over the forehead, which no doubt helps to shield the eyes from the dust storms, and its horns are twisted in spirals and not straight like those of its near relations, the Oryxes. The Leucoryx is as large as a small cow. It is whitish-grey or cream colour, darkening on the neck into russet. The long, ringed horns are curved and sweeping like a Moorish sabre.

These are the impressions recorded by Park of his glimpse of the Sahara Desert:—" In some parts of this extensive waste the ground is covered with low, stunted shrubs, which serve as landmarks for the caravans, and furnish the camels with a scanty forage. In other parts the disconsolate wanderer, wherever he turns, sees nothing around him but a vast interminable expanse of sand and sky; a gloomy and barren void, where the eye finds no particular object to rest upon, and the mind is filled with painful apprehensions of perishing with thirst. Surrounded by this dreary solitude, the traveller sees the dead bodies of birds that the violence of the wind has brought from happier regions; and as he ruminates on the fearful length of his remain-

ing journey before him, listens with horror to the
voice of the driving blast—the only sound that
interrupts the awful repose of the Desert."

On this excursion back towards Jarra, Park
believed himself to be very narrowly watched by
the Moors lest he should escape; but if the chieftain, Ali, really dreaded losing his captive, it is
difficult to understand why he restored his horse
and permitted him to ride back towards the Mandingo country. However, when Park was nearing
Jarra, and was passing the night in a village, some
Moors entered his dwelling and said they had received Ali's orders to convey him back to the
Moorish camp of Benaum. Whilst they were
sleeping, Park stole away absolutely alone, for his
ex-slave interpreter Johnson, after a whispered consultation, dared not accompany him. Alternately
riding and leading his horse, he made his way
through the wilderness on the outskirts of Bambara, constantly in terror of his life from Moors
and Fulas, robbed by the former of his cloak
(which was his one protection from cold and rain),
and occasionally having to face prowling lions who
seemed undecided which they would attack first,
his horse or himself.

He often underwent agonies of thirst; sometimes when he approached a pool of water it was
so full of frogs that he could hardly drink. At
other times, when half-mad with thirst, he would
perceive lightning near the horizon, and be encouraged by the hope of a rainstorm. The clouds
would mount the sky till it became darker and

darker with a copper tint, whilst the lightning zig-
zagged, the thunder cracked, and the wind began
to roar in the distance till it approached the traveller with the force of a hurricane.   But the wind
brought no rain with it at first; only clouds of sand
and dust which nearly suffocated him and his horse.
This would last perhaps for an hour, then there
would be still more vivid lightning, and, finally,
torrents of rain would descend; and the weary,
exhausted man could spread all his clean clothes
out on the sand.   After they were soaked, he could
quench his thirst by wringing the moisture from
them.

Very often Park was obliged to keep travelling
through the dark night, lest if he stopped to rest he
might fall asleep and be eaten by a lion.   Sometimes, when the sky was covered with heavy clouds,
he would only be able to move by groping and
feeling his way; at others he would look at his
compass by the glare of the lightning to satisfy
himself that he was walking in the right direction,
leading with him his stumbling horse.   Perhaps he
discerned a light in the distance, and made towards
it in the hope of coming to a negro village where
he might get food, shelter, and rest; but it would
turn out to be fires burning in a Moorish encamp-
ment of cattle and herdsmen passing the night
round some well or fountain.   Even though suffering from thirst, he dared not put himself in the
power of these people, in case he was sent back
to his cruel tyrant the Moorish Sultan.   On one
occasion he approached so near to the Moorish

tents that he was seen by a woman, who began to scream, and no doubt told extraordinary stories of the apparition whilst Mungo Park hurried back into the dark wilderness.

At last he reached the more settled country to the east, and was able occasionally to obtain food for himself and his horse. As long as he travelled through a country which was at all under the influence of the Moors he ran narrow risks of recapture, besides the danger of starvation; for the men usually refused to give him any food, and he owed his existence to the pity of kindly women. Amongst the Fula shepherds there was more hospitality. They would give him dates and kūskūs, or boiled corn. He seems to have had a remarkable number of brass buttons on his garments, and whenever he wished to reward hospitality would cut off one or more and bestow them on his hosts, to whom they were objects of wonder and beauty. He was nearly worn out when he reached the town of Wora, on the outskirts of Bambara.

At the door of a hut in Wora an old motherly-looking woman sat spinning cotton. Park made signs to her that he was hungry, and begged for food. She immediately laid down her distaff, and asked him in Arabic to come in. When he had seated himself upon the floor, she set before him a dish of kūskūs left over from the preceding night, and with this he was able to assuage his hunger. She also provided a little corn for his horse, and he gave her one of his pocket handkerchiefs.

After this he felt that there was a chance that he

might survive to complete his journey. His heart swelled with gratitude as he lifted up his eyes to heaven. It was not, indeed, until he had reached Wora—a small town surrounded by high clay walls —and found himself once more amongst negroes, that he could feel fairly safe as regards recapture by the Moors. In Wora he was kindly treated,[1] though he was an object of much wonderment, some thinking him an Arab, others a Moorish chief who had got detached from his followers. But the headman of the town had visited the Gambia, and knew what white men were.

From this place he managed, with no very serious difficulties, to travel to the Niger at Sego, generally consorting with negro fellow travellers on the way. Much of the journey had to be done on foot, for his horse was too weak to ride, and he would drive it before him, to the great amusement of the people, who laughed heartily at his poverty-stricken appearance, taking him for a pilgrim who had been to Mecca and lost all his goods. In fact, at last he was so jeered at that even slaves felt ashamed to be seen with him.

Sometimes the slave caravans that he passed going in the opposite direction were in charge of Moors, who fortunately were civil to him. These slaves were tied together by the necks with thongs of bullocks' hides twisted like a rope. Seven of the slaves were usually tied together, and placed in

---

[1] "The villagers would ask me a thousand questions about my country, and in return for my information would bring corn and milk for myself and grass for my horse; then kindle a fire in the hut where I was to sleep, and appear very anxious to serve me."

charge of a man with a gun. Some of them were nearly skin and bone from semi-starvation. Many were women and children, and only a small proportion of these were likely to survive the terrible journey of several hundred miles that lay between the Upper Niger and Morocco.

CHAPTER VI

Mungo Park Discovers the Niger

AT last, on 20 July, 1796, Mungo Park arrived opposite Sego, the capital of Bambara, and saw the "majestic Niger, glittering in the morning sun, as broad as the Thames at Westminster, and flowing slowly to the eastward". Unless he had been forestalled three or four hundred years ago by a Spanish monk or a Portuguese adventurer, he was the first European who ever saw the Niger River in the far interior of West Africa. It is probable that his predecessors of the fifteenth century got no farther than the Senegal, and described that as being the Niger or the Nile.

Information was at once sent to the King of Bambara at Sego that a white man was waiting to cross the river in order to come and see him. But the King sent a messenger back to beg Mungo Park not to cross the Niger until the King knew for what purpose he had come to the country. He was told to lodge at a distant village which was pointed out to him. When he reached this place no person would admit him into their house. " I was regarded with astonishment and fear, and was obliged to sit all day without victuals, in the shade of a tree, and the night threatened to be very uncomfortable, for the wind rose, and there was great appearance of a heavy rain; and the wild beasts are so very numerous in the neighbourhood, that I should have been under the necessity of climbing up a tree, and resting among the branches. About sunset, however, as I was preparing to pass the night in this manner, and had turned my horse loose, that he might graze at liberty, a woman, returning from the labours of the field, stopped to observe me, and, perceiving that I was weary and dejected, inquired into my situation, which I briefly explained to her; whereupon, with looks of great compassion, she took up my saddle and bridle, and told me to follow her. Having conducted me into her hut, she lighted a lamp, spread a mat on the floor, and told me I might remain there for the night. Finding that I was very hungry, she said she would procure me something to eat, and accordingly went out, returning in a short time with a very fine fish; which, having caused to be half-broiled upon some embers, she gave me for supper. The rites of hospitality being thus performed towards a stranger in distress, my worthy benefactress (pointing to the mat, and telling me I might sleep there without apprehension) called to the female part of her family, who had stood gazing on me all the while in fixed astonishment, to resume their task of spinning cotton; in which they continued to employ themselves great part of the night. They lightened their labour by songs, one of which was composed extempore; for I was myself the subject of it. It was sung by one of

MUNGO PARK'S FIRST SIGHT OF THE NIGER AT SEGO, 1796

the young women, the rest joining in a sort of chorus. The air was sweet and plaintive, and the words, literally translated, were these. 'The winds roared, and the rains fell. The poor white man, faint and weary, came and sat under our tree. He has no mother to bring him milk; no wife to grind his corn. Chorus: Let us pity the white man; no mother has he, &c.' Trifling as this recital may appear to the reader, to a person of my situation, the circumstance was affecting in the highest degree. I was oppressed by such unexpected kindness; and sleep fled from my eyes. In the morning I presented my compassionate landlady with two of the four brass buttons which remained on my waistcoat; the only recompense I could make her."

The fact was that Mansong, the King of Bambara, had received unfavourable accounts of this wandering Christian from the spiteful Moors and Arabs residing at Sego, who were very suspicious about the motives of his journey. When the King learnt, further, that Mungo Park was too poor to give him any present, he was still less desirous of seeing him. Yet he was not a bad-hearted man, and actually sent the white traveller a bag containing five thousand kauri shells, worth then about 10s. 6d. in our money; but in those days sufficient to carry a person a long way through these lands of cheap food and negro hospitality. In fact, Mungo Park reckoned that with these five thousand kauris he might be able to travel about fifty days and purchase provisions for himself and corn for his horse.

So Park set out from the vicinity of Sego and travelled eastwards along the banks of the Niger through a beautiful and highly cultivated country, "bearing a greater resemblance to the centre of England than to what was really the interior of Africa". This country was celebrated for the abundance of the Shea trees,[1] which produced a kind of vegetable butter. They were not planted by the natives, but grew naturally in the woods. The tree resembled an oak in appearance, and the fruit had a kernel or nut which, after being dried in the sun, was boiled in water, and the vegetable fat which rose to the surface was skimmed off, drained, and pressed into a white butter. This would keep a whole year without turning rancid, and required no mixture of salt for its preservation. Mungo Park found it of a richer flavour than the best butter he had ever tasted made from cow's milk. It is the chief fat used in cooking amongst negroes and Fulas who live to the north of the forests where the oil palm grows, and to the south of the desert regions, or those scrub countries where large herds of cattle and goats can be kept.

At several places he passed through, he found Moors who attempted to force him to take part in

[1] The Latin name of this tree is *Butyrospermum parkii*. Its common native name in Senegambia is *Karita*; in Northern Nigeria it is usually known as *Mikadania*. It is described by Clapperton as having a fruit like a peach in shape and size, but slightly more pointed at the end. When ripe the outer rind is eaten, and the vegetable fat surrounding the kernels is pressed and strained into a hard, white butter. The kernels are bruised and then boiled in water. As the fat they contain rises to the surface it is skimmed off and looks like dirty lard. This grease derived from the nuts is not used for food generally, but for burning in the clay lamps.

religious services in mosques, but generally he was protected from any actual ill-usage by the kindly negroes. His worn-out horse, which had been through such adventures and vicissitudes (being, indeed, so weary a day or two before, that it would not trouble to walk out of the way of a large lion which lay within a few feet of the road), completely broke down at a place near Kea, on the banks of the Niger. Park handed him over to his negro guide, promising him on his return to reward him if the horse was still alive. He then embarked in the canoe of a negro fisherman, his wife and son, and in this way reached a place called Silla, which proved to be the end of his journey.

Some days' travel in front of him lay the far-famed town of Jenné, so famous, in fact, that it may possibly, by its renown as a centre of trade and wealth, have given rise in varying forms of its name to "Guinea", a term we now apply to so much of West Africa. Here Park was informed that he would find people speaking a language quite different to any of the Mandingo dialects. They were fanatical Muhammadans, he was told, and the city contained many Moors and Arabs. At Silla he reviewed his position. Was it any use going farther down the river into countries still more fanatical than those he had passed through with such difficulty? He had only the value of ten shillings in kauri shells: when those were exhausted he would be in the heart of Africa entirely dependent on the hospitality of the natives, and might easily perish at the hands of some truculent Moor or Arab, and be unable to return to Europe with his wonderful story of the discovery of the Niger. Whereas, if he were to turn west from Sego he might possibly find a slave caravan starting for the upper waters of the Gambia River, and travel under its protection; even if he could not as a harmless wanderer make his way through the countries of the kindly Mandingos until he reached the court of some potentate sufficiently alive to the importance of the European trade to take him under his protection and send him to the Upper Gambia. He decided to return along the north bank of the Niger; and his adventures on his westward route deserve to be read in the original: they are thrilling in their escapes from hungry lions and hostile men.

Although Park had left his horse behind in charge of a kindly negro at a place called Modibu, or Madibu, he still carried about with him his saddle and stirrups, having picked them up on his return journey from the place where he had left them. The saddle he thought might be useful to give as a present to some king or chief, and he therefore induced the negroes he obtained as guides to carry it for him. One of these, however, scared by a lion, threw down the saddle and went away. Unable to carry this himself, Park took off the stirrups and girths and threw the saddle into the river. His negro guide no sooner saw this than he ran out of the bushes, jumped into the river, and by means of his spear hoisted out the saddle and ran away with it. Nevertheless, when Park reached Modibu he found his saddle had been left there by the guide for fear of what might befall him if his chief were told of the theft; and whilst discussing this matter with the *duti* or headman of the town, Park heard the neighing of a horse. It was actually his own faithful steed, which he had scarcely expected to see again, as he had left it almost dying in the charge of a negro. However, there it was, and most thankfully he resumed possession of it, riding once more on the saddle which had been so nearly lost altogether.

This horse of Park's, on which he had originally started from the English factory at Pisania (where he had purchased it for £7, 10s.), went through such surprising adventures and recoveries that its further history might be set forth here. Although after he escaped from the Moors in Ludamar he had more often than not to drive the horse before him instead of riding it, owing to its weakness, nevertheless it seems to have been a source of comfort and even protection to him. Sometimes, on the return journey westwards along the Niger banks, it would fall into deep clay pits or swamps, and be nearly drowned or buried in the mud before it could be dragged out. Once the horse fell right down a well, and had to be hoisted out by the negroes. In traversing the steep mountains between the Upper Niger and the Senegal, the horse was obliged to climb places that a goat might have decided were impassable, and in so doing hurt his legs very much. In this mountainous region the horse was taken from him by force by Fula robbers, but afterwards recovered through the good offices of a Mandingo chief, to whom Park eventually presented the saddle and bridle, while he gave the horse to the headman of the village whose people had so cleverly hoisted it out of the well into which it had fallen. It is to be hoped that the horse which had gone through such wonderful adventures, and had had such narrow escapes from lions, from starvation and thirst, and from Moorish or Fula robbers, lived at any rate a few years longer in peace and comfort among the kindly Mandingo people.

As to Park himself, in his return journey along the Niger, he was shunned by the King of Bambara more than ever owing to the hostile attitude of the Moors who frequented all the principal towns as merchants and slave-traders. At one time he thought of swimming with his horse across the flooded Niger, and trying to make his way due south across the utterly unexplored country heard of as " Kong ", to the British forts in the western part of the Gold Coast. Such an attempt must almost certainly have ended in disaster. After a time he would have left the relatively civilized countries of the Mandingo and Fulas, and have entered the vast forests of what is now the French Ivory Coast Colony. Here he might very well have been destroyed by the herds of savage elephants which frequently range through these forests, attack, and often kill human beings, whose presence they discern by their sense of smell. Or, more probably, he would have been killed by the cannibal negroes still inhabiting those regions;

besides which, he would have had to travel through vast wildernesses and forests without any human inhabitants whatever, and with only such food as the monkeys lived on—occasional fruits, nuts, or edible roots and fungi.

But owing to the kindness of the Mandingo negroes he journeyed up the Niger as far as Bamaku (now an important French town), and then made for the steep mountains which separate by a short distance the watershed of the Niger from that of the Upper Senegal. Here, however, he narrowly escaped perishing. He was stopped by some robbers armed with muskets, who stripped him of nearly all his clothing, and boots, and his pocket ·compass, and took away his horse. They left him his tall-crowned hat because the inside of its crown was stuffed with his written memoranda, which savoured in their eyes of magic. There the unfortunate traveller remained with naked feet, clad only in a shirt and a hat, without a compass, and with *five hundred miles* to traverse on foot before he could reach any European settlement. For some minutes he surrendered himself completely to despair: his condition seemed absolutely hopeless. Yet at this moment, painful as were his reflections, his eye was caught with the extraordinary beauty of a small moss in fructification. "I mention this," he afterwards wrote in his book, "to show from what trifling circumstances the mind will sometimes derive consolation; for though the whole plant was not larger than the top of one of my fingers, I could not contemplate the delicate conformation of its roots, leaves, and capsula, without admiration. Can that Being (thought I), who planted, watered, and brought to perfection, in this part of the world, a thing which appears of so small importance, look with unconcern upon the situation and sufferings of creatures formed after His own image?—surely not! Reflections like these, would not allow me to despair. I started up, and, disregarding both hunger and fatigue, travelled forwards, assured that relief was at hand; and I was not disappointed. In a short time I came to a small village, at the entrance of which I overtook the two shepherds who had come with me from Kuma. They were much surprised to see me; for they said, they never doubted that the Fulas, when they had robbed me, had also murdered me. Departing from this village, we travelled over several rocky ridges, and at sunset arrived at Sibidulu, the frontier town of the kingdom of Manding."

At Sibidulu, Park was brought by the people to the presence of the *duti*, or chief, who listened, whilst smoking a pipe, to the story of his adventures and misfortunes. When he had finished, the chief took his pipe from his mouth, told the weary traveller to sit down and to take a draught of water, and then swore that everything he had lost should be returned to him, to the "poor white man, the King of Bambara's stranger, who had been robbed by the people of the King of Fuladu". Messengers were at once sent to effect this purpose. Eleven days afterwards Park received back his horse and clothes, and even his pocket compass, though he found this last was broken to pieces. During these eleven days, however, he was racked with fever.

As already related, he gave away his horse to the headman of Wonda, a village where he had stayed whilst awaiting the return of his clothes, and set forth on foot to continue his journey westwards. In spite of a severely strained ankle and attacks of fever which often left him in a fainting condition, he managed to reach an important town called Kamalia, midway between the Niger and the Kokoro branch of the Senegal. This was a place situated at the bottom of some rocky hills where a good deal of gold was collected by the natives. The inhabitants were partly heathen negroes, and partly Muhammadans, who lived separately from the heathen, and who were mostly concerned with the slave trade. To the house of one of these Muhammadan Mandingos—a man named Karfa Taura —Mungo Park was conducted. He had made the acquaintance of Karfa's brother at a village farther back on the road. The introduction was most valuable, and probably saved the traveller's life. When he reached Karfa's house, at Kamalia, he found him reading aloud to a circle of slave-traders from an Arabic book, and seeing Park interested in this, he sent one of his friends to fetch a "curious little book which had been brought from the west country". This, on being opened by Park, turned out to be the Church of England Book of Common Prayer! Of course he read it aloud fluently, to the great joy of his new friend, who was anxious to help him, but also to prove at the same time to the sneering slave-traders around him that this was a genuine white man and not an Arab mendicant, as they alleged. For Park, having been so frequently naked, and so worn out with fever, was no longer white-skinned, but tanned and yellow, wearing a very long beard, and having the appearance of extreme poverty in his tattered clothes.

But Karfa, convinced of his being European by his ability to read the Prayer Book, promised him every assistance in his power, and carried out his promise to the letter in the months that followed, though he was often urged by the Muhammadans to abandon Park or allow him to be killed. He explained, however, that it would be impossible to set out for the Gambia in the autumn season during the heavy rains, when all the rivers would be in flood. Moreover, after that, they would have to wait for the dry season to parch the vegetation, especially the long grass, so that it might be burnt by the natives, and progress through the country become possible to a caravan of slaves. He convinced Park that it would be madness for him to set out alone and cross so many rivers in full flood, especially with no trade goods to pay his way and no means of transporting them. If, on the other hand, he would remain as Karfa's guest at Kamalia, and be content to eat the food of the country (on which, of course, Park had been subsisting for many months), he would eventually conduct him safely to the Gambia. Here Park could make him any return he thought proper, for instance, the value of one prime slave (which would probably be about twenty pounds' worth of trade goods).

Park, of course, accepted, and was at once provided with a hut, a mat to sleep on, an earthen jar to hold water, and a small calabash to drink out of, while Karfa sent him from his own dwelling two meals a day, and ordered his slaves to supply him with firewood and water. During the five weeks of fever which followed Park's arrival, this good-hearted man visited the poor stricken European every day. Then the dry season began to set in, and Park slowly recovered. He remained at Kamalia till 19 April, 1797. During this time his host, Karfa, was making journeys to various places to complete his supply of slaves. The great Muhammadan Fast of Ramadhan had also to be observed; provisions had to be prepared and collected to cross the Jallonka wilderness, where they would have to travel for more than five days without seeing any human habitation. During this long sojourn, however, Park heard some news from the outer world, and the incident is worth alluding to because it shows what extraordinarily long journeys were taken in those days by Arab traders from North Africa. A merchant from Fezzan, which lies to the south of the Turkish province of Tripoli, reached this town of Kamalia, near the sources of the Niger, and told Park that the French fleet had captured an important British convoy in the Mediterranean in October, 1795, about fourteen months previously!

The Mandingos and the people of Bambara, in fact most of the negroes at all in contact with Moors, Arabs, and Muhammadanism generally, had an immense reverence for "the written word". They thought—and think so still—that there is some wonderful virtue in anything which could be written.   No doubt this arose from the reverence with which Muhammadans regard their sacred book, the Koran.   They believe that verses from the Koran written on paper or parchment, and sewn up into small leather packets and hung round the neck, will preserve them from death or defeat, or cure them if they fall sick.   These charms are usually known in the Mandingo countries as safi. In the Ashanti countries they were enclosed in cases of gold.   Park was frequently asked to write sentences to be used as charms; and so were his successors in Nigerian exploration.   Sometimes the European would inscribe the words on the wooden boards used by negroes and Moors for writing exercises.   The inscription was made in charcoal, or else by means of a reed pen dipped into an ink manufactured from burnt corn stalks. On one occasion Park wrote a number of sentences in English from top to bottom on both sides of the writing-board.   His landlord, for whom he did this in lieu of payment for board and lodging, washed the writing off from the board into a calabash with a little water; and, having said a few prayers over it, drank this powerful draught; after which, lest a single word should escape, he licked the board until it was quite dry.

Whilst staying at Kamalia, and on the journey thence to the Gambia, Mungo Park noticed that some of the slaves of Karfa's caravan had a habit of eating clay. He was much surprised at this practice, and could no more account for it than could other observers for more than a hundred years afterwards. It prevails widely throughout negro Africa, and also occurs amongst whites and blacks in the West Indies, and in the Eastern States of North America. We now know that it is due to the presence in their bodies of a terrible intestinal worm, the eggs of which are hatched in dirty, moist places. The tiny, almost invisible, worm enters the human skin through the pores, generally on the hands or feet, passes into the body and establishes itself in the intestines. Here it snips the small bloodvessels, and even injects a poison into them to keep the blood from coagulating and the bleeding from coming to an end, so that the person afflicted by these worms goes on bleeding, bleeding internally till he becomes weak in body and quite unhinged in mind. For some reason, in their sickness, they are very anxious to eat soft, wet clay, perhaps with the instinctive feeling that as it passes through the digestive organs it may carry the worms away with it. For two hundred years at least this intestinal worm has afflicted the white people of Eastern North America and the West Indies who were poor, and lived in a dirty, careless fashion; above all, those who went about with bare feet, like the Negroes. All this time people from healthier regions wondered why these white people were so lazy, just as they wondered why so many negro men and women would not do any work. In reality, these "lazy" people were suffering all the time from these intestinal worms, and the whole mystery was only revealed a few years ago by the joint labours of Italian, American, German, and British doctors, who now know the right medicine to administer to expel this dreadful worm from the body, and have also pointed out that it is only a thoroughly dirty, uncivilized mode of life which gives the worm its opportunity.

Leaving Kamalia on 19 April, 1797, Park finally reached his fellow countrymen on the Upper Gambia on 10 June, 1797. Karfa Taura was suitably rewarded for his extraordinary kindness to the traveller. Although a slave-trader, as were all Africans of position at that day and all Europeans visiting Africa for commerce, Karfa Taura was, as Park says, a really good-hearted man. But for his intervention, it is probable that Park would have shared the fate of Major Houghton and other of the early explorers, and that many years would have elapsed before any definite knowledge of the Niger River was brought to Europe.

But Park's trials and troubles were not over with his arrival at Pisania. The Gambia River of 1797 had no weekly communication with England by fast and comfortable steamers, taking perhaps about ten days between the mouth of the Gambia and an English port. Park considered himself lucky when an American sailing-ship, the

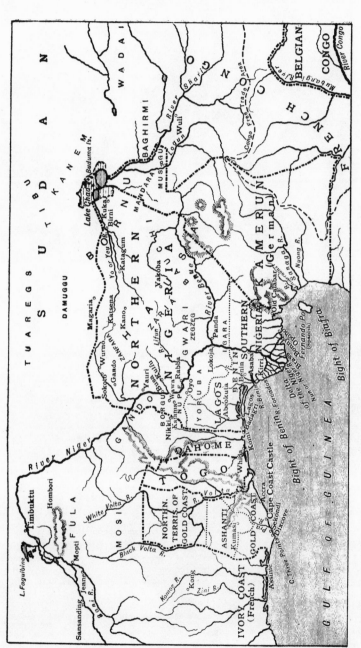

MAP OF NIGERIA AND GOLD COAST

Charlestown, came to the mouth of the Gambia
for a cargo of slaves, which were to be transported
to South Carolina. Park started in this vessel,
therefore, for America. But the ship took a long
time to reach the little island of Goree, then held
by the English (who had captured it from the
French), and during this interval four of the
American sailors, the surgeon of the ship, and three
of the slaves died of fever. The ship hung about
Goree waiting for provisions till the beginning of
October, and then started for America with about
one hundred and thirty slaves. On her way across
the Atlantic she sprang a leak and was so unsea-
worthy that her course was directed to the West
India Islands. Park was landed at Antigua, and
embarking at this island on a mail-ship, reached
England in another twenty-eight days, voyaging
across the Atlantic, and arriving in London on
the morning of Christmas Day before daylight.
As it was too early an hour to visit his brother-
in-law, Dickson, who was employed at the British
Museum, he wandered about the streets of Blooms-
bury. At last he entered the gardens, which then
surrounded the British Museum. Whilst looking
at the shrubs in the early daylight of the Christmas
morning, his brother-in-law, who had charge of
these gardens, came out also for an early inspec-
tion, and there saw to his intense surprise his
brother-in-law, Mungo Park, looking more like a
ghost than a being of flesh and blood. This, of
course, was long before the days of ocean cables
and telegraphs. Park had been absent two years

and seven months, and everyone connected with him had given him up as lost.

Park brought back the news to England of this wonderful Niger River flowing in great volume and depth to the east, and perhaps, after some considerable distance, to the south. He thought himself that it really found its outlet into the sea as the Congo. He knew that the Congo was called by the natives in its lower course Nzadi, and already European geographers had heard of the mysterious lake or great sheet of water in the heart of Africa called Zad or Chad. Mungo Park jumped to the conclusion that the Congo and Lake Chad were one and the same thing with the Niger, and he was most anxious to be allowed to go back properly equipped and descend the Niger in a boat till he came to its outlet into the sea.

But it was not until nearly eight years afterwards that his wish was granted. On 29 April, 1805, he reached Pisania on the Upper Gambia, accompanied by two other Scotchmen (like himself, natives of Selkirk county), by Lieutenant Martyn, a Royal Artillery officer, and thirty-five English and negro soldiers belonging to the Royal African Corps, which in those days was stationed at Goree to protect these West African settlements from the French.

This large party of white men left the Upper Gambia to cross over to the Niger on 4 May, 1805. Three weeks afterwards the expedition was nearly wrecked by the attack of a large swarm of

bees.   Mungo Park, on his previous journey, had
noticed how dangerous bees can be to the passing
traveller in Tropical Africa, especially if their hives
in the tall trees have recently been disturbed by
the negroes searching for honey.   They are then
ready to attack, without warning, any persons who
come within a few hundred yards of their hives.
In this particular instance nearly all the people
with Mungo Park were severely stung; seven of
the beasts of burden died from the stings, or bolted
into the bush and were never recovered, while the
confusion and upset in some way set fire to the
grass—no doubt some of the negroes attempted
to drive away the bees by the use of flaming
bundles of dry grass.   But from this fire it was
with great difficulty that the baggage of the expedition was saved.   " For half an hour it seemed
as though the bees would put an end to the expedition."

Between the Gambia and the Niger the expedition suffered sorely, though the natives generally were friendly.   The soldiers died of what
seemed to be epileptic fits, no doubt a kind of
sunstroke.   Others perished from dysentery.   The
rains set in with violence, and soon afterwards the
soldiers became affected by some mysterious disease, almost like sleeping-sickness.   They would fall
asleep in the road, or walk as if half-intoxicated,
and when they reached camp fell into such a sound
slumber they could scarcely be roused to change
their wet things.   It could not have been real
sleeping - sickness, because Mungo Park was af-

fected in the same way himself, and afterwards quite recovered.   When they entered the mountains about the Upper Senegal, though the scenery was most romantic,[1] the troubles increased.   The ascent was steep and rocky.   The asses of the expedition were heavily loaded, and most of the soldiers were too sick to walk.   Sometimes the caravan got into a state of terrible confusion on these rocky staircases which overhung tremendous precipices.   Certain of the negroes following the expedition took advantage of the soldiers' sickness to steal their pistols, greatcoats, and knapsacks from them.   At several villages extortionate demands were made for customs duties, the natives thinking that the Europeans, being so sick, would be unable to fight; but with firmness Mungo Park got over these difficulties.

"There is in these countries a species of acacia gum tree, which is called by the natives *Nitta*, the pods of which are filled round the seeds with a yellow powder, which is said to be very nutritious. In times of hunger, when the corn and pumpkins are not ripe, the people sustain themselves largely on the powder derived from this nitta pod, and in

---

[1] "The villages on these mountains are romantic beyond anything I ever saw.   They are built in the most delightful glens, and have plenty of water and grass at all seasons.   The people have cattle enough for their own use, and their superfluous grain purchases all their little luxuries; and while the thunder rolls in awful grandeur over their heads, they can look from their tremendous precipices over all that wild and woody plain which extends from the Faleme to the Black River. . . . There are no lions on the hills, though they are very numerous in the plain.   On this plain we observed some hundreds of a species of antelope of a dark colour with a white mouth; they are called by the natives *dakwi*, and are nearly as large as a bullock."   [These were evidently the roan antelope.]

order that this resource may not be wasted, the tree is put under a kind of tabu, or what is called locally, *tung*. This is done so that the women and children may be frightened of gathering the pods without permission. Some of Mungo Park's soldiers collected the fruit of the nitta and began eating the powder, whereupon the chief of the village was extremely angry. But after apologies he calmed down and explained how his people were obliged to preserve very carefully this supply of food to stave off intervals of famine. This incident brings home to us one of the many terrors of life in uncivilized lands — the uncertainty of a continual food supply.[1]

Park was cheered for a time by travelling through a country "beautiful beyond imagination", with all possible diversities of rock, some projections towering up like ruined castles, spires, and pyramids. One place they passed was so like a ruined Gothic abbey that they halted in order to satisfy themselves that the niches, windows, and ruined staircase were all natural rock. "A faithful description of this place would certainly be deemed a fiction," wrote Mungo Park. The villages were romantically situated along the edges of tremendous precipices. This was the country

---

[1] The *Nitta* or *Natta* was afterwards described by botanists and called *Parkia africana*, after its discoverer. In Hausaland the same "Nitta" tree was recorded by Clapperton. Here it was called "Durau". The beans or seeds were roasted, bruised, and allowed to ferment in water. When rotted they were washed clean and pounded into a powder which was made into cakes not unlike chocolate. A very pleasant drink was made of the farinaceous matter in which the seeds were embedded. Or this sweet flour was pressed into confections and sweetmeats.

between two affluents of the Upper Senegal, the
Ba Li, and the Ba Fing.[1] These rocks and mountains swarmed with baboons.

The soldiers began gradually to fall away from
the expedition. They would get lost and perhaps
were devoured by lions, or they would be too ill
to move when the camp was struck in the morning, and so had to be left behind in the care of
the natives. Very often they were too ill to ride,
fell off their horse or donkey, and were left behind.
Sometimes they were stripped of their clothes by
the natives while in a state of delirium, and rejoined the expedition quite naked. Mungo Park
and the officers of the expedition were constantly
ill themselves, sometimes too faint to stand.

Crossing one of the many affluents of the
Senegal (the Ba Wulima) their guide, Isaaco, a
Muhammadan Mandingo, was seized by a crocodile
as he was wading through the river in charge of
six of the asses. The crocodile laid hold of him
by the left thigh and pulled him under the water.
With wonderful presence of mind, while under
water, Isaaco felt for the head of the reptile and
thrust his fingers into its eyes, upon which it
quitted its hold and the man attempted to reach
the shore, calling out all the time for a knife.
The crocodile returned, seized him by the other
thigh, and again pulled him under water. Once
again he had recourse to the same expedient,
thrusting his fingers into its eyes with such violence

---

[1] *Ba* in all these geographical names between the Niger and the Gambia
means river.

that it finally left him. The poor man when he reached the shore was bleeding terribly and was much lacerated, some of his wounds being four inches deep. But Mungo Park patched him up somehow or other with sticking-plaster.

Mungo Park purchased all the milk that he could for his suffering men, and also used to boil cinchona bark in the camp kettles, and thus make a decoction of quinine for the fever-stricken. Nevertheless, the men on the march to the Niger dropped off, died, disappeared, were left behind, fell asleep by the wayside, and were devoured by hyenas. Mungo Park's own exertions were heroic. One of the innumerable streams which they had to ford, or rather swim, he crossed *sixteen times*; on one occasion carrying over his brother-in-law, Anderson, who was apparently dying.

As they neared the Niger they were constantly attacked by lions on the road, but managed to drive them off by the firing of muskets and the blowing of whistles. Near Bamaku on the Upper Niger, Park met once more his former benefactor, Karfa Taura.

By the time he did at last reach the Niger at Bamaku and saw its immense stream rolling along the plain, he had lost three-fourths of the men of his expedition. Only six soldiers and one carpenter had reached the Niger. Park conveyed his expedition from Bamaku to Marabu, a little bit lower down the river, and from this point he sent forward Isaaco, his guide, with a present to the great Mandingo king, or " Mansong", at Sego, who had refused to see him on his first journey, but had given him five thousand kauri shells for his travelling expenses. It may be interesting to set forth the articles which were now given to the Mansong for a present: A handsome silver-plated soup tureen; two double - barrelled guns, silver-mounted; two pairs of silver-mounted pistols; a sabre, with morocco-leather scabbard; 32 yards of scarlet broad cloth; 12 yards of blue broad cloth; 12 yards of yellow and 12 yards of light-green cloth; and two kegs and a half of gunpowder. To the eldest son of this great chief was sent a double-barrelled gun, silver-mounted, a pair of pistols, and a sabre.

Whilst waiting the return of Isaaco, Mungo Park was very ill with dysentery, and to cure himself took such a quantity of calomel that he could not speak or sleep for six days; but this dreadful remedy apparently stopped the dysentery, and presently his anxieties were relieved by the arrival of one of the Mansong's court musicians or "singing men", who brought with him friendly messages and six canoes with which to transport what remained of Park's expedition to Sego.

"Nothing could be more beautiful than the views of this immense river—sometimes as smooth as a mirror, at others ruffled with a gentle breeze, but at all times wafting us along at the rate of 6 or 7 miles an hour."

Though the great King of Bambara refused to see Mungo Park out of fear and superstition (and, in fact, whenever much was said about him

in his hearing, used to make squares and triangles
with his finger in the sand as a protection against
magic), he nevertheless offered no opposition to his
plans for exploring the Niger, and perhaps bringing these countries into direct communication with
the trade of the white man. Mungo Park made
a most sensible address to his envoys and minis-
ters, explaining that most of the trade goods
brought to them by the Moors, who were so
bitterly opposed to the coming of Europeans,
were goods made in Europe, and that it would be
a considerable gain to the black people of the
Niger if they got into direct relations with the
Europeans, instead of having to carry on their
trade through the Moors.

Park selected a town called Sansanding for his
experiment of building a boat with which to navigate the Niger, and here he settled himself. This
was a typical town on the Muhammadan Niger,
and at that time contained about 11,000 inhabitants. Like all the great buildings of Nigeria, the
mosques were built of dried mud on a wooden
framework, and, at a distance, looked like tall
buildings of masonry with towers and peaks.
"The marketplace is a large square," wrote
Mungo Park, "and the different articles of merchandise are exposed for sale on stalls covered with
mats to shade them from the sun. The market
is crowded with people from morning to night.
Some of the stalls contain nothing but beads,
others indigo in balls, others wood-ashes in balls,
others Hausa and Jenné cloth. I observed one

stall with nothing but antimony[1] in small bits, another with sulphur, and a third with copper and silver rings and bracelets. In the houses fronting the square are sold scarlet cloth, amber, silks from Morocco, and tobacco which looks like Levant tobacco, and comes by way of Timbuktu. Adjoining this is the salt market, part of which occupies one corner of the square. A slab of salt is sold commonly for eight thousand kauri shells (about equal then to £1, 15s.). A large butcher's stall, or shed, is in the centre of the square, and as good and fat meat sold every day as any in England. The beer market is at a little distance, under two large trees; and there are often exposed for sale from eighty to one hundred calabashes of beer, each containing about two gallons. Near the beer market is the place where red and yellow leather is sold."

Whilst his schooner was being built by himself, by Lieutenant Martyn, and a private soldier named Abraham Bolton who had some knowledge of carpentry, Park himself set up a shop at Sansanding, which was crowded with customers. Here he sold such of his goods as he could no longer transport with him, and realized a hundred thousand kauri shells (about £20), then the cash of all the Niger regions. But during his stay at Sansanding he lost not only Mr. Scott, the artist who accompanied the expedition to draw the scenery and people, and who died at a village two or three

---

[1] Used by the Moors and Fulas for darkening the skin round the eyes to make them more brilliant.

days distant from the Niger, but also Alexander Anderson, his brother-in-law. Park was now left with only Lieutenant Martyn, Abraham Bolton, two other private soldiers, three negro slaves, and a Mandingo interpreter called Amadi Fatuma.

The "schooner" in which Mungo Park intended to descend the Niger till he reached the sea was really made of the two best halves of two canoes, joined together in the middle. Its length was 40 feet and its breadth 6 feet. It was flat-bottomed, with only a draught of 1 foot of water when loaded, and was presumably fitted with masts and sails. "Eighteen days hard labour changed the Bambara canoe into His Majesty's Schooner *Joliba*."[1]

On 17 November, 1805, Mungo Park's expedition left Sansanding. They passed the vicinity of the great town of Jenné, with a very short halt, and traversed the Lake Debo, where they were attacked by men in canoes, armed with pikes, lances, bows and arrows. They were again attacked at Kabara, the port of Timbuktu, but always were able to beat off their assailants by means of their firearms. These constant fights with Fulas and negroes reduced the white men to a state of panic, especially Lieutenant Martyn, who was only too eager to shoot natives whenever he saw canoes advancing towards them. He even wanted to shoot the interpreter for remonstrating with him, but Mungo Park interfered. At one place, where the Niger

[1] Joliba was the Mandingo name given to the Niger.

[2] Jenné is really situated on a long narrow peninsula between the main Niger and its great affluent the Bani. Jenné or Jene, in the Songhai language simply means "the river", the Niger.

began to turn southwards, there was a strong army of Fula infantry on one side of the river. Sometimes Park's expedition seized canoes, with the people in them, as hostages, so that the interpreter might land and buy food, though for the most part they were well provided with the provisions they had collected at Sansanding. As they neared the Hausa-speaking countries, they saw, on the banks of the river near a high mountain, an army composed of Tuaregs, with horses and camels, but without firearms.

Amadi Fatuma went with them as far as the country of Yauri, on the borders of the great Hausa-speaking countries, and here his contract came to an end. From this place he was to return to Sansanding. But the chief of the Yauri town by the waterside where Mungo Park had halted, hearing that the white men would not return, but would work their way to the sea, withheld from the king of the country the handsome present which Mungo Park had left for him; therefore Amadi Fatuma was made to suffer for this, for the King of Yauri not only sent an army to oppose Park at the rapids of Busa,[1] but also put Fatuma in irons and kept him thus for three months. Then he made his way back to his native town in the kingdom of Bambara, and was able nearly five years afterwards to give an account to Isaaco about what had happened to Mungo Park. Isaaco

[1] This was Fatuma's story, but the King of Yauri told Clapperton he sent men, not to oppose the "white Christians", but to show them how to descend the rapids.

THE BUSA RAPIDS ON THE LOWER NIGER, WHERE MUNGO PARK AND LIEUTENANT MARTYN WERE DROWNED IN 1806

accompanied Park's expedition as interpreter to the Upper Niger, and then resumed his trading journeys between that river and Senegambia, and so kept in touch with the British authorities. When after some years nothing more was heard of Park after he had left Sansanding, the British Governor of Sierra Leone got hold of Isaaco and sent him to the Niger to make enquiries. Thus he learnt that Park, when he reached the rapids of Busa, where the Niger contracts into a single turbulent channel between high rocks, found these rocks covered with men who were armed with bows and arrows, spears and muskets. The King of Yauri is alleged to have wished to have helped Park, in spite of his being puzzled and offended at not getting his present. He stated that he had despatched people to help him through the rapids. However that might be, the armed natives who were on the spot, seemed to have manifested hostility, while Park too hurriedly shot at them in return. Then they closed on him and directed a furious fire of arrows and bullets into his long, narrow boat. The boat, badly steered in the panic, bumped up against a rock. Park and the only other white man who was with him took hold of each other's hands and jumped into the water, and, according to the native account, were drowned. Several of the negroes in the boat were killed, but one of them pleaded for mercy and his life was spared.

Yet, although the explorer had reached a point on the Lower Niger where he was at no great distance from the sea in a straight line, it is doubtful whether he would ever have won through to the sea. From Busa southwards there would have been many rapids and shallows difficult of navigation. The powerful people of Nupe, Yoruba, Igara, and the Ibo countries, would have been greedy for presents and tolls. The unhealthy climate of the forest belt would have finished the worn-out white men, even if they had been allowed by the turbulent, suspicious people to pass through the countries of Nupe, Igara, and Ida to the Niger Delta, a region then visited rarely by any ships that were not engaged in the slave trade or in piracy.

H.M.S. *Joliba*, though partially capsized, was drawn by the Busa people on to the rocks and some of her contents were saved and sent up to the King of Busa or distributed amongst the people of the town. They obtained thus a quantity of preserved or salted beef, packed in tins or small casks. This was eagerly devoured; but it had putrefied, and those who ate of it suffered from what we should now call "ptomaine" poisoning. Consequently many who shared in the plunder of the *Joliba* died of a mysterious internal malady. Their deaths were ascribed by superstition, not to the bad beef, but to the avenging spirit of Park. From this arose a saying which lasted long in Nigeria: "Do not injure a Christian or you will share the fate of the people of Busa".

Amongst other things said to have been retrieved from the wreck of Mungo Park's expedition was a magnificent tobe[1] of red damask silk, richly embroidered with gold—so heavy, indeed, with its gold adornments, that it could scarcely have been worn by Park himself. If it was really part of his baggage, he must have been carrying it along as a very special present for some great chief or sultan.

But the King of Busa, in 1831, told the Landers that his father many years ago had bought this tobe from a " white man who came from the north ". This white man may have been the German explorer, Friedrich Hornemann, born at Hildesheim in Hanover, in 1772, who had been one of the first pioneers engaged by the African Association of Great Britain to find the outlet of the Niger. Hornemann is reported to have crossed the Sahara Desert from Egypt to Fezzan and Bornu, and to have died in Nupe about the year 1800, whilst following the Niger seawards. If so, he came very near to snatching the glory of the discovery from British explorers. Quite possibly he passed through Busa, and there disposed of this magnificent garment to the Hausa king of that country. It was thought to be so splendid, indeed, that the young King of Busa, who told the story to Richard Lander, added that he dared not wear the tobe, lest the display of so much wealth in costume should provoke neighbouring potentates to go to war with him. Indeed, he afterwards gave the gold-and-crimson tobe away to Richard Lander,

[1] The word tobe (or taub), which will often recur, is the Hausa name for the great smocklike garment worn by men in Nigeria.

to whom it proved very useful, as you will see in a later portion of this book.

But the young, handsome, and friendly King of Busa (who enabled the brothers Lander to complete that tracing of the Niger which was so nearly accomplished by the great Scottish explorer) had preserved an undoubted relic of Mungo Park; and this, we are told, he valued " as a household god ". Eighty years ago or so, print or hand-writing amongst these negroes of Northern Nigeria was full of a wonderful unexplained magic. This treasure of mystic potency was an old nautical almanac, and between its leaves was reverently kept (amongst other papers) the following letter:—

" Mr. and Mrs. Watson would be happy to have the pleasure of Mr. Park's company at dinner on Tuesday next, at half-past five o'clock.

" An answer is requested.

"Strand, 9 November, 1804."

CHAPTER VII

Pioneers in the Gold Coast Hinterland

WHEN the Portuguese reached the Gold Coast in 1471, and Benin in 1485, natives of these regions do not seem to have been as much astonished at the sight of white men as would have been the case if they had never heard of such beings. But we may assume that they were not unfamiliar with the idea through the penetration into their countries of Moors and Arabs from the north.[1] At any rate, the Portuguese found the natives all prepared for a trade in gold.

In the seventeenth century the Dutch first, and the English second, replaced and drove out the Portuguese, and established many fortified trading posts on the Gold Coast, partly in order to collect slaves, and partly for the sake of the gold.

Until we opened up this trade with the Gold Coast in the reign of Charles II, we could only obtain gold for the English coinage through our uncertain trade with Spain. As soon as we were able to export gold from West Africa, however, Charles II was able to issue a new British gold coinage, which on account of its origin bore the

[1] See Chapter I. They were far from being the naked cannibal savages of the Ivory Coast or the Niger Delta.

name of "Guinea", and was worth approximately twenty-one shillings.

The British, represented by a Chartered and subsidized Corporation called the African Company of Merchants, possessed at the close of the eighteenth century the strong fort of Cape Coast Castle as their headquarters on the Gold Coast. They had seven other fortified trading-stations between Dixcove on the west and Accra on the east. The Dutch Chartered Company ruled in between or to the westward of Dixcove; and the Danes held the coast between Accra and the mouth of the Volta River.

In 1807, however, the kingdom of Ashanti thrust itself on the notice of the European nations trading with the Gold Coast by forcing its way through the Fanti tribes to the sea, attacking, capturing and destroying the English fort of Anamabú and the celebrated Dutch fort of Cormantyn (Koromanti), from which so many thousand slaves had been shipped to America.

In 1811, and again in 1816, the Ashanti army invaded the Fanti country, and even blockaded the principal British settlement of Cape Coast Castle. Several times the Ashanti invading force had been bought off by the British Government, which ransomed the Fanti refugees by large sums of gold. But in 1817 it was decided to send a mission to Ashanti in order to come to a friendly understanding with the king of that powerful country. The mission was entrusted to the leadership of Mr. Frederick James, to whom was attached as assistant, Thomas Edward Bowdich; also a secretary (Mr. Hutchison), and a surgeon (Mr. Tedlie).

Afterwards, the attitude and arguments adopted by Mr. James in his intercourse with the King of Ashanti were so disagreed with by Bowdich and the other members of the mission, that James was recalled by the Governor of the Gold Coast, and his place as head of the mission taken by Mr. Bowdich.

The route followed by the mission from Cape Coast[1] Castle to Kumasi, the Ashanti capital, passed through dense forest and across numerous swamps. The ground of every camp was damp and swarmed with insects and snakes. The nights were made additionally uneasy by the screeching and wailing cries of the tree-hyrax,[2] and the caravan was sometimes disturbed by the passage through the camp of wild hogs—probably the red river hog of West Africa. Immense trunks of fallen trees obstructed the path, and every member of the caravan was forced to climb over them. The standing trees were covered with parasites

---

[1] The name was a corruption of the Portuguese *Cabo Corso.*

[2] The Hyraxes (*Procavia*) are (at the present day) little mammals about the size of a large rabbit and somewhat like a rabbit in appearance, except that they have small ears. In reality they are small ungulates of a very primitive type, no doubt resembling somewhat in structure and appearance the creatures which existed at the beginning of the Tertiary Epoch, and were the stock from which all the modern hoofed animals were derived. The hyrax is mentioned in the Old Testament; and the Hebrew word was translated "coney", which was the older English name for rabbit. Hyraxes are still found in Syria and Egypt, but elsewhere only in Tropical Africa. In all parts of Africa which are densely forested the hyraxes live in the trees; elsewhere they inhabit the crannies of the rocks. At night they utter loud cries which sound very strange and mournful.

and creepers; some of these last (no doubt, rubber vines) were like small cables ascending the trunks to some height, and abruptly falling downwards in loops, crossing to the opposite trees and threading in and out the brushwood in a perplexity of twistings and turnings. The foliage was noisy with parrots and turacos, and in the swamps were numerous crowned cranes. At night, fireflies spangled the herbage till the whole of the lower parts of the forest glittered with dancing lights. By day and by night a strong fragrance was emitted from the flowers of certain trees and creepers, while a stupefying stench would arise in other directions from decaying vegetation.

The porters of the expedition were in the greatest terror of the evil spirits of the woods, and to keep up their courage uttered discordant yells by night and by day. These, mingled with the howls and screeches of the forest birds and beasts, robbed the unfortunate Europeans of any chance of uninterrupted sleep when in camp. In the few clearings through which they passed where there had once been villages, the ground was scattered with human skulls, the relics of Ashanti butcheries.

When they attained the Assin territory their surroundings became more cheerful. The native towns presented wide and clean streets of regular houses, amongst which it was easy to find a comfortable dwelling, and fairly large, clean rooms. The fronts of the houses were usually whitewashed, while the floors were a deep red. When they crossed the Prā river and reached the country of Ashanti the land became much more hilly, with occasional outcrops of quartz.

As they entered the capital, Kumasi, they passed under its protecting "fetish", which was the cut-up body of a dead sheep, wrapped in red silk, and suspended between two lofty poles. They were received by something like five thousand warriors, and a deafening blowing of trumpets, beating of drums, gongs, and rattles, and the incessant discharges of musketry. The captains of the warriors were dancing madly in the centre of circles formed of their soldiers, some of whom waved English, Dutch, and Danish flags, and jumped and yelled around their springing leaders, who were discharging shining blunderbusses so close to the flags that they set them on fire. The dress of the captains consisted of a war cap of immense plumes of eagles' feathers, with gilded rams' horns projecting in front. The caps were fastened under the chins with bands of kauris. The arms remain naked, but each captain wore a sleeveless waistcoat of red cloth covered with fetishes and amulets in gold, silver, or embroidered cases. These were intermixed with small brass bells, the horns and tails of animals, and bright-coloured shells. Long knives were stuck into the belts, and leopards' tails hung down over the back of each captain, who wore in addition loose cotton trousers tucked into immense Moorish boots of red leather, reaching halfway up the thigh, and having their tops attached by small chains to the waistbelt. A small quiver of poisoned arrows hung from the right wrist, an assagai was carried in the left hand (with its stem swathed in red cloth and silk tassels), round each arm were hung the white plumes of Colobus monkey tails, and the tails of horses. Each captain held by his teeth the end of a long steel chain, to the other extremity of which was fastened a charm, consisting of a piece of parchment inscribed with Arabic writing.

"This exhibition continued about half an hour, when we were allowed to proceed, encircled by the warriors, whose numbers, with the crowds of people, made our movement as gradual as if it had taken place in Cheapside; the several streets branching off to the right, presented long vistas crammed with people, and those on the left hand being on an acclivity, innumerable rows of heads rose one above another: the large open porches of the houses, like the fronts of stages in small theatres, were filled with the better sort of females and children, all impatient to behold white men for the first time; their exclamations were drowned in the firing and music, but their gestures were in character with the scene. When we reached the palace, about half a mile from the place where we entered, we were again halted, and an open file was made, through which the bearers were passed, to deposit the presents and baggage in the house assigned to us.

" Here we were gratified by observing several of the caboceers (chiefs or headmen) pass by with their trains, the novel splendour of which astonished us. The bands, principally composed of horns and flutes, trained to play in concert, seemed to soothe our hearing into its natural tone again by their wild melodies; while the immense umbrellas, made to sink and rise from the jerkings of the bearers, and the large fans waving around, refreshed us with small currents of air, under a burning sun, clouds of dust, and a density of atmosphere almost suffocating. We were then squeezed, at the same funeral pace, up a long street, to an open-fronted house, where we were desired by a royal messenger to wait a further invitation from the King. Here our attention was forced from the astonishment of the crowd to a most inhuman spectacle, which was paraded before us for some minutes; it was a man whom they were tormenting previous to sacrifice; his hands were pinioned behind him, a knife was passed through his cheeks, to which his lips were noosed like the figure of 8; one ear was cut off and carried before him, the other hung to his head by a small bit of skin; there were several gashes in his back, and a knife was thrust under his shoulder blade; he was led with a cord passed through his nose, by men disfigured with immense caps of shaggy black skins, and drums beating before him; the feeling this horrid barbarity excited must be imagined. We were soon released by permission to proceed to the King, and passed through a very broad street, about a quarter of a mile long, to the marketplace.

"Our observations *en passant* had taught us to conceive a spectacle far exceeding our original expectations, but they had not prepared us for the extent and display of the scene which here burst upon us: an area of nearly a mile in circumference was crowded with magnificence and novelty. The King, his tributaries, and captains were resplendent in the distance, surrounded by attendants of every description, fronted by a mass of warriors which seemed to make our approach impervious. The sun was reflected, with a glare scarcely more supportable than the heat, from the massy gold ornaments, which glistened in every direction. More than a hundred bands burst out on our arrival, with the peculiar airs of their several chiefs; the horns flourished their defiances, with the beating of innumerable drums and metal instruments, and then yielded for a while to the soft breathings of their long flutes, which were truly harmonious; and a pleasing instrument, like a bagpipe without the drone, was happily blended. At last a hundred large umbrellas, or canopies, which could shelter thirty persons, were sprung up and down by the bearers with brilliant effect, being made of scarlet, yellow, and the most showy cloths and silks, and crowned on the top with crescents, pelicans, elephants, and arms and swords of gold; they were of various shapes, but mostly domed; and the vallances (in some of which small looking-glasses were inserted) were fantastically scalloped and fringed; from the fronts of some, the proboscis and small teeth of elephants pro-

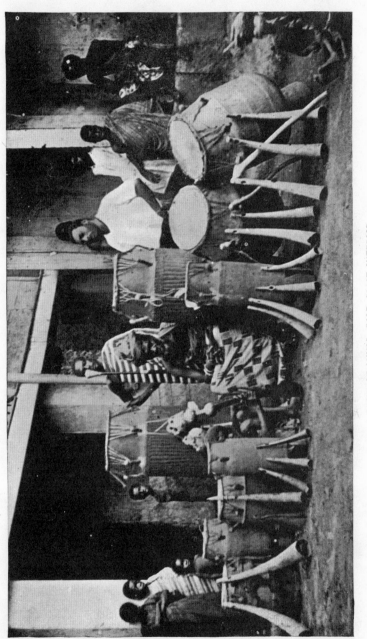

A BAND OF MUSIC, GOLD COAST INTERIOR

jected, and a few were roofed with leopard skins, and crowned with various animals naturally stuffed. The state hammocks, like long cradles, were raised in the rear, the poles on the heads of the bearers; their cushions and pillows were covered with crimson taffeta, and the richest cloths hung over the sides. Innumerable small umbrellas, of various coloured stripes, were crowded in the intervals, whilst several large trees heightened the glare, by contrasting the sober colouring of nature.

" The King's messengers, with gold breastplates, made way for us, and we commenced our round, preceded by the canes and the English flag. We stopped to take the hand of every caboceer, which, as their household suites occupied several spaces in advance, delayed us long enough to distinguish some of the ornaments in the general blaze of splendour and ostentation.

" The caboceers and their superior captains and attendants wore Ashanti cloths of extravagant price, from the costly foreign silks which had been unravelled to weave them in all the varieties of colour, as well as pattern; they were of an incredible size and weight, and thrown over the shoulder exactly like the Roman toga; a small silk fillet encircled their temples, and massy gold necklaces, intricately wrought, suspended Moorish charms, dearly purchased, and enclosed in small square cases of gold, silver, and curious embroidery. Some wore necklaces, reaching to the navel, entirely of agri beads[1]; a band of gold and beads encircled the knee, from

[1] See page 21.

which several strings of the same depended; small circles of gold like guineas, rings, and casts of animals were strung round their ankles; their sandals were of green, red, and delicate white leather; manillas[1], and rude lumps of rock gold, hung from their left wrists, which were so heavily laden as to be supported on the head of one of their handsomest boys. Gold and silver pipes, and canes, dazzled the eye in every direction. Wolves' (hyænas') and rams' heads as large as life, cast in gold, were suspended from their gold-handled swords, which were held around them in great numbers; the blades were shaped like round bills, and rusted in blood; the sheaths of leopard skin, or the skin of a fish, like shagreen[2]. The large drums, supported on the head of one man and beaten by two others, were braced around with the thigh bones of their enemies, and ornamented with their skulls. The kettledrums, resting on the ground, were scraped with wet fingers, and covered with leopard skin. The wrists of the drummers were hung with bells and curiously shaped pieces of iron, which jingled loudly as they were beating. The smaller drums were suspended from the neck by scarves of red cloth; the horns (the teeth of young elephants) were ornamented at the mouthpiece with gold, and the jawbones of human victims. The war caps of eagles' feathers nodded in the rear, and large fans, of the wing feathers of the ostrich, played around the dignitaries. Immediately behind

---

[1] Iron bracelets.
[2] Probaby a lizard skin from the large Monitor lizard.

their chairs (which were of a black wood, almost covered by inlays of ivory and gold embossment) stood their handsomest youths, with corslets of leopard's skin covered with gold cockle shells, and stuck full of small knives, sheathed in gold and silver, with the handles of blue agate; cartouche boxes of elephants' hide hung below, ornamented in the same manner; a large gold-handled sword was fixed behind the left shoulder, and silk scarves and horses' tails (generally white) streamed from the arms and waist cloth: their long Danish muskets had broad rims of gold at small distances, and the stocks were ornamented with shells.

"Finely grown girls stood behind the chairs of some chieftains, with silver basins. Their stools (of the most laborious carved work, and generally with two large bells attached to them) were conspicuously placed on the heads of the favourites; and crowds of small boys were seated around, flourishing elephants' tails curiously mounted. The warriors sat on the ground close to these, and so thickly as not to admit of our passing without treading on their feet, to which they were perfectly indifferent; their caps were of the skin of the pangolin[1] and leopard, the tails hanging down behind; their cartouche belts (composed of small gourds which hold the charges, and covered with leopard and pigs' skin) were embossed with red shells, and small brass bells thickly hung to them; on their hips and shoulders was a cluster of knives; iron chains and collars dignified the most daring, who

---

[1] The scaly ant-eater or manis (*Manis gigantea* probably).

were prouder of them than of gold; their muskets had rests affixed of leopards' skin, and the locks a covering of the same; the sides of their faces were curiously painted in long white streaks, and their arms also striped, having the appearance of armour.

"We were suddenly surprised by the sight of Moors, who afforded the first general diversity of dress; there were seventeen superiors, arrayed in large cloaks of white satin, richly trimmed with spangled embroidery, their shirts and trousers were of silk, and a very large turban of white muslin was studded with a border of different coloured stones. Their attendants wore red caps and turbans, and long white shirts, which hung over their trousers; those of the inferiors were of dark-blue cloth; they slowly raised their eyes from the ground as we passed, and with a most malignant scowl.

"The prolonged flourishes of the horns, a deafening tumult of drums, and the fuller concert of the interval, announced that we were approaching the king: we were already passing the principal officers of his household; the chamberlain, the gold-horn blower, the captain of the messengers, the captain of the royal executions, the captain of the market, the keeper of the royal burial ground, and the master of the bands, sat surrounded by a retinue and splendour which bespoke the dignity and importance of their offices. The cook had a number of small services covered with leopard's skin held behind him, and a large quantity of massy silver plate was displayed before him, punch bowls,

waiters, coffee pots, tankards, and a very large
vessel with heavy handles and clawed feet, which
seemed to have been made to hold incense. The
executioner, a man of an immense size, wore a
massy gold hatchet on his breast; and the execution stool was held before him, clotted in blood,
and partly covered with a caul of fat. The king's
four linguists (interpreters) were encircled by a
splendour inferior to none, and their peculiar in-
signia, gold canes, were elevated in all directions,
tied in bundles like *fasces*. The keeper of the
treasury added to his own magnificence by the
ostentatious display of his service; the blow pan,
boxes, scales, and weights, were of *solid gold*."

The King of Ashanti appeared to be about
thirty-eight years of age, rather stout, but with
a benevolent countenance. He wore a fillet of
agri beads round his temples, a necklace of four
cockspur shells strung by their largest ends, and
over his right shoulder a red silk cord suspended
three amulets in gold cases. His bracelets were
the richest mixture in beads and gold, and his
fingers were covered with rings. His long waist
cloth was of dark-green silk, a pointed diadem
was elegantly painted in white on his forehead,
also an imitation epaulette on each shoulder, while
a gold ornament, like a full-blown rose, one leaf
rising above another, covered his whole breast.
Round his knees were bands of agri beads, and
from each ankle hung strings of whole ornaments
of the most delicate workmanship. His sandals
were of a soft white leather, embossed across the

instep band with small gold and silver cases of
amulets.   He was seated in a low chair richly
ornamented with gold, and he wore a pair of
gold castanets on his finger and thumb, which he
clashed together to enforce silence.   Behind his
chair stood negro guards, whose cartridge belts
were cased in gold, and further covered with small
imitation jawbones of the same metal.   Some of
his attendants waved elephants' tails spangled with
gold, and others agitated fans of birds' feathers.
Close by the King was placed the royal stool or
traditional throne of the Ashanti kings.   It was
entirely cased in gold, and stood under a huge
and gorgeous umbrella, surrounded with drums
and other musical instruments also cased in gold.
The swords of state carried by the courtiers were
sheathed   in   golden   scabbards,   their   handles
mounted in gold, and from these handles were
suspended large circles of gold by a ribbon of
scarlet cloth.   The breasts of the leading attendants and courtiers around the king were adorned
with large stars, wings, imitation stools, and crescents of solid gold.

Bowdich concluded a treaty with the King of
Ashanti, who swore with the utmost solemnity to
execute its provisions.   Yet shortly afterwards the
Mission nearly came to a fatal termination.   Bowdich, who, though an able, was a rather pompous
man, determined to leave at once for the coast
before certain minor questions had been settled to
the satisfaction of the King of Ashanti, amongst
them being the installation of Mr. Hutchison as

British Resident at Kumasi. Bowdich insisted on going when he pleased, and on trying to start with his Fanti carriers and English soldiers he was forcibly prevented from doing so by the Ashanti captain in whose house he lodged. They came to blows, and the Ashantis used stones and clubs freely, but were careful to avoid guns. Nevertheless, Bowdich was nearly killed in the struggle, and was obliged to appeal to the King to restore peace. Then followed a reconciliation, and they became better friends than ever. When Bowdich and his Mission did leave, it was under the charge of Ashantis who took the utmost care of him and his companion.

It was now the height of the rainy season—September. The rivers were swollen, but Bowdich, who was on several occasions needlessly obstinate, insisted on pursuing the journey. He was accompanied by an Ashanti headman, who refused to leave him, saying, that if any disaster happened to the white men he and the other Ashanti guides would be decapitated when they returned to their own land. "We lost some time" (writes Bowdich) "in trying to make torches to keep off the wild beasts, and to direct us in the right track, for we were walking through a continued bog, and before long had lost our shoes. A violent tornado ushered in the night, we could not hear each other hallo, and were soon separated; luckily I found I had one person left with me (the Ashanti headman) who, after I had groped him out, tied his cloth tight round his middle, gave me the other end, and thus plunging along pulled me after him through

bogs and rivers exactly like an owl tied to a duck
in a pond! The thunder, the darkness, and the
howlings of the wild beasts were awful; but the
loud and continuing crash of a large tree which
fell very near us during the storm was even more
so to my ear. The Ashanti had dragged me along
or rather through in this manner until I judged it to
be midnight, when, quite exhausted, with the rem-
nants of my clothes scarcely hanging together, I let
go his cloth, and, falling on the ground, was asleep
before I could call out to him. I was awaked
by this faithful guide, who had felt me out and
seated me on the trunk of a tree with my head
resting on his shoulder; he gave me to understand
that I must die if I sat there, and we pursued the
duck-and-owl method once more. In an hour we
had forded the last river, which had swollen considerably above my chin, and spread to a great
width. This labour I considered final, and my
drowsiness became so fascinating that it seemed
to beguile me of every painful thought and apprehension, and the yielding to it was an exquisite
though momentary pleasure. I must have slept
about an hour, lifted by this humane man from
the bank of the river to a drier corner of the forest,
more impervious to the torrents of rain; when, being
awoke, I was surprised to see him with a companion
and a torch. He took me on his back, and in
about three-quarters of an hour we reached Akrofrum. This man knew I carried about with me
several ounces of gold for the subsistence of my
people, not trusting to our luggage, which we

could not reckon on in such a season and journey.
Exhausted and insensible, my life was in his hands,
and, infested as the forest was with wild beasts, he
might, after such a night, without suspicion, have
reported me as destroyed by them. . . . It was
about two o'clock in the morning, and the inhabitants of Akrofrum were almost all asleep . . .
however, I was directly carried to a dry and clean
apartment, furnished with a brass pan full of water
to wash in, some fruits and palm wine, an excellent
bed of mats and cushions, and an abundance of
country cloths to wrap myself in, for I was all but
naked. After I had washed I rolled myself up
in the cloths one after the other, until I became
a gigantic size, and, by a profuse perspiration,
escaped any other ill than a slight fever."

The treaty made by Bowdich with the King of
Ashanti (Osai Tutu Kwamina) was accepted by the
British Government, but never really carried into
effect, so far as it concerned the handing over of the
Fanti people and the coast districts to the King of
Ashanti. In fact, the British authorities at Cape
Coast Castle did not behave honourably in this
matter; but the fact was they shrank from giving
effect to their envoys' agreements when they saw
what cruelties were likely to be inflicted on the
unfortunate Fanti people once the Ashantis were
masters of the Gold Coast.

Consequently, in 1823 the King of Ashanti de-
clared war on the British authority. Sir Charles
M'Carthy, the Governor-in-Chief of the West
African Settlements (Gambia River, Sierra Leone,

and the Gold Coast), hastened to take up the gage
of battle. He advanced from Cape Coast Castle
to meet the Ashantis inland with a force of only
about one hundred British soldiers and some four
thousand Fanti auxiliaries. Near the Prā River
(at Esamako), in January, 1822, he encountered an
army of over ten thousand Ashanti warriors, was
defeated and killed; and only fifty white soldiers
(including two officers) returned alive to Cape
Coast Castle. Sir Charles's head was cut off and
sent to Kumasi, where the skull was made into
a royal drinking vessel. Curiously enough the
victorious Ashanti king (Osai Tutu) died—from
excitement, it is said—on the day of his victory.
Though the Ashanti army ravaged the Fanti country, it did not succeed in taking Cape Coast Castle;
and by 1826 a British force had avenged Sir Charles
M'Carthy in the battle of Dodowa, in which fight
the Ashanti army, under its new king, sustained
such a crushing defeat, that it ceased to be a serious
danger to the coast forts. In 1831 the southern
boundary of the Ashanti kingdom was fixed at the
River Prā.

Between 1850 and 1872 the British Government
bought out the Danish and Dutch Governments
from their possessions and protectorates on the
Gold Coast. These actions displeased the King
of Ashanti, who did not want to see the whole
coast line between his country and the sea pass
under the control of one European nation. In
1873 the King of Ashanti—Kofi Kalkali—invaded
the Fanti districts, and set the British at defiance.

The result was the expedition under Sir Garnet
Wolseley, which effectually humbled the Ashanti
power for twenty years. In 1895 fresh troubles
were threatened, and an expeditionary force under
Sir Francis Scott entered Kumasi and brought
away the supreme King of Ashanti (Kofi Kalkali's
son, Prempe) to the coast. In 1901, after another
military expedition, the Ashanti kingdoms (for the
King of "Ashanti" was really King of the Kumasi tribe, and only the principal monarch of a
confederation of kings) were annexed to the Gold
Coast Colony, and henceforth administered directly
by British officials.

Since Bowdich's day, when the British possessions in this part of West Africa were limited to
Cape Coast Castle and isolated forts at Accra,
Anamabu, Sekondi, Dixcove, and three other
places on the Fanti coast, the Gold Coast Colony
has expanded to an area of 80,000 square miles,
and stretches northwards far beyond Ashanti to
regions near the basin of the Central Niger and
to lands remarkable for their Muhammadan civilization, where the mode of life resembles closely the
descriptions given by Mungo Park, Clapperton,
and Lander of the Mandingo States, of Borgu,
Hausaland, and the Fula Empire.

CHAPTER VIII

The Advance on the Niger from the East:
The British in Bornu

THE death of Mungo Park was not known approximately in England till the year 1811. At that time the British Government was entirely absorbed in the climax of its struggle with Napoleon, and unable to think about African exploration. But no sooner was this struggle brought to a close by the battle of Waterloo than a renewed interest was felt in the fate of Mungo Park and the discovery of the Niger outlet.

Although a clever German geographer, Reichard, had put together all the information that could then be collected, and had proved that the Niger must find its outlet through the rivers between Benin and Old Calabar, the belief that the Congo was really the mouth of this great river was dominant. Consequently the British Government decided to send its expedition under Captain Tuckey to the mouth of the Congo, and perhaps reach the Niger or the great inland sea (Lake Chad), in which, according to some speculations, the Niger lost itself.

But Captain Tuckey's mission only progressed

about 160 miles up the Congo, and led to little or
no increase in our knowledge.

During the Napoleonic wars, however, Great
Britain had occupied, and finally annexed, the
island of Malta in the Mediterranean. Malta
carried on an important trade with Tripoli, on the
north coast of Africa. Tripoli was the capital of
one of the six Barbary States, of which the others
were the Empire of Morocco, the Deylik of Oran,
the Deylik of Algiers, the Beylik of Constantine,
and the Beylik of Tunis. Like all the other " Barbary " States, except Morocco, it was an appanage
of the Turkish Empire; but the Basha of Tripoli
in those days was practically independent, and had
become an ally of the British Government, after
Nelson's victories had given us the maritime control of the Mediterranean.

The consuls who represented Great Britain
diplomatically and commercially in Tripoli soon
sent back reports of the wonderful Sudan trade,
of the rich countries of Bornu, Hausa, and Sakatu
(Sokoto), even of "Nyffe" (which we now call
Nupe), and of the "Quorra", Kwara, or Niger
River, together with the great Lake Chad. When
Tuckey's expedition to the Congo had failed, there-
fore, the next best course seemed to be to send an
expedition across the Sahara Desert to reach the
Lower Niger in that way, and a caravan under
Mr. Ritchie and Captain George Lyon started from
Tripoli in 1818 and reached the country of Fezzan.
Here Ritchie died, and Captain Lyon was obliged
to return.

But four years afterwards—in 1822—a much stronger expedition was sent with the intention at least of reaching Bornu. It was under the command of Dr. Walter Oudney, a Scottish physician, who had been appointed political agent to Bornu, and who was to be assisted by Lieutenant Hugh Clapperton of the Royal Navy and Lieutenant Dixon Denham[1] of the British army. The expedition at first did not get much farther than Captain Lyon had done, because it was evident that, in spite of all his promises and assurances, the Basha of Tripoli was really very suspicious of the motives of Great Britain, in trying to penetrate to Central Africa, no doubt thought that what has subsequently occurred would occur—that we should take possession of these regions.

But, owing to the energy of Lieutenant Denham, he was brought to his senses, and thenceforth made the journey of the British explorers across the Sahara easy and safe. Dixon Denham and his companions left Sokna, in Southern Fezzan, in October, 1822. They travelled under the special charge of a Moorish merchant, Abu-bakr Bu-Khalum, a Tripolitan merchant of great wealth and influence who had made his fortune by trading

---

[1] Denham was born in London in 1786. He was first articled to a solicitor, then joined the army as a volunteer, and served through the Peninsular War and the Waterloo campaign; afterwards he travelled through France and Italy.

Hugh Clapperton was born in 1788 at Annan, in Dumfriesshire, and therefore, like Mungo Park, was a Scotchman of the Borders. He was thirty-seven years old when he started in 1825 on his last journey to Central Africa. As a boy he was apprenticed to the Mercantile Marine, and from that service passed into the Navy, where he rose to the rank of lieutenant. He distinguished himself on the Canadian lakes and off Mauritius.

in the Sudan. Bu-Khalum travelled with considerable pomp, and though he afterwards came to grief
(as you will see), he made the journey across the
Desert safer and more comfortable for these first
English travellers than it has ever been subsequently. He was mounted on a beautiful white
Tunisian horse, a present from the Basha of Tripoli,
who had specially commended the expedition to his
care. The peak and rear of his saddle were covered
with gold, the housings were of scarlet cloth, with a
border of gold 6 inches broad. His dress consisted
of red boots richly embroidered with gold, yellow
silk trousers, a crimson-velvet caftan with gold
buttons, a silk sleeveless coat of sky blue, and a
silk shirt underneath. A transparent white silk
barracan was thrown lightly over this, and on his
shoulders hung a scarlet burnous with wide gold
lace, a present also from the Basha. A cashmere
shawl turban crowned the whole.

Major Denham (he was afterwards promoted to
this rank, and wrote the principal account of the
expedition) had secured as his personal attendant
and interpreter a valuable individual, who had been
nicknamed "Columbus" for his extensive journeys,
but whose real name was Adolphus Sympkins! He
was a negro or mulatto of the island of St. Vin-
cent, in the West Indies, who had become a merchant seaman, and somehow or other had attracted
the attention of the Basha of Tripoli, who employed
him as an interpreter. Besides English, he spoke
French, Italian, and perfect Arabic.[1] Another

---

[1] He afterwards accompanied Clapperton to the Lower Niger.

interesting member of the expedition was William
Hillman, a native of Somersetshire, who had joined
the British navy and had become a ship's carpenter,
and later on a shipwright in the dockyard at Malta.
In spite of severe fevers, he lived to make this journey to the very heart of Africa, and afterwards returned to his native country, where it is to be hoped
he survived to a happy old age.

After they had got past the more settled regions
of Fezzan into the Desert country, inhabited—so
far as it had any resident people at all—by the
negroid Tibus, they began to have some evidence
of the slave trade across the Desert. Round most
of the wells where they halted to obtain water there
would be numbers of human skeletons scattered
on the sands. Sometimes these remains looked
as though a battle must have taken place at some
former period, the ground being covered with
whitened skulls and detached bones. But the
skulls and skeletons were simply those of slaves
who had died of thirst or starvation and been abandoned by the caravans. The road to the Sudan,
indeed, was lined on either side by human remains.
Some were partially covered with sand; other bodies,
with the hands still pressing the head, as though
to stave off some frightful headache, lay shrivelled
up like mummies. Denham counted a hundred
skeletons round one small well with the skin remaining attached to the bones. The Arabs of the
expedition, however, laughed heartily at his expressions of horror, and said: "They were only
blacks whose fathers were in Hell". They knocked

about the limbs with the butt ends of their guns,
saying: "This was a woman, this was a young-
ster", and so on. Denham was told that these
slaves often left Bornu with a very insufficient
allowance of food, so that more died from starvation than fatigue or even thirst. They were obliged
to march with heavy chains round their necks and
legs. Sometimes the horses of the riders would
crash through heaps of dead and withered bodies,
stumbling over the smooth skulls, and tripping up
over the ribs. This would be because the wind
had blown a light covering of sand over the dead
slaves, thus concealing their corpses from view.
Sometimes it seemed as though the camels in their
hunger had broken up the bodies in order to gnaw
the bones; in other cases, no doubt, the wretched
survivors amongst the slaves had attempted to make
a meal off their dead companions.

In this way *millions* of negroes must have
been sacrificed to the slave trade between the
Nigerian Sudan and the Mediterranean countries
—the Barbary States, Egypt, and Turkey—during
the nine centuries which followed the complete
Muhammadan conquest of Northern Africa.

The route across the Sahara through the Tibu
country is studded at intervals with oases, generally valleys or depressions in the desert where
there is water near the surface. Very often there
are small lakes or pools of salt or brackish water,
near to which good fresh water can be obtained
by digging. In all these cases there are inhabitants and a certain amount of cultivation. The

moisture below the surface nourishes fruitful date palms, water fowl frequent the pools; gazelles, oryxes, and wild sheep[1] come here to drink, or to lick the dry salt, and hyenas and chitas (hunting-leopards) follow in pursuit of the antelopes. Some days' journey to the south of Fezzan the traveller meets with the first sign that he is really in Tropical Africa — this the *dome* or *dūm* palm, which may be seen so commonly in Upper Egypt. It is a species of *Hyphœne* palm that branches instead of being content with a single stem; and its fronds are curved like fans into half-circles. The fruit of the dūm palm has a sweet rind with a taste of gingerbread. Another tree characteristic of " Real Africa " is the thorny Acacia genus, the flowers of which give out a most delicious scent. They are like little powder-puffs of golden-yellow or white, resembling their Australian relation, the " mimosa " which now grows so abundantly in the south of France.

The Tibu or Tubu of the Desert are a dark-skinned people. Major Denham describes the men as being usually extremely ugly, whilst the women, especially the girls, were really pretty, of a rich copper colour, and with beautiful white teeth. The men are often quite black-skinned, and their long teeth are a deep yellow; their noses resemble a round lump of flesh stuck on the face, and the nostrils are so large and open that they seem like direct passages upwards to the brain. Denham

[1] The great maned sheep of North Africa—*Ovis lervia*—of a uniform reddish-yellow, the colour of sand and sandstone.

says that the passion for snuff-taking has enlarged
the nostrils, as the men were constantly ramming
snuff up as high as it would go. Nevertheless
they were smart fellows and active, besides being
splendid horsemen. The women wore their hair
hanging down in thick plaits and streaming with
oil; coral beads were inserted into the nostrils,
and large amber necklaces were worn. Many of
them carried a fan made of soft grass or hair for
the purpose of keeping off the flies, or, for the
same reason, the branch of a tree, or bunches of
ostrich feathers which they waved over their heads
as they advanced. The men generally wore high
turbans of deep indigo blue, the ends of which
were brought under the chin and across the face,
so as to shield the mouth and nostrils from the
sand of the desert. As many as twenty charms
done up in red, green, or black leather cases
would be attached to the folds of the turban.

The travellers on this journey were often sustained in the Tibu country by draughts of camels'
milk, which, like other explorers, they described
as "perfectly delicious", perhaps the nicest-tasting
milk derived from any beast. In some parts of the
Northern Sudan, where there is very little herbage
(except the thorn trees on which the camel feeds),
the horses are fed on camels' milk, and little else.

As the expedition gradually neared the end of
the Desert towards Bornu, the face of the country improved rapidly. They passed occasionally
through what seemed to them joyous valleys smiling with flowering grasses and a variety of trees,

some of which gave a luxurious shade, while arbours were formed by creepers. Large black vultures were soaring in the heavens, troops of hyenas threatened to seize the young camels or the children of the expedition at night, and in the daytime poisonous snakes were seen—horned vipers.

At last they came in sight of Lake Chad, "glowing with the golden rays of the sun in its strength", and their hearts bounded with delight at having found the chief object of their search. The water was covered with flocks of geese and wild ducks, so little used to being disturbed by humanity that they scarcely moved away at the approach of the travellers. On the sandy shores were thousands of pelicans, flamingoes, cranes, storks, curlew, spoonbills, and plovers. The soil near the edge of the lake was a firm dark mud, with occasional patches of short grass on which big-horned cattle were feeding; the lake water was sweet and pleasant, and abounded with fish. These last were caught in a very simple fashion. A number of women would go into the shallow lake in single file and form a line of considerable length out in the water, facing the land. They would then rush through the water towards the shore and drive the fish before them, so that they were caught by hand or forced on to the dry mud.

A few days later the travellers saw elephants either swimming in the lake or standing quietly on the shore. One of these elephants kept so still in the middle of the herbage that Hillman, the carpenter, laid himself down to rest within a dozen yards of it awaiting the arrival of the rest of the caravan. He was much startled when an Arab came up and struck the elephant with a spear. The huge beast trumpeted angrily, but moved away without attacking anyone. In some places they found forests of trees broken down where the elephants had been feeding.[1] They also killed an enormous python 18 feet long, and saw droves of the red hartebeest antelope, big red and white gazelles, and occasional buffaloes, lions, and wart-hogs.

They had now got into the region of large negro towns, composed of *round* houses built of reeds or else of mud with conical roofs, looking very much like well-thatched stacks of corn. They

---

[1] Some time later Denham went on an elephant hunt by the waters of Lake Chad and saw three very large elephants, one so enormous that he guessed its height at 16 feet, feeding on the vegetation. They allowed the traveller and his negro attendants to approach quite close, taking little notice of them, but occasionally giving loud trumpetings. At last one of the negroes coming up quite close, hurled a spear at the big male elephant, which struck him just under the tail. "The huge beast threw up his proboscis in the air with a loud roar, and from it cast such a volume of sand that, unprepared as I was for such an event, it nearly blinded me." Denham goes on to relate that the elephants of Bornu rarely, if ever, attack without provocation, but when irritated they will sometimes rush upon a man who is on horseback and attempt first to choke him with a great discharge of sand or dust from the trunk, and then, whilst he is puzzled and blinded, seize him and destroy him. Denham several times fired at elephants, but apparently did them no harm with his bullets, discharged as they were from a smooth-bore gun. The elephants seemed most alarmed at the flashes made by the flint in the pan of the gun, for although we are considering a period of *less than ninety years ago*, these travellers did not even possess gun *caps*, but had to use flints that struck off a spark which then ignited a small quantity of powder in the pan and so set fire to the charge in the barrel. Denham noticed numbers of birds "resembling a thrush" perched on the backs of the elephants and engaged in picking off ticks and other vermin. These were probably the same as the well-known rhinoceros bird, which is larger than a starling and with a curiously formed beak. It belongs to the genus *Buphaga*, and the starling family.

were surrounded by neat enclosures made of reed fences, in which there were goats, poultry, and sometimes a cow. The streets or passages between the houses were very narrow. Inside the house would be a bed or sofa made of rushes lashed together and supported by six poles. This was covered by skins of wild cats or antelopes. Round the sides of the hut were hung the wooden bowls used for water and milk, together with the shield of the master of the house. A division of matwork divided the dwelling into one half for the women and children, and the other for the husband. These towns were often surrounded by walls of clay 13 or 14 feet high, with a moat. There would be two gates, east and west, defended by mounds of earth thrown up on either side. The women passed most of their time spinning cotton or preparing food for eating. [After the semi-starvation of the desert the travellers found the fish of Lake Chad most delicious eating, fresh - broiled over the embers.]

They were here within the dominions of the great sultan or king of Bornu, at one time reckoned in the Muhammadan world as a potentate equal to the Sultan of Turkey, the Shah of Persia, and the Emperor of Morocco. His negro soldiers were mostly cavalry, and rode small but perfectly trained horses. They wore coats of mail almost exactly like those of the Crusaders. In fact, the interesting part of this armour (which is still worn in the eastern half of the Sudan) is that it was copied from that of the Crusaders by the Turkish,

IN BORNU

Circassian, and Arab soldiers of Egypt, and so passed on up the Nile to Darfur, Wadai, and the country of Bornu. When Denham saw the displays of Bornu cavalry, the soldiers wore coats of mail composed of iron-chain, which covered them from the throat to the knees, but which were cut away behind so that they could sit free in the saddle. Some of them wore helmets or skull caps of chain mail with chin pieces, all sufficiently strong to ward off the shock of the spear. Their horses' heads were defended by plates of iron, brass, and silver, just leaving sufficient room for the eyes of the animal. Of course any such armour was useless as a protection against bullets driven with any force of powder; but it is evident that guns and gunpowder did *not* get a complete hold over the vast region of the Sudan between Abyssinia and Senegambia until the middle of the nineteenth century. Indeed, when Major Denham crossed the Sahara Desert, guns were a subject of great wonderment and terror to the Tibus. If an Arab were to put down his musket at the foot of a tree whilst he went to get a drink of water, the Tibu robbers would walk round and round it at a safe distance, very inquisitive, and yet much too afraid to touch the weapon.

Kuka (Kukawa) was the principal town of Bornu, and the residence of the sheikh or prime minister (the real ruler of the country). Denham thus describes the marketplace and the goods that were sold there:—

"Slaves, sheep, and bullocks, the latter in

great numbers, were the principal live stock for sale.   There were at least fifteen thousand persons gathered together, some of them coming from places two and three days distant.   Wheat, rice, and gussub (millet) were abundant.   Tamarinds . . . groundnuts, beans, okroes,[1] and indigo. The latter is very good, and in great use amongst the natives to dye their garments in stripes of deep blue alternately with white. . . . Of vegetables, only onions and small tomatoes were for sale.   We did not see any fruit, and there is none in the country except a few limes.   But there was leather in great quantities—the skins of the large snake (python), pieces of crocodile skin, used as an ornament for the scabbards of daggers; also butter, sour milk, honey, and wooden bowls. . . . Amongst other things offered to me for sale by the people were a young lion and a monkey; the latter really the more dangerous of the two.   The lion walked about with great unconcern, confined merely by a small rope round his neck held by the negro who had caught him when he was not two months old, and who, having had him for a period of three months, now wished to part with him.   The lion was about the size of a donkey colt, with very large limbs, and the people seemed to go quite close to him without much alarm, even though he had struck with his foot the leg of one man who stood in his way, and made the blood flow copiously."

[1] The buds of a mallow plant, very glutinous, and delicious when cooked in soup.

Major Denham, with some pressing, was invited to lay his hand on the lion's back, but the latter did not wait for the caress; he brushed past Denham, broke up the ring of people, and dragged his conductor away with him, overturning several people who stood in his way. The foreign merchandise most in demand at this market was amber and coral.

Denham was extremely anxious to explore the coasts of Lake Chad, so as to arrive at some correct idea of the extent of that lake. He also wished to visit the reported River Shari and the negro lands of Central Africa to the south. Nothing, of course, could be done without the consent of the Sultan of Bornu, the nominal ruler of the country, though its real chief was the sheikh, who resided at Kuka—a sort of prime minister—whose surname was Al Kanemi.[1] The sultan himself generally lived at the town of Birni, on the

---

[1] Bornu has had a regular dynasty of kings—probably of Tibu origin—for the last thousand years. Since about 1100 A.D. the dynasty has been Muhammadan. In 1808 the kingdom of Bornu, which usually included the Tibu country of Kanem, north-east of Lake Chad, was invaded by the Fulas from Hausaland. The Bornu sultan fled, but a holy man or "fakir" from Kanem offered to restore him to power and drive away the Fulas. This holy man or "sheikh (expounder) of the Koran" in Kanem, was Muhammad-al-Amin, surnamed Al-Kanemi. Muhammad-al-Amin was of Tibu origin and born in Fezzan. He had travelled much, and everywhere made himself liked by his goodness and charity, besides being very learned in the Koran. He wrote verses from that book which were regarded everywhere in the Central Sudan as powerful charms. But the magic by which—about 1810—he drove the Fulas out of Bornu in a ten-months' campaign was—gunpowder! He enlisted in his service not only thousands of Kanem bowmen, but hundreds of Arabs and Moors armed with muskets. In those days the Fulas fought only with spears and bows, and the terror of the Arab guns drove them out of Bornu.

Muhammad-al-Amin-al-Kanemi then ruled the country, but he did not abolish the native "Sefu" dynasty, though he treated the Bornu kings

River Yeu.[1] He received the Oudney expedition
seated in a sort of cage of reeds or wood near
the door of his garden, on a raised seat which
was covered with silk or satin. His courtiers were
grotesque objects, because the sultan preferred
people with large heads and inflated stomachs.
People with large heads only tried to make themselves very stout in appearance by putting quantities of wadding under their clothes. Some of
them wore eight, ten, or even twelve shirts of different colours, one over the other, to assist in
increasing his stoutness of person! Their heads
were turbaned with many folds of muslin or linen
of different colours, and the mode in fashion was
to make the turban top-heavy to one side. They
were also hung all over with charms enclosed in
little red leather parcels. To the left of the sultan,
when he gave audiences, stood a personage who
was like the singing-men of the Mandingos, whose
function it was to shout or sing loud praises of
his master, besides relating his pedigree. Every
now and then he was interrupted by a man with a
wooden trumpet, who blew blasts of distracting noise.

as puppets. He died in 1835, and was succeeded as sheikh by his son
Omar, who did abolish the old dynasty, and whose descendant is now King
of Bornu under the British. Between 1895 and 1902 Bornu was conquered
and ruled over by Rabeh, a Nubian slave of Zobeir Pasha, who broke away
from the Dervishes in the Egyptian Sudan, with a remnant of the well-
drilled Sudanese troops, and created for himself and his son, Fadl-allah, a
great Central African kingdom. But Rabeh, and after him Fadl-allah, were
both killed in battle with the French, and when the British took over the
protectorate of Bornu they recognized as king of that country Abba Gurbe
(or Kiari), the son of Sheikh Bu-bakr, and the great grandson of the Sheikh
Muhammad-al-Amin, who received with such help and generosity the first
British mission to Bornu.

[1] Also called the Yo, Yobe, and Komadugu.

Major Denham, after a considerable delay, obtained the permission of the sheikh, the real ruler of Bornu, to accompany a powerful raiding expedition which was being sent to the country of Baghirmi far to the south of Lake Chad.

This expedition was under the command of Barka Gana, an Arab commander-in-chief of the sheikh's army, and was also accompanied by the great slave-trader Bu-Khalum, under whose protection they had crossed the desert. His first experiences were most exhilarating. He had a good horse to ride, the weather was cool, the country flat and easy, he was riding with three thousand mounted spearmen and musketeers, besides a number of foot soldiers and slave-porters. The commander-in-chief, Barka Gana, had what might be called a band of kettledrums—mounted men with drums hung round their necks. One of them carried a small pipe made of a reed, another blew blasts on a buffalo horn, and all five sang extempore songs; every now and again making up special verses to illustrate incidents of the march. One of their impromptu songs was about Major Denham, and gave great delight to all the hearers. He gives a rough translation.

> " Christian man he come,
>   Friend of us and of the sheikh;
> White man, when he hear my song,
>   Fine new tobe give me.

> " Christian man all white,
>   And dollars white has he;

Kanuri [1] like him come,
    Black man's friend to be.

" See Felatah, how he run;
    Barka Gana shake his spear;
White man carry two-mouthed gun,
    That's what make Felatah fear."

Here is an account of the way in which they
fed this expedition. " As soon as the army had
halted, sheep were killed, cut in half, and laid
upon a framework of wood made of strong stakes.
. . . Under it was a fierce fire, and by this
means the meat was roasted well. When it was
ready for eating, the half of a roasted sheep would
be laid on green boughs, placed on the sand before
the leaders of the expedition. The black chiefs
then stripped off their clothing and proceeded to
act as carvers with sharp daggers, cutting off large
slices of flesh until they reached the bones, and
then sending for another half sheep and stripping
that in the same manner. The flesh thus cut off
was distributed to all assembled, and quickly eaten
without either bread or salt. Then everyone drank
huge draughts from a large wooden bowl, which
contained rice water mixed with honey, tamarinds,
and red pepper." The commander-in-chief told
Denham that he always lived on the country and
the food which it afforded, and only carried as a
reserve a kind of paste made of rice flour and
honey, which he took, mixed with water, morning
and evening, when he could get nothing better.

[1] Kanuri is the name of the ruling class of Bornu people and of the
language now used: both are of Kanem (Tibu) origin. The native name
of Bornu and of the Bornu people is Berebere or Barba.

Unfortunately, many of the Arabs that accompanied this expedition were fanatical Muhammadans. They were much puzzled by Major Denham,
because on the line of march he was never noticed
to stop, wash himself, and pray, as did the Mos-
lems, who were careful to observe the precepts of
their religion. "Where do you wash and pray?"
said to him a fanatical old Figi or Dervish. "In
my tent," said Denham. But Bu-Khalum was
cross-examined, and was obliged to admit that
Denham was a Christian, though a friend of the
great Basha of Tripoli. After that he was not
allowed to drink out of the same bowl as the
Muhammadan chieftains and leaders. When the
expedition reached the capital of Mandara, its
Muhammadan sultan asked the same questions,
who was shocked to find that the Arabs allowed
a white man who was not a Muhammadan to travel
with them, and refused to see Denham again. He
was a person, though small, of striking appearance,
for he wore a magnificent silk tobe, and had dyed
his beard a beautiful sky blue!

In this land the customary salutations between
the suite of one great man and that of another
were of a dangerous nature, for it was considered
etiquette, on visiting a great man, to gallop up to
his outer court or reception verandah at full speed,
checking your horse just as he is about to collide
with the building. Nothing must stop you; if a
man or a horse get in your way you must ride
over him. Denham occasionally saw horses' legs
broken and men killed in these dashing salutes.

Nevertheless, although the Muhammadan sultan shunned the society of the Christian white man, the latter had no cause to complain of his hospitality. Forty slaves, preceded by one of the sultan's eunuchs, came to the camp bearing wooden bowls filled with a paste of millet flour. Salt, fat, and pepper had been poured over this dough, mixed with a proportionate seasoning of onions; and this rough "pudding" was to be eaten with a liberal supply of roast mutton, also sent by the sultan. The heat at this time was frightful, so that the thermometer frequently stood as high as 113° in the shade; the camping-places swarmed with biting ants, flies, and other insects, which so afflicted Denham that his hands and eyes swelled and he was unable to see much or to use a pen. He was obliged to cover himself with all the blankets he could find, to keep off the power of the sun as well as the flies, whilst his negro attendant poured cold water over his head.

The numerous Arabs that accompanied the expedition, did so for the sole purpose of carrying out extensive slave raids amongst the negroes. The Sheikh of Bornu had allowed this expedition to go, and to join with the forces of the Sultan of Mandara, not altogether with the idea of raiding the harmless pagan Musgu negroes of the mountains, but in order to make an attack on the Fulas or Fellata, who had at different times possessed themselves of the kingdom of Mandara and carried their rule as far east as the Shari River and Lake Chad. We have already met with the Fulas in this story, when we began to consider the adventures of Jobson on the Upper Gambia and the early travels of Mungo Park. It is wonderful to think that they were as active and important 1500 miles away to the east as on the frontiers of Bornu and Baghirmi. Major Denham was already aware of this remarkable fact, because he met Fulas who could tell him about Timbuktu and the Upper Gambia, and even noticed that Fulas who came from the far west of Africa could converse easily with those who were dwelling in the country of Mandara.

The Sultan of Mandara had led all this force from Bornu to attack the Fula town of Musfeia, in the middle of extraordinarily picturesque mountains. The result was a terrible reverse which nearly cost Denham his life. Bu-Khalum, who had led these British travellers across the Sahara Desert, was wounded by a poisoned arrow. The forces of Bornu and Mandara fled precipitately after the defeat of the Arabs. Denham was unhorsed and immediately attacked by three or four Fulas with their spears. He seized a pistol from his holster and presented it at two of the spearmen, who ran away; the third he wounded. His horse rose, he jumped on its back and dashed onwards in his retreat; but again the horse fell and flung him with violence against a tree; after that the horse rose to his feet and galloped away. From the tree, Denham saw one of the court officials of Mandara and his four followers butchered to death by the Fulas. Their cries were dreadful,

whilst his own chances of life were very slight.
He was surrounded and, incapable of making the
least resistance, was stripped of his clothes, and
whilst attempting to retain either shirt or trousers,
was thrown on the ground. The Fula warriors
thrust at him with their spears, wounding his
hands and the right side of his body. But those
attacking were more anxious to secure his clothes
than to kill him until they had stripped him naked,
which they soon did. They then began quarrel-
ling over their spoil, and the naked Denham at
this moment crept under the belly of a horse and
ran as fast as his legs could carry him to the
thickest part of the wood. But he was pursued
by the Fula warriors whilst he fled in an eastern
direction, thinking in that quarter to come up with
the fugitive Arab force. In this desperate race he
dashed through thorny creepers and shrubs, so that
his naked body was torn and bleeding. Suddenly,
in plunging down a deep ravine, he saw a mountain stream before him. To break his fall into the
water he clutched at the branches issuing from the
stump of a large tree which overhung the water,
when to his horror one of the branches at which
he was clutching turned out to be a venomous
snake, probably a kind of tree cobra. It recoiled
to strike him, but at that instant Denham tum-
bled headlong into the water beneath. With three
strokes of his bleeding arms he swam to the opposite bank, crawled up, crept once more into the
brushwood, and was tolerably safe from further
pursuit.

But his feelings were not cheerful. Here he
was, quite naked, his skin scratched, torn, and
bleeding, in a thorny forest which he had already
noticed abounded in daring, man-eating leopards
and poisonous snakes. But as he pressed on
breathlessly towards the open country, he saw
two horsemen passing through the trees, and with
feelings of intense relief recognized them as Barka
Gana and Bu-Khalum, accompanied by six Arabs,
but still pursued by Fula warriors, whom they kept
at bay with their guns and pistols, whilst they
covered the retreat of what remained of the foot
soldiers. Denham cried to them with all his might,
but in the noise and confusion which prevailed from
the cries of those who were falling under the Fula
spears, and the cheers of the Arabs attempting to
rally their force and repulse the enemy, his shouts
for help were disregarded, and he would probably
have perished at the hands of the Fulas, had not
the head slave of the Bornu sheikh—a negro
named Marami—recognized him. He rode up to
the naked, bleeding white man, and assisted him
to mount his horse and sit behind his saddle. All
this time the poisoned arrows of the Fulas were
whistling over their heads, but as soon as Denham
was up, Marami galloped off as fast as his already
wounded horse could carry the double load. After
a mile or two the pursuit of the Fulas slackened,
in consequence of all the baggage of the Arabs
being abandoned to the enemies. He then again
saw Bu-Khalum, whom an hour or so before he
believed to be dead, after being shot with the Fula

arrows. But apparently he had recovered from his wounds, and he at once told one of the Arabs to cover Denham with a burnus or woollen cloak. This was a most welcome relief, for the burning sun had begun to blister the white man's neck and back, and added to the exquisite pain he already felt from his scratches and spear-thrusts. But in the very moment of experiencing this relief a fresh trouble befell him. Marami exclaimed, " Look, look! Bu-Khalum is dead!" And Denham saw this Moorish merchant, who had escorted them across the Sahara from Tripoli to Bornu, drop from his horse into the arms of his Arab attendant. He never spoke again, and expired soon afterwards.

Barka Gana then ordered a slave to bring a horse for Denham so that he might leave Marami. But the horse had been wounded in the chest, and Marami warned his companion not to mount him for he would certainly soon fall down and die, a prediction which soon afterwards was verified, and the Arabs who had taken the horse instead of Denham, and were attempting to ride away from the pursuing Fulas, were butchered by them before they could rise and escape on foot. Meanwhile Denham and Marami were riding away from the danger as fast as their horse could take them. Denham had become speechless with thirst. He was quite unable to answer Marami's remarks, as any attempt at speaking caused a painful straining in the stomach and throat. When at last they reached a stream of water the horses, with blood gushing from their nostrils, rushed into the shallow water. Then Denham, letting himself down gingerly, knelt in the stream and imbibed new life by copious draughts of water—muddy though it was. When he rose to his feet and staggered out of the stream, he fainted at the foot of a tree on the other side, and from the faint passed into a deep sleep. Whilst he slept a consultation took place amongst the Arabs. Marami had pointed out the condition of his wounded horse, and the impossibility of two men riding it for a much greater distance. The Arab commander-in-chief, irritated by his losses and defeat, and annoyed at Denham having refused the wounded horse he had previously offered him, proposed that he should be left behind to his fate. He was only a Christian, and many true believers had already perished.

Strange to say, at this juncture Denham's old antagonist, the Fiki,[1] or holy man, who had first called attention with wrath to the presence of a Christian in the expedition, and refused to eat out of the same bowl with Denham, now spoke up in his defence, saying, "God has preserved him, let us not forsake him". Accordingly Marami picked up Denham, put him on his horse, and the mounted men moved forward with such poor speed as the desperate condition of their horses permitted. More than thirty horses died at this river from the effect of the poisoned arrows. Immediately after drink-

---

[1] Fiki, Faki, Figi, is an Arab word much employed in the Sudan, which reappears in India as *Fakir* (Fakeer), and which means a holy man, an ascetic, a saint, a person learned in the Koran.

ing they dropped down and died, blood gushing from their noses, mouths, and ears.

However, after riding more than forty-five miles, they reached the territory of the Sultan of Mandara in the middle of the night. All this time Denham, naked except for the woollen cloak, had been obliged to ride on the bare back of a lean horse, with consequences that may be imagined. His body was covered with flesh wounds and scratches, and these were irritated to a maddening degree by the friction of the woollen burnus; and, worse than this, the Arab cloak was teeming with vermin, the bites of which drove Denham nearly frantic, and perhaps worried him more than the smarting pain of the wounds. He had to endure this for another whole day until he could borrow a shirt from an Arab who had two, and who lent him one on his promising to pay in exchange a new shirt when they reached Kuka. There was no tent to shelter him, and he would have been without food had it not been for the kind negro Marami, who supplied him at intervals with a drink made of parched and bruised corn, which he found not only grateful to his thirst, but sufficiently nourishing.

Migammi, the dethroned sultan of a country to the south-west of Lake Chad now subject to the Sheikh of Bornu, noticed the desperate condition of the Englishman, and leading him to his leather tent, with a countenance full of commiseration, lent him his own pair of voluminous Moorish trousers. "Really," wrote Denham, "no act of charity could exceed this! I was exceedingly affected at so unexpected a friend, for I had scarcely seen or spoken three words to him." The negro sultan, however, was moved to tears at Denham's condition, and having obtained another pair of trousers from one of his slaves, he insisted on dressing Denham in his own garments. From that time onwards, Denham and Migammi were fast friends, until the former's departure from Bornu to return to Tripoli and England.

It was found that on this expedition forty-five of the Arabs had been killed in the fighting, nearly all the survivors were more or less wounded, and several of these died after they had reached the country of Mandara. As in the case of Bu-Khalum, the effect of the poisoned arrows was that after a few hours they died suddenly, blood issuing from the nose and mouth, while the body instantly became swollen and black. The few surviving Arabs were completely humbled, and had to go round begging for a little corn to save them from starvation, having lost their camels and everything they possessed. The Sultan of Mandara, who had sent them on this expedition against the Fulas, now treated them with great harshness, and set to work to defend his own country against Fula reprisals. No doubt, neither he nor the Sheikh of Bornu were at all sorry at the disaster which had overtaken the Arab and Moorish raiders, who, if they succeeded, might have turned their armies against either Mandara or Bornu. The Sheikh of Bornu, however, treated Denham with the greatest kindness and consideration, and attempted, as far as possible, to make up to him for the sufferings he had endured, sufferings which were, of course, much due to his own recklessness in being so ready to accompany an expedition that he must have known was chiefly got up for the purpose of slave-raiding.

CHAPTER IX

Denham in Bornu

THE next expedition on which Denham departed was commanded by the sheikh in person, and was directed against a people in the west of Bornu called Munga. The expedition was intended to collect their tribute. Of course, it was really another slave raid. This sheikh, or prime minister of Bornu, having come from Kanem, and, by means of the Shawa Arabs and his own forces, driven the Fula people away from Bornu (of which he had become practically the ruler), the Munga tribe of negroes affected to reserve their allegiance for the Sultan of Bornu only, and refused to give tribute to the sheikh. He, in his turn, alleged that they were unbelievers, heathen, and that therefore he was justified in making slaves of them if they resisted him. For throughout Muhammadan Africa there is a pretence that a Muhammadan cannot be a slave to a Muhammadan. It is only a pretence, but the Arabs, Moors, and Muhammadanized negroes whenever they wanted to conduct a slave raid on a large scale accused the negroes of being heathen and then made slaves of them. Accordingly, the sheikh's expedition consisted of over

5000 warriors, Arabs, Tibu, and negroes.   They travelled westwards along the Yeu River.

The negroes of Northern Bornu at that period were frequently raided by the Tuaregs from the north, and to defend their country from being overrun by these marauders (as also, no doubt, to catch elephants and other big game) they were in the habit of digging huge perpendicular pits, which they called *blakwa*, in the high grass and jungle near the banks of rivers, and in the vicinity of their towns.   These pits were generally circular in shape, and at the bottom were placed six to eight sharp-pointed stakes of wood, hardened in the fire.   The top of the pit was cleverly disguised with a layer of slender reeds or sticks on which grass and herbage was laid, so that to the eye there was only a tempting, smooth piece of ground which looked like a little clearing in the bush; but any large animal—especially a horse with its rider —stepping on to one of these traps would be quickly precipitated to the bottom of the pit, and probably transfixed and killed on the sharp stakes. The kindly negroes warned Denham of the risk he was running just in time, for he found that he had passed within a yard of several of the pits. Later on, his West Indian servant, Adolphus Sympkins (" Columbus "), was less careful, and in riding a mule fell into one of these *blakwa* and received very severe wounds, whilst his mule was killed.

Occasionally a lion was caught in these *blakwa*, though this beast was much more wary and cautious about pitfalls than even the elephant. About the time of Denham's visit, a large man-eating lion, measuring from the tail to the nose fourteen feet and two inches, which had previously devoured four slaves, was thus disposed of. The natives had dug a very deep *blakwa*, of circular shape (with its sharp-pointed sticks at the bottom), and had cunningly covered it over with millet stalks or straw. Then a bundle of straw enveloped in a tobe was laid on the spot, to which a gentle motion, like that of a man turning in his sleep, was occasionally given by means of a line carried to some distance and held by the negroes who were lying in wait. Other negroes with loud cries and noises had driven the lion from his lair, where he had been feasting on the last of his human victims. When they saw that he was entering the clearing where the trap was dug, they went away, and everything became perfectly quiet. For seven or eight hours the human watchers in the distance, who held the end of the line which was attached to the dummy, observed the lion approach closer and closer to the pitfall. At last, having made up its mind that it really was a sleeping man that lay on the supposed path in front of him, he made a spring on to his supposed prey and was precipitated to the bottom of the pit. The negroes now rushed to the spot, and before the lion could recover himself despatched him with their spears.

But this journey along the Yeu was a pleasant experience. On the banks of the river there were large tamarinds, and other trees bearing fruits that were edible and pleasant to the taste, some of the fruits resembling a medlar, while others were the jujube berries mentioned by Mungo Park (p. 123). These groves, in consequence, were the home of innumerable monkeys, who fed on the fruits and who were very indignant on seeing their domain invaded by an army of human warriors. They pelted the riders as they passed, with fruits and nuts. Some of the negroes wished to fire at the monkeys, but Denham very rightly restrained them, as "considering their numbers they were not sufficiently presuming to deserve such punishment". The waters of the river in shallow places were covered with flocks of geese, and were frequented by numbers of marabou storks. The thick woods were inhabited by lions, jackals, and hyenas. Huge lions crossed the path every now and then in sight of the expedition. Sometimes the travellers encountered a bundle of wood and a hatchet lying on the ground, and a short distance farther on the skull and bones of some unfortunate negro or negress who had been seized and eaten by a lion, and finished up by hyenas and jackals. Elephants were most abundant, but not particularly aggressive. The natives preferred catching them occasionally in pitfalls, and therefore seldom attacked them direct. Denham relates that the negroes of this part of Bornu would sometimes beat brass pans or vessels, and that the elephants would dance and frisk to the noise "like so many goats".

The sheikh's expedition camped beside small lakes of great depth swarming with hippopotami

BORNU TRUMPETERS SOUNDING THE "FRUM-FRUMS"

and fish. Sometimes the dry brushwood by the
lake shores would be set fire to, and the scene was
then splendid at night with the hippo rising, snorting, splashing, and gleaming in the reflection of
the blaze, and the naked negro warriors entering
the lake with torches to drive the fish ashore for
capture. There was little silence during the hours
of darkness: what with the shouting people, the
grunting hippos, the neighing of the tethered
horses, and, perhaps, in the distance, the roaring
of lions and the laughing of hyenas.

Denham gives the following description of his
march with the Bornu army:—"But little order
is preserved previous to coming near the enemy:
everyone appears to know that at a certain point
the assembly is to take place; and the general
instructions seem to be to everyone to make the
best of his own way thither. The sheikh takes
the lead, and close after him comes the Sultan of
Bornu, who always attends the army on these occasions, although he never fights. The sheikh is preceded by five flags—two green, two striped, and
one red—with extracts from the Koran written on
them in letters of gold, and he is attended by about
a hundred of his chiefs and favourite slaves. A
negro, high in confidence, rides close behind him,
bearing his shield, jacket of mail, and wearing his
skull cap of steel; he also bears his arms. Another,
mounted on a swift *maherhi* (dromedary), and fantastically dressed with a straw hat and ostrich
feathers, carries his timbrel or drum, which it is
the greatest misfortune and disgrace to lose in

action. On the expedition, which cost the Sultan Denhama (the late Sultan of Bornu) his life,[1] the timbrel and the sheikh were supposed to have fallen in a sudden rush of the Baghirmi warriors; almost everyone near him suffered. The people, however, firmly believe that he was saved by a miracle; they say: 'He became invisible; that the Baghirmi chiefs scoured the field, calling out for the sheikh; that the drum sounded at intervals, but could not be seen any more than the sheikh himself.' Close in the rear of the *maherhis* follow the eunuchs and the harem; the sheikh takes but three wives, who are mounted astride on small trained horses, each led by a boy slave or eunuch, their heads and figures completely enveloped in brown silk burnuses, and a eunuch riding by the side of each.

"The Sultan of Bornu has five times as many attendants as the sheikh, and his wives were three times as numerous; he is attended also by men bearing trumpets (*frumfrum*) of hollow wood ten and twelve feet long; with these a kind of music is constantly kept up. As this instrument is considered an appendage of royalty alone, the sheikh

---

[1] The Sultan Denhama of Bornu (the similarity of his name to that of Denham was only a coincidence), who always accompanied the sheikh to war, lost his life owing to his immense size and weight. The horse he rode, from fatigue refused to move on with him, although at the time not more than five hundred yards from the gates of the city of Angala. Thus Denhama fell into the hands of the enemy. He died, however, with great dignity; and six of his eunuchs and as many of his slaves, who would not quit him, shared his fate. A sultan of Bornu carried no arms, and it was considered beneath his dignity to defend himself. Denhama, therefore, sat down under a tree, with his people around him, and thus received his enemies. He hid his face in the shawl which covered his head, but was pierced with a hundred spears.

has no *frumfrums*; the *keigomha*, or standard-
bearer, rides in front of him, carrying a very long
pole, hung round, at the top, with strips of leather
and silk of various colours in imitation, probably, of
the bashaw's *tigue* or tails; and two ride on each
side of him, called *Mistrumha dundelma*, carrying
immense spears, with which they are supposed to
defend their sultan in action, whose dignity would
be infringed by any attempt to defend himself; but
the spears are so hung round with charms, and the
bearers so unwieldy, that the idea of such weapons
being of any use in the hands of such warriors is
absurd. Indeed, the grotesque appearance of the
whole of this prince's train—with their heads hung
round with charms, and resembling the size and
shape of a hogshead—their protruding stomachs
and wadded doublets, is ridiculous in the extreme.
. . . The sheikh was attended by four sultans who
accompanied the expedition under his orders, and
a circle was formed by the Arabs and the Bornu
horse. The sheikh's principal slaves and com-
manders were dispersed in different parts, habited
in their scarlet burnuses with gold lace, and surrounded also by their followers. His own dress
was, as usual, neat and simple: two white, figured,
muslin tobes, very large, with a burnus of the same
colour, and a Kashmir shawl for a turban. Over
the whole, across his shoulders, hung the sword
which, as he repeatedly said, 'the Sultan Inglese
(English king) had sent him'. He was mounted
on a very beautiful bay horse from Mandara, and
took his station on the north side of the circle;

while the Kanembu were drawn up on the opposite
extremity in close column to the number of nine
thousand.   On the signal being made for them to
advance, they uttered a yell, or shriek, exceeding
anything in shrillness I ever heard; then advanced
by tribes of from eight hundred to one thousand
each.   They were perfectly naked, with the exception of a rather fantastic belt of goat or sheep's
skin, with the hair outwards, round their middles,
and a few *gubkas* (narrow strips of cloth, the money
of the country) round their heads, and brought
under the nose.   Their arms are a spear and shield,
with a dagger on the left arm reversed, secured by
a ring which goes on the wrist, the point running
up the arm, and the handle downwards.   The
shields are made of the wood of the *fogo*, a tree
which grows in the shallow waters of the great
lake,[1] and are so extremely light as to weigh only
a few pounds; the pieces of wood of which it is
formed are bound together by thongs of the hide
of bullocks with the hair on, which is also carried
along the edge of the outside of the shield in van-
dykes, and forms an ornament.   The shields are
something in the shape of a Gothic window, and
most of them slightly convex.   Under cover of
these the Kanembu attack the bowmen with good
order, and at a slow pace.   Their leaders are
mounted, and are distinguished merely by a tobe
of dark blue and a turban of the same colour.

"On nearing the spot where the sheikh had

---

[1] Probably the Ambatch also found on the Nile (*Herminiera*, a tree of
the Bean order).

placed himself they quickened their pace, and, after striking their spears against their shoulders for some seconds, which had an extremely grand and stunning effect, they filed off to the outside of the circle, where they again formed, and awaited their companions, who succeeded them in the same order. There appeared to be a great deal of affection between these troops and the sheikh; he spurred his horse onwards into the midst of some of the tribes as they came up, and spoke to them, while the men crowded round him, kissing his feet and the stirrups of his saddle. It was a most pleasing sight; he seemed to feel how much his present elevation was owing to their exertions, while they displayed a devotion and attachment deserving and denoting the greatest confidence. I confess I was considerably disappointed at not seeing these troops engage, although more than compensated by the reflection of the slaughter that had been prevented by that disappointment."

The Munga submitted to this show of force, and the almost bloodless victory of the Bornu army was greatly assisted by a device then absolutely new in the history of Central Africa. Denham had brought with him a small number of rockets, and when these were discharged on a very dark night they created wonder, even stupefaction, amongst the natives. Some fell on their faces, and began to pray when the rockets burst into stars.

The result was that a rival sheikh or "figi", who had rebelled against the Prime Minister of

Bornu, and had associated himself with the rebel
Munga, came in to tender his submission with
fully one thousand followers. He was superbly
mounted on a white horse, but dismounted at the
door of the sheikh's tent, humbled himself in the
dust, and attempted to pour sand over his head.
His victorious rival, however, was generous, and
prevented this extreme humiliation. The figi was
brought into his presence expecting to have his
throat cut. As was customary, in tendering submission, he was simply clad and with an uncovered
head. Instead of being ordered to execution, however, he was clothed with eight handsome tobes,
one over the other, and his head made as big as
six with turbans from Egypt.

Before the army returned to Kuka, an incident
took place which illustrated the ups and downs
of life in Muhammadan countries. Barka Gana,
the favourite general of the Sheikh of Bornu,
whose acquaintance we made over that unfortunate
expedition into the Mandara country, was the
governor of six large districts, with a large
number of wives, and a household of one hundred
male slaves, the general-in-chief and the special
favourite of the Sheikh of Bornu. But in distri-
buting presents and plunder after the victory over
the Munga people, the sheikh had unintentionally
given away to Barka Gana a horse which he had
really promised to another chief. He therefore
asked his general to give it up; but the latter took
such offence at this request that he returned all the
horses that the sheikh had previously given him,

saying that he would in future walk if he could not
ride horses of his own. Thereupon the sheikh sent
for him, had him stripped naked in his presence,
and a leather girdle put round him. After re-
proaching him with his ingratitude, he ordered
that he should be sold forthwith to the Tibu merchants as a slave. Barka Gana fell on his knees
and acknowledged the justice of his punishment.
He begged for no forgiveness for himself, but en-
treated that his wives and children might be provided for by the sheikh.

On the following day, when Barka Gana was to
be handed over to the merchants, his black soldiers
and the Arab chiefs fell at the feet of the sheikh,
and, notwithstanding the arrogance of Barka Gana
towards them in the past, begged pardon for his
offences and that he might be restored to favour.
Barka Gana appearing at this moment to take
leave, the sheikh threw himself back on his carpet,
wept like a child, suffered Barka Gana, who had
crept close to him, to embrace his knees, and, then
calling his retinue "his sons", pardoned the re-
pentant general. There was a great deal of weep-
ing all round, followed by explosions of joy. In
the evening the timbrels were beaten, the Kanem
people yelled and struck their shields, and Barka
Gana, in new robes and a rich burnus, rode round
the camp followed by all the chiefs of the army.

The situation of the four Europeans—Dr. Oudney, Denham, Clapperton, and William Hillman—
was not very happy in the months that followed the
return from the Munga expedition. All were ill,

chiefly from fevers. Dr. Oudney had been suffering for months from the chest complaint of which he ultimately died. Moreover, they were almost entirely dependent for their subsistence on the kindness and hospitality of the Sheikh of Bornu, and quite unable without funds to pursue their investigations of Central Africa. They had paid large sums to Bu-Khalum (the Moorish merchant who had died from a poisoned arrow) to hold for them, and in the disposal of his goods after his death their funds had not been recovered. They were told that a brother of Bu-Khalum—called Hajji, from his having made a pilgrimage to Mekka—would be arriving shortly from Kano in Hausaland, and would acknowledge the debt owed by his brother and repay them. But when Hajji Bu-Khalum arrived he evaded the question, or only admitted a small portion of the debt.

A message was sent to England asking for further funds and assistance, but no answer could be expected for months. Indeed, for a time, communications with Tripoli were cut off, owing to a Moorish caravan having robbed the Tibu, and the latter, in revenge, having filled up the wells and stopped the road. Meantime, the situation of the British explorers was becoming very uncomfortable. They were peculiarly harassed with disease. Life, in fact, was a positive martyrdom. It was the long summer or rainy season of Bornu, when mosquitoes swarm. Quite unaware (as everyone was, down to about ten years ago) that it is certain kinds of mosquito which inoculate human beings with

malarial fever and other diseases, they probably
took no precautions to prevent mosquitoes getting
access to them at night. Consequently they were
martyrs to malarial fever. The "white ants" (or
termites, as they should properly be called) devoured much of their furniture and clothing; the
black ants, whose bites are as bad as the stings
of scorpions, nipped them all over the body. Although the sheikh continued his kindness to them
(and in exchange Hillman, the shipwright, made
him wonderful things like guncarriages, and Denham showed him how to manufacture cartridges,
and drilled his troops), his people, being Muhammadans, by degrees became scornful of these Christians, and even hostile, especially of Christians who
had no money, and whose wonderful medicines
were impotent to cure themselves.

Nevertheless, during this long and dreary wait,
almost amounting to an imprisonment, Denham
recorded some interesting observations and experiences. From his writings we obtain the following
information regarding the *Kanuri* people of Bornu,
or *Barebare* as they are properly called. "They
have large, unmeaning faces, with flat negro noses,
and mouths of great dimensions, with good teeth
and high foreheads. They are peaceable, quiet,
and civil. . . . In their manner of living they are
simple in the extreme. Flour made into a paste
sweetened with honey and fat poured over it, is
a dish for a sultan. The use of bread is not
known. . . . The grain most in use amongst the
people of all classes is a species of millet called

gussub (this is probably a kind of *Pennisetum*). The poorer people eat this grain raw, or parched in the sun, and are satisfied with no other nourishment for several days together. Bruised and steeped in water, *gussub* forms the travelling stock of all pilgrims and soldiers. When cleared of the husk, pounded, and made into a light paste, in which are mixed okroes (see p. 73) and melted fat, it forms a favourite dish. There is also a wild rice (*Zizania*) which grows in abundance near the water. This is parched in the sun, and when boiled is eaten as rice or made into flour." The Bornuese cultivated four kinds of beans in Denham's day, and made a paste from them. This, together with fish and fowls,[1] was the only form of food which travellers could find in the towns near the Shari; elsewhere, in these countries, rice and Indian corn were cultivated, besides, of course, cotton and indigo.

The Bornuese had twenty cuts or lines on each side of the face, which were drawn from the corners of the mouth towards the angles of the lower jaw and cheekbone. It was quite distressing to these English travellers to witness the torture the poor little children underwent who were thus marked. They endured not only the heat, but the attacks of countless flies on the festering wounds caused by this slashing of the face. The adults exhibited also one cut on the forehead in the centre, six on each arm, six on each thigh, four on each breast, and nine on each side just above the hips. These cuts

---

[1] In Denham's day, as many as forty fowls would be purchased in Bornu markets for the value of four shillings in trade goods.

often rose into prominent weals or scars of shiny, raised skin.

The people of Bornu still rode bullocks in Denham's time, a far older method of progression than the use of camels. The bullock was also the principal draught animal of Bornu in those days, and carried large burdens fixed to a small saddle of plaited rushes. This saddle was made additionally comfortable by cushions of leather filled with corn for the women-riders of bullocks. A leather thong was passed through the cartilage of the ox's nose, and served as a bridle. The man, or more often the woman, who rode the bullock, would usually sit cross-legged on this roomy and comfortable saddle. When the rider was the daughter or the wife of a Shawa Arab, a handsome carpet or an embroidered robe would be spread over the leather cushions, and the girl herself would be extravagantly adorned with amber, silver rings, coral, and all sorts of finery, her hair streaming with melted fat, and a rim of black dye an inch wide painted round her eyes to enhance their beauty.

The towns of Bornu in that day were large and well built, with clay walls, nearly 40 feet in height and 20 feet in thickness. Each town usually had four entrances through the walls, with a succession of three separate gates to each, made of solid planks, 8 or 10 inches thick, and fastened together with heavy clamps of iron. The houses still consist of several courtyards between four walls, with apartments leading out of them for slaves. Then there is a passage and an inner court leading to the habitations of the different wives, who each have a square space to themselves enclosed by walls, and a handsome thatched hut. From the centre of the house space there is usually a wide staircase of five or six steps leading to the apartments of the husband. These may consist of two buildings like towers, with a terrace of communication between them looking into the street. The walls in Denham's day were made of reddish clay as smooth as stucco, and the roofs were tastefully arched on the inside with branches, and neatly thatched on the outside with a long and wiry grass. Into the walls are fixed the horns of gazelles, oryx, and other antelopes, which serve as substitutes for nails and pegs. On to them are hung the arms—quivers, bows, spears, and shields—of the house-owner, and such of his clothes as are not in use. The pinnacle of each thatched roof belonging to a man of quality is surmounted by an ostrich egg.

The Shawa, or Shua Arabs of Bornu, are described by Denham as bearing a strong resemblance in features and habits to the English gipsies, though much darker in complexion. They were a distinctly handsome people, but deceitful and arrogant. Eighty years or so ago they easily imposed themselves on the black people of Bornu and the surrounding countries, by pretending to have a natural gift of prophecy, and by being able to write sentences in Arabic, which they sold as charms. They were great breeders of cattle and horses, and annually supplied the Sudanese trade with two or

three thousand horses. The Shawa were divided
into tribes, some of which still bore the names of
Arab tribes in Egypt and Arabia. They were probably descended from that great Arab invasion of
North-east Africa which occurred in the middle of
the eleventh century.

Denham noted the way in which the Shawa
Arabs killed buffalo on the shores of Lake Chad.
They would chase them in the swamps and ride
close up to them on horseback, so that at last
the rider was able to get one foot well fixed on
the buffalo's back. Then with singular skill he
pierced the animal just behind its shoulder with one
or two spears. The buffalo was thus only able to
run a short distance, after which he was easily
despatched. But, of course, it occasionally happened that the buffalo before being struck by the
spear would wheel round and upset both horse and
rider, and in such circumstances gore both of them
to death.

Denham also tells us about the Buduma islanders
of Lake Chad. Lake Chad at the present day is
reduced to a small and a large lake connected with
each other by meandering streams, and separated
by a considerable tract of marshy country, which
is studded with sandy tracts of raised soil. These
were possibly islands in Denham's day, and Lake
Chad may have been then one huge sheet of water,
with this great Buduma Archipelago in the middle.
The Buduma are now a peaceful folk on the best
of terms with the English. But in the last century
they held themselves as independent, and refused

to be subdued by any of the surrounding peoples. When this English expedition visited Bornu, the Buduma were accustomed to snatch the natives of the mainland and hold them up to ransom, demanding sometimes a payment of two or three thousand bullocks, or a proportionate number of slaves for any person of rank whom they might kidnap.

The Buduma or Yedima islands lie on the eastern side of the Chad, and between them and the Bornu shore there used to be, when the rainy season had filled Lake Chad, a canoe voyage of five days of open sea. The islands are very numerous, but vary much in size and numbers as the lake rises or falls. Sometimes they are merely peninsulas or isthmuses of dry land. The Buduma people have a language of their own, although it resembles that of Kanem. Their arms are still spears and shields, and in Denham's day they fought with every body around them—Wadai, Baghirmi, and Bornu. They believe in a divine power, which rules everything, but are not Muhammadans even now. They used to boast of their strong arms and cunning heads which were given to them instead of a large country and much cattle; consequently they argued, "we must take from those who are richer than ourselves". Eighty years ago they were reported to have nearly one thousand large canoes. The Buduma are most friendly with the British now, but even in Denham's day they were not considered a sanguinary or cruel people. When prisoners were taken in battle, they did not kill, but cured them; and if no ransom was offered, the

prisoners were given Buduma wives, and allowed
to remain on the islands as free as their captors.

During this long and sometimes dreary deten-
tion in Bornu, amongst the few distractions of the
Englishmen were the wrestling competitions of the
negro slaves. Quickness and main strength were
the qualifications which ensured victory: the wrestlers struggled with a bitterness which could scarcely
have been exceeded in the armed contests of the
Roman gladiators, and which was greatly augmented
by the voices of their masters, urging them to the
most strenuous exertion of their powers. A rude
buffalo-horn trumpet sounded to the attack, and the
combatants entered the arena naked, with the exception of a leathern girdle about the loins. Those
who had been victorious on former occasions were
received with loud acclamations by the spectators.
Slaves of all nations were first matched against
each other; of these the natives of Hausaland were
the least powerful, and seldom victors. The most
arduous struggles were between the Musgowi and
the Baghirmi[1] negroes: some of these slaves, and
particularly the latter, were beautifully formed, and
of gigantic stature; but the feats of the day always
closed by the matching of two Baghirmi against
each other—and dislocated limbs, or death, were
often the consequence of these kindred encounters.
The wrestlers would commence by placing their
hands on each other's shoulders. They made no
use of their feet, but frequently stooped down and

[1] The Musgu people came from the Logun branch or tributary of the
Shari.

practised a hundred deceptions to throw the adversary off his guard. At length one would seize his
antagonist by the hips, and after holding him in the
air, dash him against the ground with stunning
violence, where he might lie covered with blood
and unable to pursue the contest. A conqueror of
this kind was greeted by loud shouts, and garments
would be thrown to him by the spectators; he on
his part would kneel at his master's feet, and the
proud master cause him to be clothed with a tobe
of the value of 30 or 40 dollars (£6 to £8). Denham writes that he has seen the wrestlers foam and
bleed at the mouth and nose from pure rage and
exertion, their owners all the time vying with each
other in using expressions most likely to excite their
fury: one chief would draw a pistol, and swear by
the Koran that his slave should not survive an instant his defeat, and, with the same breath, offer him
great rewards if he conquers. Both these promises
were sometimes too faithfully kept; and one poor
wretch, who had for more than fifty minutes with-
stood the attacks of a ponderous negro from some
country to the south of Mandara, turned his eye
reproachfully on his threatening master, only for an
instant, when his antagonist slipped his hands down
from the shoulders to the loins, and by a sudden
twist raised his knee to his chest, and fell with his
whole weight on the poor slave (who was a Hausa),
snapping his spine in the fall. Former feats were
considered as nothing after one failure; and a slave,
that a hundred dollars would not have purchased
to-day, might, after a defeat, be sold at the market

for a few dollars, to anyone who would purchase
him.

Another relief to the monotony (so far as Denham was concerned) was the collection of a men-
agerie. The Sheikh of Bornu sent Denham three
specimens of the Ground Hornbill, which had
been taken in their nests on the Logun river far
to the south. They were much esteemed amongst
the natives, as their flesh was thought to be a
medicine for many disorders if cooked and placed
against the part affected, especially as a remedy
for enlargement of the spleen. These Ground
Hornbills feed on insects, fish, snakes, and serpents.
They have a particular instinct for discovering
snakes, especially when the snake is incubating its
eggs in anthills or burrows. The hornbill digs out
the snake with its immense beak and eats it, together with the eggs. Ground Hornbills are larger
than a turkey cock in size, with much longer legs
than the Tree Hornbills.

Surrounded by his monkeys, parrots, civets,
ichneumons, hyenas, and hornbills, Denham felt
that his circumstances resembled those of Robinson
Crusoe; but as the cooler weather of the autumn set
in, his solitude was less apparent, as Dr. Oudney
and the other two white men recovered their health
to a certain extent and were able to join him.

On 14 December, 1823, Dr. Oudney and
Captain Clapperton left Kuka[1], the capital of

[1] The name of Kuka is probably derived from the local name for the
great baobab tree, which throughout Bornu is called *Kuka*. The place is
now called Kukawa.

Bornu, to accompany a caravan of twenty Moorish merchants, who were proceeding to Kano, probably the largest city of Central Africa even at the present day, and the capital or principal town of the extensive domain of the Hausa people. The Sheikh of Bornu gave them all the facilities at his command, and Dr. Oudney was determined to go on this journey, although in an almost dying condition—indeed, he died not long afterwards.

Major Denham remained in Bornu a little longer, and then, having been joined in December, 1823, by a new assistant, Ensign Toole of the 80th Regiment, he decided to accompany a Bornu expedition to the country of Baghirmi, far to the south of Lake Chad. This Mr. Toole was a handsome, energetic young officer (only twenty-two years old), who deserved a better fate than what befell him. He had volunteered at Malta at only twenty hours' notice to join this research party in the Sudan, and had made the long, dangerous, and difficult journey from Tripoli to Bornu (alone and unattended, except for such small parties of Arabs or Moors as he accompanied) in the short space of three months and fourteen days. He had only lost five camels out of the caravan, and had brought ample supplies of money and trade goods to the expedition.

Denham and Toole travelled up the Shari River to the country of Logun. This was a region of civilized negroes, with large, populous towns mostly on the banks of the Shari River, which was here a wide, handsome stream. But this country was infested to an extraordinary degree, even for Central Africa, with flies, mosquitoes, and bees. The houses of Kusseri (for example) were built like one cell within another, the innermost sanctum being perhaps surrounded by as many as five or six outer covered courts. These dwellings were thus constructed in order that the inhabitants might find some escape from the attacks of flying insects. During several hours of the day it was dangerous to go out into the open air, and those who did so returned with their head and eyes so stung and poisoned that they nearly died from the effects.

The principal town of Logun itself was surrounded by high walls which rose picturesquely from the banks of the broad river. The main street was as wide as Pall Mall, and had large dwellings on each side, built with great uniformity, each having a courtyard in front, surrounded by walls and a handsome entrance through a strong door hasped with iron. The house in which Denham and Toole took up their residence for a few days consisted of four separate huts within an outer wall, together with a large entrance hall for the servants.

The next morning the travellers were summoned to appear before the sultan. Ten immense negroes of high birth, most of them grey-bearded, bareheaded, and carrying large clubs, preceded them through the streets, and the white men were received with considerable ceremony. After passing through several dark rooms they were conducted to a large square court, where some hundred

persons were assembled, all seated on the ground
—in the middle was a vacant space, whereon the
white men were requested to sit down also. Two
slaves, in striped cotton tobes, who were fanning
the air through a lattice-work of cane, pointed out
the covered "cage" in which the sultan was concealed. On a signal, the covering was removed,
and something alive was discovered on a carpet,
wrapped up in silk tobes, with the head enveloped
in shawls, and nothing but the eyes visible. The
whole court then prostrated themselves and poured
sand on their heads, while eight frumfrums and
as many horns blew a loud and very harsh-sound-
ing salute.

The Musgu people of Logun had a metal currency, which at that period was a great novelty
to European travellers in Central Africa, who were
more used to seeing kauri shells, kola nuts, cotton
cloths, or even slaves quoted as a standard of value.
The currency in Logun consisted of thin plates of
iron like an imperfect horseshoe in shape. These
would be tied up into parcels of ten or twelve according to weight, and thirty of these parcels were
equal in value to about 4s. 2d.

However, at this point Denham's explorations
were brought to a full stop by the advance of the
Baghirmi army. This so frightened the Sultan of
Logun that he forced the travellers with their
Bornu escort to return at once to the north. This
hurried departure, no doubt, was the immediate
cause of Toole's death, which occurred on
26 February, 1824. He was buried at a place

called Angala, on the Shari, and if his grave could be identified, it is to be hoped that a permanent memorial might be raised over it. Such a lovable young man was he that his loss was regretted by every native, as well as European, with whom he had come into contact, from Tripoli to the Shari River.

Denham returned to Bornu in time to witness the great and decisive battle between the forces of the Sheikh of Bornu and the powerful army of the Baghirmi negroes, who were invading Bornu from the Shari River, five thousand strong, with two hundred chiefs at their head. The guns and the cavalry possessed by the Bornuese and their Arab allies gained the day. Two or three thousand of the Baghirmi, including many notable persons, were killed, and the remainder fled back to their own country.

In the late summer of 1824, Denham having been rejoined by Clapperton (who had returned from his remarkable expedition to the Niger, which I shall next describe), made his way back across the desert to Tripoli and so to England. As a reward for his remarkable exploring work he was sent out in 1827 to assist the natives of Sierra Leone in improving their villages, making roads, and advancing their agriculture. In 1828 he was also sent as government inspector to Fernando Pô, but returned to Sierra Leone as lieutenant-governor, and died at Freetown, May, 1828.

CHAPTER X

Clapperton in Hausaland

CAPTAIN HUGH CLAPPERTON, in company with
Dr. Oudney, left Kuka, the capital of Bornu, on
14 December, 1823, to explore what they called
the "Soudan", namely, the regions between Bornu
and the Niger. Some parts of Western Bornu
were then under Fula domination: others were
still liable to Tuareg raids. But at the time of
Oudney's and Clapperton's passage through this
part of the northern Sudan there was a truce to
fighting, and trade flourished. In every big town
there was a market, and Clapperton has left us a
good description of one of these centres of eager
trade:

"The goods were exposed for sale in booths
or houses open at the side next the street. The
different wares were arranged each in its particular
quarter: knives, scissors, beads, silken cords, and
pieces of silk, sword slings, and dagger cases,
men's robes, and women's dresses; beef, mutton,
and fowls; millet and sorghum, beans, Indian corn,
&c. There were four different kinds of Indian
corn: the yellow, the red, the white, and the
Egyptian. The last is reckoned the best. There
were stalls besides, for making and mending every-

COMMANDER HUGH CLAPPERTON, R.N.

(From the picture in the National Portrait Gallery)

thing in common use. Bands of music, composed
of drums, flutes, and a kind of guitar with strings
of horse hair, were parading from booth to booth
to attract the attention of customers."

At one of these stalls Captain Clapperton
bought a pound of coffee[1] for the value of twelve
shillings! It was the only nourishment or stimu-
lant that his unfortunate dying companion — Dr.
Oudney—could take.

At the important city of Katagum, which is
situated close to the banks of the Yeu River,
the travellers were met by a servant of the Fula
governor on horseback. He presented them with
a small basket of kola nuts from far-off Ashanti.
After delivering this present, the servant returned
at full speed to a party of horsemen at a little distance. This troop of cavalry then rode up to the
travellers at a gallop, brandishing their spears.
The horsemen, after saluting them, wheeled round
and rode on before, the drummers beating their
drums, and two bards singing the praises of their
master, the governor, in the following song which
Clapperton took down in writing. One of the
two singers bawled the sentiments of the song,
whilst his companion responded with the chorus.
This song, the original of which was apparently
in the Hausa language, is translated as follows
by Captain Clapperton:—

" Give flesh to the hyenas at daybreak:
    Oh! the broad spears.

[1] See p. 74.

The spear of the sultan is the broadest:
    Oh! the broad spears.
I behold thee now—I desire to see none other:
    Oh! the broad spears.

" My horse is as tall as a high wall:
    Oh! the broad spears.
He will fight against ten, he fears nothing:
    Oh! the broad spears.
He has slain ten—the guns are yet behind:
    Oh! the broad spears.
The elephant of the forest brings me what I want:
    Oh! the broad spears.

" Like unto thee—so is the sultan:
    Oh! the broad spears.
Be brave! be brave! friends and kinsmen!
    Oh! the broad spears.
God is great!—I wax fierce as a beast of prey:
    Oh! the broad spears.
God is great!—to-day those I wished for are come:
    Oh! the broad spears."

On 12 January, 1824, Dr. Walter Oudney died
at the village of Murmur in an advanced stage of
consumption. He was only thirty-two years old.
Clapperton himself was ill, but so eager for discovery that he pushed on westwards as soon as
he had buried his companion. After leaving
Katagum he entered the country of Hausa proper,
though for some time past he had been travelling
through the new Fula empire of Sokoto wherein
the governors of the towns were mostly Fulas.[1]

---

[1] Clapperton gives this description of a Fula governor: " Tall and
slender, with a high arched nose, broad forehead, and large eyes—as fine a
looking black man as ever I had seen." He shrewdly remarks that he sees
nowhere in the Sudan—not even amongst the Fulas—any sign of a *plough*.

According to Clapperton, the Fulas were in features and in the manner of wearing the turban, very like the inhabitants of Tetuan in Morocco.

Hausaland[1] Clapperton describes as "a beautiful country with numerous plantations, as neatly fenced as in England. The roads are thronged with travellers, and the shady trees by the roadside serve to shelter female hucksters. The women who were not engaged in the retail of their wares were busy spinning cotton, and from time to time surveyed themselves with whimsical complaisancy in little pocket mirrors."

The soil was a strong red clay, large blocks of granite frequently appearing above the surface. The towns were always surrounded by clay walls, and in the larger towns Clapperton found markets that were finer and more important in the produce sold than the bazaars of Tripoli. In one such place Clapperton, who was ill with fever, stopped to rest all through the heat of the day under the shade of a tree.

"A pretty Fellata (Fula) girl going to market with milk and butter, neat and spruce in her attire as a Cheshire dairymaid, here accosted me with infinite archness and grace. She said I was of her own nation; and, after much amusing talk, I

There is no plough, he remarks, in use by the natives farther south than in Fezzan. No negro race (until taught recently by the white man) knew anything of the plough, and the absence of this agricultural implement (possessed by the ancient Egyptians, the Abyssinians, and the Galas) from the Fula communities show that the migration of these strange "semi-white men" from the white man's countries of the north and east must have been very ancient.

[1] That is, the Hausa-speaking provinces of Kano, Katsena, Zanfara, Zaria and Gwari.

pressed her, in jest, to accompany me on my journey, while she parried my solicitations with roguish glee by referring me to her father and mother. I don't know how it happened, but her presence seemed to dispel the effects of the ague. To this trifling and innocent memorial of a face and form, seen that day for the first time and last time, but which I shall not readily forget, I may add the more interesting information, that the making of butter such as ours is confined to the nation of the Fellatas, and that it is both clean and excellent. So much is this domestic art cultivated, that from a useful prejudice or superstition it is deemed unlucky to sell new milk; it may, however, be bestowed as a gift. Butter is also made in other parts of Central Africa, but sold in an oily fluid state something like honey."

Of Katagum and its vicinity he says:—

"The land, everywhere the eye turned, looked beautiful; the grain was just high enough to wave with the wind; little villages were numerous; the trees full of foliage, none being left hardly but such as were fit for use, such as the mikadania or butter tree (*Butyrospermum*), the natta or durau (*Parkia*), and the tamarind; herds of fine white cattle were seen grazing on the fallow ground; horses and mares were tethered in the small spaces left between the plantations in cultivation; women, to the amount of a hundred, were threshing out corn with large sticks on the flat rock at the base of the mount, the wind, blowing fresh from the westward, serving them as a winnowing machine."

" The town was below, in the form of an oblong square, the four sides facing the four cardinal points; the headman's house in the centre of the town, and like one of the old keeps or castles in Scotland, near the borders; it is also of the Moorish form, and the general one for all the governors' houses in Hausa. A high clay tower, through which is the gate or entrance from each side, overtops a wall of clay about twenty feet high, in the form of a square; inside are huts and *kuzis* (courtyards) for the women, eunuchs, domestics, and horses; the governor occupying the upper part of the three-storied tower in times of alarm and danger, and his men-slaves and armed retainers the lower. In the middle storey, at each side, and above the gate, are oblong holes, which serve for archers to shoot their arrows through. The windows of the houses are either shut by a mat on the side next the wind, or by a number of coloured and plaited lines of grass strung over a small rod, which is hung across the top of the window; the ends falling down admit sufficient air and light, and keep out the flies. This plan is also used for the doors of inner apartments in the lower houses, and requires no opening or shutting. Rainwater is conveyed from the flat roofs of the big houses, clear of the walls, by long, baked, clay funnels, which look like great guns mounted on the tops of the walls. The smaller houses of the town are like the generality of Hausa dwellings outside the capital towns: circular thatched huts within a high, square, clay wall; frequently there is in addition a single room, with a flat roof, used by the master of the house as a safe repository for his goods.

"Every house has two or three date trees within this wall or enclosure which bear fruit twice a year, like those of Katsena and Kano. The people use two pieces of flat board or gourd-husk, one fixed, the other movable, to which is attached a line for the purpose of clapping one against the other to frighten the fruit-bats and a kind of jay (roller-bird) which lodge on the trees and destroy a great quantity of fruit. The ibis, adjutant stork, crane, and several other birds, build their nests in the shady trees of this town.

"The market of Katagum is held daily, and is well attended: grain, oxen, sheep, and all the necessaries of life, abound. A tame ostrich is kept in the marketplace to avert the evil eye—a Bornu custom. There are several places of prayer in the Katagum, but one principal mosque or *jama* stands on the right of the governor's house." In Katagum there were four kinds of pigeons: the domestic or blue rock pigeon, a large handsome wood pigeon, claret-coloured with white spots; a fruit pigeon with a fleshy substance round the outside of the eye; and a small dove with purple breast and black ring round the neck. The inhabitants offered no objections to Clapperton shooting at these pretty birds in their courtyards; at least he says not, but being Muhammadans who hold pigeons as semi-sacred they probably did not like his killing them.

"In the shady tree close to the house in which I lived were birds (weaver birds) a little larger

than our sparrows, with a jet-black head, and a
bright yellow in the neck, breast, belly, and under
the wings, and the back a dusky green. They
chirped just like the sparrow. Hundreds were
building their nests in this and other trees, which
they do at the extreme branches or twigs. The
nests are leaves sewn together, but they are also
plaited with grass and have their entrance at the
bottom. Both male and female work at the nest,
and the hen lays six or seven eggs. During this
season they are very busy, and keep up a constant
chirruping, and flutter under their nests and about
the trees."

In the districts of Hausaland near the Niger,
Clapperton notices the enormous hills of the termites, or white ants, which are between twenty and
thirty feet high, and look "like Gothic steeples".

When Clapperton was near the great town of
Kano, he believed it to be such an important place,
that to make a good impression he dressed himself
in full naval uniform. But when he entered this
great emporium of Hausaland he was grievously
disappointed. He had expected to see a city of
surprising grandeur from the accounts given by
the Arabs; in reality, he found a vast area of
ground enclosed within the high clay walls, but
the houses scattered about in detached groups between large stagnant pools of water. "I might
have spared all the pains I had taken with my
toilette, for not an individual turned his head
round to gaze at me."

The marketplace was bordered on the east and

west by an extensive swamp covered with reeds and water, and frequented by wild ducks, storks, cranes, and vultures. These last-named birds swarmed over all the area of Kano, as they were town scavengers protected by public opinion. The house which had been hired for Clapperton was situated close to this morass, and he had to endure the horrible smells from the public sewers which opened into the streets, together with the odour of decaying vegetation and stagnant water arising from the swamp. His house had six rooms on the upper story, extremely dark, and five rooms below, with a dismal-looking entrance or lobby, a backcourt, a well, and other conveniences. Little holes or windows admitted a glimmering light into the apartments.

Whilst residing in Kano, the Arabs who had travelled with Clapperton attempted to get him into trouble with the Fula authorities by appealing to him when they complained of the Governor's exactions. But he replied wisely by one of their own exaggerations, "Whatever the Sultan does is beautiful"; for he knew they only wanted to entrap him into making some foolish remark, and then denounce him as a Christian spy to the rulers of Hausaland. After this he was no more troubled with their complaints.

Kano city eighty years ago was of an irregular oval shape, about fifteen miles in circumference, and surrounded by a clay wall thirty feet high, with a dry ditch on either side of the wall. There were fifteen gates of wood, covered with sheet iron.

regularly opened and shut at sunrise and sunset.
Not more than a fourth of the ground within the
walls was occupied by houses: the vacant space
being laid out in fields and gardens. The houses
were built of clay, mostly in the shape of a square;
with a central room, the roof of which was supported by the trunks of palm trees, which served
as a hall for the reception of visitors. A staircase
led to an open gallery overlooking the hall, and
serving as a passage to the chambers of the second
story, which were lighted with small windows.
On the north side of the city there are two remarkable hills, each about two hundred feet in height.
Kano is very similar to Clapperton's description at
the present day.

In the world-famed market of Kano, particular
quarters were appropriated to distinct articles; the
smaller wares being set out in booths in the middle,
whilst cattle and bulky commodities were exposed for sale in the outskirts of the marketplace.
Wood, dried grass, bean-straw for provender;
beans, guinea corn (sorghum), Indian corn, wheat,
&c., were stored in one section; goats, sheep,
asses, bullocks, horses, and camels in another;
earthenware and indigo in a third; vegetables and
fruit of all descriptions, such as yams, sweet
potatoes, water and musk melons, pappaw fruit,
limes, cashew nuts, parinarium plums, mangoes,
shaddocks, dates, &c., in a fourth, and so on.
Wheaten flour was baked into bread of three
different kinds: one like muffins, another like our
twists, and the third a light puffy cake, with honey

and melted butter poured over it. Rice was also
made into little cakes. Beef and mutton were
killed daily. Camel flesh was occasionally to be
had, but was of poor quality; the animal being
commonly killed, as an Irish grazier might say,
"to save its life": it is esteemed a great delicacy,
however, by the Arabs, when the carcass is fat.

The native butchers of Kano seemed to Clapperton "fully as knowing as those at home", for they
made a few slashes to show the fat, blew up meat,
and sometimes even stuck a little sheep's wool on
a leg of goat's flesh, to make it pass with the
ignorant for mutton! When a fat bull was brought
to market to be killed, its horns were dyed red
with henna; drummers attended, a mob soon collected, the news of the animal's size and fatness
spread, and all ran to buy. [The colouring of the
horns is effected by applying the green leaves of
the henna shrub, bruised into a kind of poultice.]

Near the shambles there were a number of
cookshops in the open air; each consisting merely
of a wood fire, stuck round with wooden skewers,
on which small bits of fat and lean meat, alternately mixed, and scarcely larger than a penny-
piece each, were roasting. Everything looked
very clean and comfortable; and a woman did the
honours of the table, with a mat dish-cover placed
on her knees, from which she served her guests,
who were squatted around her. Ground millet and
water gruel was retailed to those who could afford
this beverage at their repast: the price, at most,
did not exceed twenty kauris (then worth about

a halfpenny in English money). Those who had
houses ate at home; women never resorted to cookshops, and even at home ate apart from the men.

The interior of the great market was filled with
stalls of bamboo, laid out in irregular lanes. Here
the more costly wares were sold, and articles
of dress, ornaments, &c., made and repaired.
Bands of musicians paraded up and down to attract
purchasers to particular booths. Here the merchants displayed coarse writing-paper of French
manufacture, brought from Algeria and Tunis;
scissors and knives, of native workmanship; crude
antimony and tin, both the produce of the country;[1]
unwrought silk of a red colour, which the people
wove into belts and slings, or into long stripes to
be inserted into the finest cotton tobes; armlets
and bracelets of brass; beads of glass, coral, and
amber; finger rings of pewter, and a few silver
trinkets, but none of gold; tobes, or men's garments, and turkadis, or women's robes; also turban
shawls, coarse woollen clothes of all colours, coarse
calico, Moorish dresses, the cast-off gaudy garbs
of the Mameluke soldiers of Egypt and Barbary;
pieces of Egyptian linen, checked or striped with
gold; sword blades from Malta, &c. The market
was crowded from sunrise to sunset every day, not
excepting the Muhammadan Sabbath, which is
Friday.

The slave market was held in two long
sheds, one for males, the other for females. Here

---

[1] Long afterwards tin mines were discovered by the Royal Niger Company in Southern Hausaland, and are now being worked.

the slaves were seated in rows, and carefully decked out for exhibition; the owner, or one of his trusty slaves, sitting near them. Young or old, plump or withered, beautiful or ugly, would be sold without distinction; but the buyer generally inspected his intended purchase with the utmost attention, and somewhat in the same manner (writes Clapperton) as a volunteer seaman would be examined by a surgeon on entering the navy. The slave-buyer would look at the tongue, teeth, eyes, and limbs, and endeavour to detect any weakness or defect. If the slaves were afterwards found to be faulty or unsound, they might be returned within three days. When removed from the market they were stripped of their finery, which was then sent back to their former owner.

In this wonderful market of Kano, Clapperton bought for three Spanish dollars (12s. 6d.) an English green cotton umbrella, an article he little expected to meet with, yet one which was by no means uncommon in the marketplaces of the Sudan.

At Kano, Clapperton saw an exhibition of Hausa boxing. He offered prizes worth two thousand kauri shells (4s. 2d.) to induce the people to get up a match, but he expressly stipulated that they should not fight in earnest, because he had heard that it occurred so frequently that one or other of the combatants was killed.

"The boxers arrived, attended by two drums and the whole body of butchers who here compose 'the fancy'. A ring was soon formed, by the

THE FULAS

master of the ceremonies throwing dust on the spectators to make them stand back. The drummers entered the ring and began to drum lustily. One of the boxers followed, quite naked, except for a skin round the middle. He placed himself in an attitude as if to oppose an antagonist, and wrought his muscles into action, seemingly to find out that every sinew was in full force for the approaching combat; then coming from time to time to the side of the ring, and presenting his right arm to the bystanders, he said, 'I am a hyena;' 'I am a lion;' 'I am able to kill all that oppose me.' The spectators, to whom he presented himself, laid their hands on his shoulder, repeating, 'The blessing of God be upon thee;' 'Thou art a hyena;' 'Thou art a lion.' He then abandoned the ring to another, who showed off in the same manner. The right hand and arm of the pugilists were now bound with narrow country cloth, beginning with a fold round the middle finger; after which, the hand being first clenched with the thumb between the fore and mid fingers, the cloth was passed in many turns round the fist, the wrist, and the forearm. After about twenty had separately gone through their attitudes of defiance, and appeals to the bystanders, they were next brought forward by pairs. If they happened to be friends, they laid their left breasts together twice, and exclaimed, 'We are lions;' 'We are friends.' The one then left the ring, and another was brought forward. If the two did not recognize one another as friends, the set-to immediately commenced. On taking their stations, the two pugilists stood at some distance, parrying with the left hand open, and, whenever opportunity offered, striking with the right. They generally aimed at the pit of the stomach, and under the ribs. Whenever they closed, one seized the other's head under his arm and beat it with his fist, at the same time striking with his knee between his antagonist's thighs. In this position, with the head *in chancery*, they are said sometimes to gouge or scoop out one of the eyes. When they break loose, they never fail to give a swinging blow with the heel under the ribs, or sometimes under the left ear. It is these blows which are so often fatal. The combatants were repeatedly separated by my orders, as they were beginning to lose their temper. When this spectacle was heard of, girls left their pitchers at the wells, the market people threw down their baskets, and all ran to see the fight. The whole square before my house was crowded to excess. After six pairs had gone through several rounds, I ordered them, to their great satisfaction, the promised reward, and the multitude quietly dispersed."

Clapperton in due course reached the town of Sokoto (a name which should probably be pronounced *Sakatu*[1]). He was immediately sent for by the great Fula sultan of that kingdom, who had become a kind of emperor over all the provinces of Hausaland and the regions south of the River

[1] According to Clapperton the word means in the Fula language "a resting-place". By degrees it became applied to the whole dominion of the Eastern Fulas. This native capital was abandoned later in favour of Wurno, higher up the Sokoto river.

Benue, in addition to the territories conquered by his predecessors in the basin of the Central Niger. The name of this sultan was Muhammad Bello. He was a noble-looking man, forty-four years of age, though much younger in appearance; five feet ten inches in height, and portly in person; with a short, curling black beard, a small mouth, a fine forehead, a Grecian nose and large black eyes. He was dressed in a light-blue cotton tobe, with a white muslin turban, the shawl of which he wore over his nose and mouth in the Tuareg fashion. When he first received Clapperton, he was seated on a small carpet between two pillars supporting the roof of a thatched house. The walls and pillars were painted blue and white, and on the back wall or screen was sketched a sort of fire-screen ornament, a rough Moorish design of a flowerpot. An armchair with an iron lamp affixed to it was placed on each side of the screen.

In Muhammad Bello, the Fula sultan or emperor of Sokoto, Clapperton found a wonderful personage. Although a copper-coloured negroid monarch of West Central Africa, ruling, or at any rate dominating, an area almost equivalent to the British Protectorate of Northern Nigeria at the present day (his descendant is still recognized as the Sultan of Sokoto by the British Government), he was through his position as an enlightened Muhammadan in touch with the world beyond the Sahara Desert. The merchants of Morocco, Algeria, Tunis, and Tripoli, and the pilgrims passing to and from Mekka across the Egyptian territories, kept him informed of what was going on in the Mediterranean, even amongst the countries of Europe and Asia. Bello had some considerable knowledge of the early sects in Christianity, and though he was not clearly informed as to the differences between Protestants and Catholics, was able to ask Clapperton "whether he was a Nestorian or a Socinian". He had heard about the British bombardment of Algiers (1818), and the insurrection of the Greeks against the Turks (1821). He knew about the ancient Moorish kingdoms in Spain, and was pleased to hear that the British had been for some time past in possession of Gibraltar. He also made many enquiries regarding the British Empire which was being built up in India. Questioned as to the course of the Niger, he related with accuracy the fate of Mungo Park, drew a rough map of the course of the Niger and its affluents; and although this map omitted to give the lower part of the river between Lokoja and the sea, the verbal description which accompanied it clearly pointed to the fact of which English geographers were not yet satisfied, that the outlet of the Niger was in the Gulf of Guinea. Clapperton found at Sokoto various articles of English manufacture which he was assured were received from the sea coast and the country of "Yarba" (Yoruba). Clapperton naturally desired to penetrate to the Niger, and perhaps thus to reach the sea coast. But Bello was not very anxious he should do so, and although he professed to find guides, every time one of these was brought for-

ward he cried off at the last moment, saying that
the journey was too dangerous. So at last Clapperton, as his health was failing, had to resign himself to returning to Bornu, whence he proceeded to
England with Major Denham.

CHAPTER XI

Clapperton and Lander Reach the Niger Through Yoruba

AT this point in the narrative mention should be made of the brilliant achievement of Major Alexander Gordon Laing, born in Edinburgh in 1794. Major Laing had been aide-de-camp to the governor of the West African Settlements at Sierra Leone, and carried out most successfully in 1823 an exploration of the hinterland of this region, in the course of which he managed to locate with approximate correctness the actual source of the Niger near Falaba. Mungo Park had made the mistake of placing the Upper Niger on the map much too far to the east. Laing, though he did not actually see (in the distance) more than the mountains where the Niger rose, nevertheless gave a generally correct account of its origin and direction. Many years later, and mainly through the explorations of the French, it was realized that the head streams of the Niger are two great rivers of nearly equal length and volume which do not join till they meet at Mopti, east of Jenné. The Western Niger rises in the Kissi country, to the northeast of the Sierra Leone protectorate, the Eastern

Niger or Bani rises just beyond the north-eastern frontier of Liberia.

Major Laing returned to England from Sierra Leone, got permission to make a journey over-land from Tripoli to Timbuktu, and left Tripoli at the close of 1825. On his way to the oasis of Ghat, he was attacked and left for dead by the Tuaregs. In spite of his twenty-four wounds he struggled to life, continued his journey, passed through Ghat, and (first and last of British ex-plorers, so far) through the great oasis of Twat, reaching Timbuktu in August, 1826. Here he ex-cited the suspicions of the Fulas and Moors, and was ordered to leave the city. He did so after making arrangements to accompany a Moorish caravan across the Desert to Morocco. But the leader of the caravan had been requested by the authorities of Timbuktu to kill Laing as soon as he was well away from the neighbourhood. He was therefore murdered by the Berabish Moors at dawn, on the morning of the third day's journey north from Timbuktu.

Less than two years *before* this sad event, Commander Hugh Clapperton had left Sokoto (May 4, 1824), taking back with him to England a letter from the Fula sultan, Muhammad Bello, to George IV. This letter asked that a British consul and a physician might be sent to reside at a place on the sea coast near the delta of the Niger, in regions which (according to the belief of this Fula prince) were under Fula influence or sove-reignty.

Accordingly, in their desire to open up a legitimate trade with Africa, the British Government despatched Commander Hugh Clapperton to West Africa in the autumn of 1825. With his expedition was associated Dr. Dickson, Dr. Morrison, and a Captain Pearce. Dr. Dickson, for some reason, insisted on travelling alone to Timbuktu and Sokoto, and landed for this purpose at the port of Whida (Hwida), on the coast of Dahomé. He was never heard of any more after he quitted the capital of that sanguinary kingdom. Commander Clapperton himself proceeded with Pearce and Morrison, and with his servant Richard Lander (who was afterwards to become famous as the man who finished the Niger problem), to the river of Benin, as it was believed that at its mouth must be the trading station on the coast indicated by Sultan Bello. But when they reached this river a British merchant established there—Mr. Houtson —warned them against the difficulty of going any farther in that direction.

The kingdom of Benin has had a celebrated history. Possibly it was founded six or seven hundred years ago by some adventurer from the north, from Yoruba, who may have been of Negroid type, like a Fula, Songhai, or Hausa; and who imposed his rule on the savage, cannibal, naked negroes of these dense forests. Some degree of Upper Niger civilization seems to have been imported into these westernmost parts of the Niger Delta. When the Portuguese coasted along the Bight (or "Bay") of Benin in the latter part of

THE NIGER RIVER NEAR FALABA AND NOT FAR FROM ITS SOURCE

the fifteenth century, they heard stories of this powerful kingdom and its commerce, and very soon got into relations with the people of Benin. The Portuguese furnished the Bini or Edu tribes with the metals for making bronze, namely, copper and tin (though they may have got both from Eastern Nigeria). The Benin people seem to have brought from their ancestral home in Yoruba the art of modelling objects in clay—the Portuguese taught them to use wax for the mould and to cast in bronze. They acquired these arts very rapidly from the Portuguese, because before the fifteenth century was finished they had made in this way remarkable productions in bronze, as well as in carved ivory, of the Portuguese soldiers, seamen, and merchants. These can now be seen in the British Museum.

But the King of Benin, after first trading with Europeans in pepper and ivory, found that the most profitable commerce lay in the slave trade. He sent his warriors in all directions to raid the savage negroes around him, and the men, women, and children who were captured in these slave raids, together with all the criminals of Benin, were sold to the ships of the Portuguese, English, and French who visited the Benin River. Large numbers of slaves were also massacred every year in connection with the ceremonies of the Benin religion.

So when the British Government put a stop, as far as possible, to the slave trade at the beginning of the nineteenth century, the King of Benin was very angry. Therefore this country, from that time onwards till the end of the nineteenth century, was practically closed to Europeans, and if Clapperton had attempted to travel through it he would almost certainly have been killed.

Mr. Houtson advised him to start on his journey towards the Niger from a place called Badagri,' in the modern British colony of Lagos. Badagri was evidently the place called "Tagra" by Sultan Bello, and the seaport at which he had advised that an English consul should reside, because from thence there might be an overland trade with Sokoto. But Bello had exaggerated greatly his own power in these coast countries when he wrote this letter to George IV. At Badagri nobody had ever heard of the Fula emperor.

However, Clapperton's party reached without any difficulty the Muhammadan country of Yoruba, where Clapperton himself felt that he was once more in touch with the Sudan, for he met natives of Bornu and Hausaland, and most of the chiefs of Yoruba rode horses. Clapperton noticed how fond the Yoruba people were of *dogs*, whom they treated with great respect (but whom they also ate). No great man was without a pet dog, which had a boy-slave told off to look after it, and which wore a handsome collar ornamented with kauri shells. In this country, however, both Dr. Morrison and Captain Pearce died; but Clapperton had the assistance of Mr. Houtson, who was of the greatest service to him in appeasing the suspicions of the Yoruba people.

The Yoruba country proved to be very moun-

tainous in its central portion. The road to the
Niger led through winding and beautiful valleys
meandering between gigantic blocks of granite,
which in some places rose to a height of six or
seven hundred feet above the road. Along the
rivers tall trees were growing, but the sides of the
mountains were bare, except in the crevices. In
some districts it appeared as though a great con-
vulsion of nature had thrown the immense masses
of granite into wild and terrific confusion. The
scenery of these mountain passes was grand and
imposing. The road would sometimes ascend
almost perpendicularly and then descend through
masses of rocks into deep dells; or it would wind
picturesquely round the side of a steep hill, under
rocks overhanging the track in fearful uncertainty.
In every cleft of the hills, wherever there appeared
the least soil, were cottages surrounded by small
plantations of millet, yams, or plantains, giving a
beautiful variety to the rude scenery. The road
continued rising, hill above hill, till the travellers
arrived at the large and populous town of Chaki,
situated on the top of the highest hill (about
2500 feet above sea level). On every hand, on
the hills, on the rocks, and crowding on the road
the inhabitants were assembled in thousands; the
women welcoming the caravan by holding up their
hands and chanting choral songs, and the men
with the usual salutations and every demonstration
of joy. The headman of the town was seated on
the outside of his house, surrounded by his ladies,
his singing men and singing women, his drums,

fifes, and gong-gongs. He was a good-looking man, about fifty years of age, with a pleasing countenance. His house was all ready for the white men; and he immediately ordered a large supply of goats, sheep, and yams for the benefit of the expedition. Clapperton was so ill as they passed through Yoruba, and the English medicines of that day were so inefficient in dealing with the African maladies, that in his despair he had recourse to native remedies. The pain in his side was relieved by the skin being rubbed with a chewed-up mess of pepper seeds. After this application a cord or rope was rubbed backwards and forwards over the place, and the friction took the pain away. A little later on he was given a drink, which was like lime-juice mixed with pepper. This made him so sick that he could not stand for half an hour, after which he got suddenly well, and was so delighted at his recovery that he took care to give a present of six coral beads to the native medicine-man.

The capital of Yoruba in those days was called Eyeo, Oyo, or (by the Hausas) Katunga. The king or principal chief of Yoruba (Mansola) received the travellers sitting under the veranda of his house, between two huge red-and-blue umbrellas rising from tall poles held by slaves. The British explorers walked up to the king's verandah, and the king lifted up his hands; then raised the hands of the Europeans in his own three times, saying, "Aku, Aku!" which was the Yoruba greeting. Whilst he did this the large gathering of women ranged at the back of the sovereign, and his male attendants in front, stood up and shouted, "Oh, oh, oh!" It was impossible to count the number of his wives; they were so densely packed and so very numerous. To judge by their smiles they were as glad to see the white men as their master. The king was dressed in a white tobe or large shirt, with a blue one underneath. Round his neck he wore three strings of large, blue, cut-glass beads, and on his head the imitation of a European crown cut out in pasteboard and covered with blue calico.

But although the principal chief of Yoruba was so friendly the usual irritating delays occurred, which in the nineteenth century baffled so many patient explorers. The Yoruba ruler and his advisors hesitated to let Clapperton go on to the Niger, either because they were afraid he might be killed by the Fulas, or, more likely, because already some anxiety was felt lest if the white people knew too much about the country and its means of communication they might come in and dispossess the black rulers.

At this period—some eighty-five years ago—the people of Yoruba were not converted to Muhammadanism as they are now. They were still pagans of much the same type as those of Benin, Dahomé, and Ashanti, though not so bloodthirsty. Their religion consisted of the worship of a Supreme Spirit, to whom they offered sacrifices of horses and cows, sheep, goats, and fowls. At the principal yearly feast, all these animals were sacrificed at the fetish house, and some of their blood was spilt on the ground.   The flesh was then cooked, and the king and all the people, men and women, assembled in a state of nakedness to partake of the meat, and also to drink at the same time a fermented wine made of palm sap, and probably also beer from crushed grain.   Occasionally, human beings were sacrificed, but they were always criminals, and only one was killed at a time.   The king spoke with horror of the killing of human beings in the lavish style of Benin and Dahomé.

On the occasion of these great sacrifices the chiefs and headmen of the various districts of Yoruba were visiting the king, and they usually took advantage of their stay at the capital to act what Clapperton calls a play or pantomime.   Here is a description of one of these performances as seen by Clapperton and his companions in the winter of 1825.

The place chosen for this pastime was the king's park.   A fetish house occupied the left side; to the south were two very romantic and large blocks of granite, by the side of which was an old withered tree.   On the east were some beautiful shady trees; and on the north the king's house, from whence he viewed the scene.   In the centre were two clumps of trees, in one of which was a tall fan palm, overlooking the whole area, a space that may include some seven or eight hundred yards square.   Under these trees were seated the actors, dressed in large sacks, covering every part of the body; the head fantastically decorated with strips of rags, damask silk, and cotton, of many glaring colours.   The king's servants attended to keep the peace, and to prevent the crowd from breaking into the square in which the actors were assembled. Musicians also attended with drums, horns, and whistles, which were beaten and blown without intermission.

The first act consisted of dancing and tumbling in sacks, which the actors performed to the admiration of Clapperton, who remembered they could not see, and had not the free use of their feet and hands. The second act consisted of "catching the python snake". First, one of the sackmen came in front and went down on his hands and feet, then approached a tall, majestic figure, having on a head-dress and mask difficult to describe. It was a glossy black colour, sometimes like a lion couchant over the crest of a helmet; at another like a black head with a large wig: at every turn the man made it change its appearance. This figure held in its right hand a sword, and by its superior dress and motions appeared to be the director of the scene (for not a word was spoken by the actors). This director in the black mask then came up to the man who was crawling on his hands and feet; by his orders another sack-dancer was dragged forward in his sack and laid down at the crawling man's head or feet. Then the ends of both sacks, having been unsewn, were united in such a way as to make one long cover for the two men to occupy. There was now great waving of the director's sword; and the sacks being united the two men inside imitated the gliding motion of a large, fat snake. Something like the head of a python was protruded from

the front end of the united sacks; the jaws opened
and it attempted to bite the director, but at a wave
of the latter's sword the python threw its head in
another direction to avert the blow.

The imitation python then began gradually to
creep out of the sacks, as though sloughing its skin,
and went through the motions of a real snake in a
very natural manner, "though it appeared to be
rather full in the belly". It opened and shut its
mouth (which Clapperton suspected was made by
the front performer's two hands) "in the most
natural manner imaginable". The length of the
python was spun out to about 14 feet; and the two
men inside were tightly covered with a painted
cloth which well imitated the colour and markings
of the snake. After following the director round
the park for some time and attempting to bite him,
a sign was made for the body of actors to come up.
Then the director of the sports pretended to hack
the python in pieces, while the pretended snake
gasped, twisted, and seemed as if in great torture.
When nearly dead, it was shouldered by the
masqued actors, still gasping and making attempts
to bite, and was carried off in triumph to the fetish
house.

The third act of the performance was called
"the white devil". The bulk of the actors having
retired to some distance in the background, one
of them was left in the centre. His sack falling
gradually down, exposed a white head, at which
all the crowd gave a shout that rent the air; they
appeared indeed to enjoy this sight, as the perfec-

THE MASKED MUMMERS OF YORUBA, AS SEEN BY CLAPPERTON AND LANDER

tion of the actor's art. The whole body was at
last cleared of the encumbrance of the sack, when
it exhibited the appearance of a human figure cast
in white wax, of the middle size, miserably thin,
and starved with cold. It frequently went through
the motion of taking snuff, and rubbing its hands;
when it walked, it was with the most awkward gait,
treading like the most tender-footed white man
would do in walking barefoot for the first time over
rough ground. The spectators often appealed to
Clapperton to confirm the excellence of the imitation, and he thought it politic to pretend he was
pleased and amused. He admits in his diary
that the negro actor "burlesqued the part to
admiration".

The performance being concluded, the actors
retired to the fetish house. Between the acts,
there were choral songs by the king's women, in
which the assembled crowd joined their voices.
Therefore Clapperton was hardly far-fetched in
comparing this entertainment with an English
pantomime.

At last, after many delays and disappointments,
Clapperton got permission from the King of Yoruba
to leave on his journey to the Niger River. Mr.
Houtson remained behind at Oyo (Katunga). The
next halt of importance was at the principal town
of the Kaiama country, a province of Borgu[1]. The

[1] Borgu or Bariba (also Barba), which Clapperton and Lander were
probably the first Europeans to enter, is a very remarkable African state.
Nowadays, it is divided into two portions: Kaiama (Clapperton's Kiama)
and Nikki. The Nikki or western half is French, and the Kaiama section
is British. Even in Clapperton's day Borgu was subdivided among three

chief of this town and district was a man named
Yarro. He was a stout, good-looking man, past
middle age, dressed in a large white tobe, with
a red cap on his head. His courtiers lay about
him on the ground resting on their stomachs or
sides, and talking to him from that posture. When
this chief went out to visit Clapperton he rode a
splendid roan horse, and was attended not only
by a number of armed men on horseback and on
foot, but also by six young female slaves, absolutely
naked, except for long ribbons of narrow white
cloth tied round their heads, the ends flying out
behind as they ran. They carried each a light
spear in the right hand and followed their chieftain
on foot, running alongside his horse. They also
attended on him as a kind of guard when he entered
Clapperton's house. Before doing this, each put
on a blue cloth. After the visit was over, the chief
mounted his horse, the young ladies undressed, and
away went the most extraordinary cavalcade Clapperton had ever seen.

or four important chieftains, of whom the principal one was the King
of Nikki. Borgu, according to its legendary history, was founded as an
organized state by a light-skinned people who came from the north (Tuaregs,
in fact) more than a thousand years ago, and who were *Christians*. They
settled down as rulers among the black people, and their descendants were
soon merged in the negro multitude. But they are said to have converted
the Bariba people to the distorted version of Christianity which the Bariba
still profess, under the name of "Kisra". They believe that Kisra was a
Jew, who died for the sins of the world. The legendary men from the north,
who founded Borgu civilization, were possibly Tuaregs or Berbers (hence
Bariba, the native name of Borgu), converted to Christianity in Roman
North Africa, and driven across the Desert by the spread of Muhammadanism. The Fulas also settled very early in Borgu, but the indigenous Bariba
people repudiated Muhammadanism and remained followers of "Kisra".
They fought the advancing Fula empire with success. The Bariba
language is distantly related to Ashanti, far away to the west.

The present which Clapperton gave to this chief,
Yarro, consisted of a large blue silk umbrella, an
immense sword, a good deal of blue and red cloth,
red beads and coral, an imitation gold chain, two
bottles of rum, two "phosphorus boxes" (the pre-
cursor of our matches), some knives, scissors, and
calico prints.   On seeing the sword the chief could
not restrain his delight, and brandishing it round
his head, called out: "Ya baturi! Ya baturi! Oh
my white lord! Oh my white lord!" His eyes
sparkled with joy, and he shook Clapperton's hand
about a dozen times.

One of this chief's most treasured possessions,
which had been some time in his family, was a re-
presentation in English earthenware of a certain old
Toby Philpot, with a jug of flowing ale in his hand.

At the next big town of Wau or Wawa, Clapperton and Lander[1] were pursued by the attentions
of a wealthy widow named Zuma, who had inherited
the great possessions in slaves and lands of her
husband and her father.   Apparently she was of
mixed race, half-Arab[2] and half-negro, and con-

[1] The other members of the expedition (Morrison and Pearce) had died
in Yoruba, Houtson did not go farther than Katunga, and Clapperton and
Lander constituted the "expedition".

[2] Richard Lander subsequently recorded the following information about
Zuma's father: "The King of Kiama, in the latter part of the eighteenth
century (father and predecessor of Yarro), during his lifetime enjoyed the
friendship of an Arab from the Sahara Desert, and this friendship was
returned with equal warmth and sincerity.   A similarity of dispositions and
pursuits produced a mutual interchange of kind actions; their friendship
became so great that the King was never happy except when in the Arab's
company; and, as a proof of his esteem and confidence, he gave him his
favourite daughter in marriage.   The fruit of this alliance is the restless
widow Zuma, and hence her relationship to the present monarch of Kiama.
To return to his father and the Arab: their friendship lasted until the death
of the latter.   The King, however, was inconsolable for his loss, and looked

sidered herself equivalent to a white woman, though her skin was a yellowish-brown. She had once been very handsome, but had grown enormously fat, "almost like a walking water-butt". When Clapperton visited her she received him in a square house surrounded by a veranda with screens of matting all round, except in one place where there was hung a tanned bullock's hide. To this spot he was led up, and on the hide being drawn to one side he saw this very stout lady sitting cross-legged on a small Turkey carpet, with a large leather cushion under her left knee, a mug of kola nuts by her side, and a calabash of water with which to wash out her mouth: alternately she ate the bitter kola nuts and chewed tobacco. Zuma wore on her head a white muslin turban, and her limbs were swathed in a fine striped silk and cotton cloth; but her enormously fat shoulders and bosom were without any covering except many necklaces of coral and gold chains, and one which seemed to be of uncut rubies and gold beads. Her hair was dyed *dark-blue* with indigo! and her hands and feet were stained a deep red with henna. When Clapperton sat down on the carpet, this well-disposed lady sent her humpbacked maid (a hideous, naked female dwarf) to fetch her finery for him to inspect. It consisted of four gold bracelets, two large *paper* dressing cases with looking-glasses, and many

around him in vain for some one to supply the place of his friend; but the ardour of his affections was too strong, and led by the hope of following his friend to another world, he committed suicide. This is the most affecting instance of genuine friendship, and, indeed, the only one, that has come to our hearing since we have been in the country."

strings of coral, silver rings, and silver bracelets. Clapperton was then made to visit all the apartments of her house. They were "cool, clean, and ornamented with pewter dishes and bright, brass pans".

But in spite of all these advantages, and her offer to send for a Muhammadan priest to read the marriage service over them, Clapperton declined the match.

At this place—Wawa—he gives an interesting description of one of the travelling musicians, of the type to be met with between the Upper Gambia and Lake Chad.

"The man was attended by two boys. His instrument was a violin made of a gourd, with three strings of horse hair, not in single hairs, but a number for each string untwisted; the bow the same; the body of the violin was formed of half a long gourd; the bridge, two cross sticks; the top, the skin of a guana (Monitor lizard) stretched tightly over the edges; the neck was about 2 feet long, ornamented with plates of brass, having a hollow brass knob at the end. To this instrument was hung a diminutive pair of sandals to denote his wandering occupation, a piece of natron salt, strings of kauri shells, and strips of cloth. He said he would accept anything that was given to him. The boys had hollow gourds with stones or beans in them, with which they kept time by holding them in one hand and beating them against the other. The minstrel sang songs (made up as he went along) to his own accompaniment, and the boys

contributed a chorus." Clapperton describes him
as of the middle age (his beard being tinged with
grey) and middle height, but spare in figure. His
face was rather long than oval, with a nose slightly
hooked, a high forehead, sensitive mouth, good
teeth, and large, bright, and clear eyes, with a
kind of indefinable expression in them of half-rogue
and half-merry fellow. But when the minstrel sang
in a "clear and melodious voice, he sometimes
looked sublime". He was dressed in a white turban
and a large sky-blue tobe.

When staying at the town of Wawa Clapperton
was taken to see the *konkoni* tree from which the
poison is obtained for the arrows of the warriors
and hunters. This was really a species of *Strophan-
thus* (so far as we can judge from his description). The tree grows as a parasite or creeper,
which supports itself against the trunks of larger
trees, twisting itself round the stem and branches.
The five petals of the flower have their points
prolonged into pendent ringlets. The leaves of
the tree are rough and furry, exuding a gum which
sticks to the fingers. The twin seedpods are closely
joined together by their ends, and grow out at right
angles to the flower stalk. The seeds (of this
species) are rather like the caraway seeds of a seed-
cake. Inside the pod they are embedded in a silky
substance. The seeds and the silky fibre are boiled
until the whole is turned into a paste, which is afterwards smeared on the arrows.[1]

[1] Richard Lander, writing of the same district some years later, says:
"The inhabitants of Leoguadda, having probably no vegetable poison,

Some of the tribes of Fulas or Fellatas met with by Clapperton in Wawa were as fair as the lower class of Portuguese or Spaniards. They led a pastoral life, shifting from place to place as they found grass for their horned cattle, and living in temporary huts of reeds or long grass.

From Wawa, Clapperton reached without difficulty the town of Busa, situated on the rocky bank of the Niger, where that great river is narrow, turbulent, and deep. Above Busa the Niger divides into three branches, the westernmost of which is called the Menai, a slow and sluggish stream; but the other two branches have a very strong current, with eddies and whirlpools breaking over rocks.

It was here that Clapperton for the first time saw the Niger, and it is remarkable that he should give vent to no sentiment on the subject in his well-written diary.

He found the Sultan of Busa to be a fine-looking young man descended originally from the family of the sultans of Bornu. He was about twenty-six years of age, five feet ten inches tall, with a high forehead, large eyes, Roman nose, thin lips, good teeth, and an inch and a half of beard growing from his shapely chin. When he gave his interviews to Clapperton he was usually accompanied by his "midaki" (midiki) or queen consort. The fat widow Zuma of Wawa had strongly advised Clap-

make use of the venom of snakes on the tips of their arrows. The heads of those serpents from which they extract this deadly substance are exposed on sticks which are thrust into the inside of the thatch of their dwelling as a kind of trophy."

perton to pay particular court to this personage, as she wielded a great influence over her husband. She was nothing much to look at, except that she had a very pleasant voice and "winning, womanish ways". When she accompanied her husband to these audiences she usually sat on his left side a little behind him, with one arm round his neck. She approved much of Clapperton, because he told them people in his country were punished if they married another wife whilst the first one was living.

To this queen of Busa he gave an imitation gold chain. "She first put it round her own neck; then taking it off, placed it round the sultan's, and looked up in his face with as sweet an expression of countenance as ever I saw." The sultan, whose name was Muhammad, belonged ostensibly to the faith of Islam, as did most of the people of Busa; but many of them, including their sovereign, had relapsed in their practices into paganism. The sultan, for example, had as "totem" (crest or sacred emblem of his clan), the ox; and milk therefore was his "fetish", or prohibited to him by religious scruple. Therefore he was unable to drink it. But he and his people ate monkeys, dogs, cats, rats, fish, and mutton; and those who had no family scruples about the ox added beef to their dietary. As a rule, however, sheep were only eaten on great occasions, or as religious sacrifices. One day when Clapperton took breakfast with the sultan, it consisted of a large grilled water-rat with the skin on, some very fine boiled rice eaten with dried fish steeped in palm oil, and fried or stewed crocodile's eggs. For drink they had the fresh water of the Niger.

Clapperton found that the real indigenes of this Busa country belonged to a negro tribe called Kámbari, or Kámbali, though the townsfolk were mostly of Borgu, Yoruba, and Hausa origin. The Kámbari lived mostly in the woods, and were (in his day) in a more or less naked condition. They spoke a language of their own, and were pagans, chiefly worshipping the hippopotamus and the crocodile. With the skulls and bones of these animals they decorated their temples, piling them high on platforms.[1]

[1] Richard Lander afterwards described these aboriginal water-people of the middle Niger—the Kámbari—as harmless and good-natured, but dirty in their persons, and singular in their manners. Their language was different from that spoken at Busa. (It is allied to Gbari, and even very distantly to the Bantu languages.) Most of the villages on the islands, as far as Yauri, were inhabited by the same Kámbari people, and they were also scattered along the banks of the river. The women daubed their hair with red clay, but the men wore no ornaments. They were partial to agriculture, and cultivated large areas with corn, rice, and onions; besides which fishing was carried on by them extensively, and numbers of the men went three days' journey up the Niger to catch fish. Most of their small beehive huts were supported on clay pillars wonderfully small, or on stone slabs not more than an inch in thickness. The walls of the huts were only two or three inches in thickness, and were furnished with a small single aperture near the roof, up to which their owners were obliged to climb; and even then they could not enter without great exertion.

The most unfavourable trait in the character of the Kámbari was the extreme dirtiness they displayed in their habits. They disfigured themselves by boring immense holes in the lobe of the ear for the admission of bits of bright-coloured wood; and the soft part of the septum of the nose was perforated in like manner, in order to receive a long piece of blue glass. When the females had a mind to appear with unusual smartness and effect, a crocodile's tooth was inserted through both lips, and projected upwards as far as the nose. These singular ornaments imparted to their countenances an unnatural and barbarous expression, which their gentle, amiable natures belied; for in their intercourse with Clapperton and the brothers Lander, the Kámbari behaved with civility, hospitality, and kindness.

After his detour to visit Busa, Clapperton journeyed along the Niger till he reached the ferry of Komi, where he expected to meet with his servant Lander and his baggage, so that he might cross the Niger and continue his journey to Kano. His one idea—it is not clear why—was to get back to Bornu, and thence apparently to cross the desert to Tripoli; and as he had been sent specially on an expedition to trace the course of the Niger to the sea, it is not clear why he was so ready to abandon a task which he could apparently have fulfilled (in his circumstances) without great difficulty. On reaching Komi, however, he found to his extreme annoyance that his baggage was detained at Wawa, owing to the vagaries of the fat widow Zuma. This lady had followed Clapperton to Komi. He was so anxious about baggage and servant that he returned to Wawa, and was there told that his luggage would not be allowed to leave the place until Zuma came back. "What have *I* to do with the widow?" he asked the governor indignantly. After some palaver, however, he gave the governor his umbrella as a token so that she might be summoned back to the city, which she had left a few days before, declaring that she would follow the white man to Kano, and afterwards come back with many soldiers and make herself Queen of Wawa.

"This morning the widow arrived in town with a drummer beating before her, whose cap was bedecked with ostrich feathers; a bowman walking on foot at the head of her horse; a train behind armed with bows, swords, and spears. She rode astride on a fine horse, whose trappings were of the first order for this country. The head of the horse was ornamented with brass plates, the neck with brass bells, and charms sewn in various coloured leathers, such as red, green, and yellow; a scarlet breastpiece, with a bright brass plate in the centre; scarlet saddlecloth trimmed with lace. She was dressed in red silk trousers and red morocco boots, on her head a white turban, and over her shoulders a mantle of silk and gold. Had she been somewhat younger and less corpulent, there might have been great temptation to head her party, for she has certainly been a very handsome woman, and such as would have been thought a beauty in any country in Europe."

However, peace was patched up between the widow and the governor; Clapperton recovered all his baggage, and crossed the Niger at Komi in canoes. The river at this place was about a quarter of a mile in width, and ten to twelve feet deep.

Clapperton had arrived in the province of Yauri; but he was now obliged to make a great detour to the south to see the king of Yauri, who had gone to a large camp in the Nupe or Nife country—the region which extends (with some overlappings) between the rivers Lifun (Kaduna) and Gurara, and includes the opposite bank of the Niger. The King of Yauri was a very greedy personage, who begged to be given everything he saw in Clapperton's possession. But at last his desires were appeased, and Clapperton was able to turn again to the north and resume his journey to Kano. He stayed some time at a place near the Kontakora River named Kulfu.

"The house in which I live is one of the best in Kulfu. I have three separate kuzis (courtyards) parted off from the rest of the house. . . . My landlady is a widow (named Laddie) large, fat, and deaf, with an only child, a daughter, about five years old. She is considered to be very rich, and is a merchant; sells salt, natron,[1] and various other articles: but what she is most famed for is her *buza* (beer) and *roa-būm* (as the palm wine is called). Every night the large outer hut is filled with the topers of Kulfu, who are provided with music as well as drink, and keep it up generally till the dawn of morning separates them. Their music consists of the drum, *erbal* or guitar of the Arabs, the Nupe harp, and the voice. Their songs are mostly extempore, and allude to the company present. The buza (beer) is made from a mixture of durra corn (sorghum), honey, Chili pepper, the root of a coarse grass on which the cattle feed, and a proportion of water: these are thrown in equal proportions into long earthen jars, open at top, and are allowed to ferment near a slow fire for four or five days, when the buza is fit to drink, and is put into earthen jars. It is a very fiery and intoxicating beverage; but, whether Muhammadan or pagan, they all drink, and agree very well together when in their cups. . . .

---

[1] Natron, which is so often mentioned by these early explorers of the Sudan as an article of commerce, is a glassy, white carbonate of soda found in the beds of dried-up lakes on the borders of the Sahara Desert.

"My landlady had thirteen pieces of wood, on each of which was written by the Bornu *malem*[1] the word 'Bismillah' ('in the name of God'), the only word he could write. These boards she then washed, and drank the water, giving it also to her family to drink. She offered some of it to me; but I said I never drank dirty water. And I thought that if she and her servants had taken a cup of comfortable buza or būm it would have done them more good than drinking the washings of a board written over with ink, for the man was a rogue who had made her pay for such stuff. 'What!' says she. 'Do you call the name of God dirty water? It was good to take it.'

"These rogues, who call themselves malems, impose on the poor ignorant people; and the pagans are as fond of having these charms as the Muhammadans. These dirty draughts are a cure for all evils, present and to come, and are called by the people *dua*. Some of their fighting men will confine themselves to their houses for thirty or forty days, fasting during the day, and only drinking and washing with this dirty stuff. If a man is fortunate, or does any feat above the common, it is attributed to the *dua* or medicine; neither his wit nor the grace of God gains a man anything."

Most of the people of this region of Yauri and Northern Nupe were Muhammadans. They had just been going through the fast of the Ramadhan. Upon the sight of the new moon the fast was at an end, and great rejoicings began.

[1] *Malem* means in Arabic "learned man".

"Everyone was dressed in his best, paying and receiving visits, giving and receiving presents, parading the streets with horns, guitars, and flutes; groups of men and women seated under the shade at their doors, or under shady trees, drinking roa-būm or buza. I also had my share of visitors — the headman of the town came to drink 'hot water', as they call my tea. The chief of Ingaski, the second town in Yauri, only a few days' journey distant, sent me a present of a sheep, some rice, and a thousand gora (kola) nuts, for which he expects double the amount in return. The women were dressed and painted to the height of Nife (Nupe) perfection; with the wool on their heads plaited and dyed with indigo; their eyebrows painted with indigo, the eyelashes with kohl, the lips stained yellow, the teeth red, and their feet and hands dyed red with henna; their finest and gayest clothes on; all their finest beads on their necks; their arms and legs adorned with bracelets of glass, brass, and silver, their fingers with rings of brass, pewter, silver, and copper. Some had Spanish dollars soldered on the back of the rings. They, too, drank of the buza and roa-būm as freely as the men, joining in their songs, whether good or bad. In the afternoon, parties of men were seen dancing—free men and slaves—all were alike; not a clouded brow was to be seen in Kulfu. But at nine in the evening the scene was changed from joy and gladness to terror and dismay; a tornado had just begun, and the hum of voices and the din of people putting

their things under cover from the approaching
storm had ceased.   All was silent as death, except
the thunder and the wind.   The clouded sky appeared as if on fire; each cloud rolling towards
us like a sea of flame, and only surpassed in
grandeur and brightness by the forked lightning,
which constantly seemed to ascend and descend
from what was now evidently the neighbouring
town of Bali on fire, only a short distance outside
the walls of Kulfu.

"When this was extinguished a new scene began,
if possible worse than the first.   The wind had
increased to a hurricane; houses were blown down;
roofs of houses going along with the wind like
chaff, the shady trees in the town bending and
breaking; and, in the intervals between the roaring of the thunder, nothing heard but the war-cry
of the men and the screams of the women and
children, as no one knew but that an enemy was
at hand, and that we should every instant share
in the fate of Bali. . . . At last the rain fell—the
fire in Bali had ceased by its being wholly burnt
down!   In our house we escaped with the roof
blown off one kuzi, and a shed blown down.   All
was now quiet; and I went to rest with that satisfaction every man feels when his neighbour's house
is burnt down, and his own, thank God! has
escaped."

The Nupe country, the northern limits of which
were visited by Clapperton, is a most interesting
and important part of Nigeria.   It is inhabited by
pure negroes, but has long had a Muhammadan

civilization. Clapperton describes thus the "manner
of life" in Nupe.[1]

The food of the free and the slave is nearly
the same; perhaps the master or mistress may have
a little fat, flesh, fish, or fowl, more than their
slaves, and have their meat served to them in a
separate place and dish; but the greatest man or
woman in the country is not ashamed at times to
let their slaves eat out of the same dish, though
a woman is never allowed to eat with a man. The
principal food in Nupe consists of ground maize
("corn flour") made into puddings or loaves, about
half a pound in weight, and sold at five kauris each
in the market; and of flummery, or, as they call
it in Scotland, "sowens", made from the ground
millet, which is allowed to stand covered with
water until it gets a little sour. This flummery
(or, as the Nupe people call it, *koko*) is then well
stirred and strained through a sieve of basket-work
into another vessel, when it is left to settle, and
the water being strained off, it is dried in the sun.
When perfectly dry, it is broken into lumps and
kept in a sack or basket. Prepared for eating by
being put into boiling water and well stirred it
makes a pleasant "porridge", which is eaten for

---

[1] All the earlier travellers wrote the name of this country as "Nyffe" or
"Nife". But the correct name now in force is Nupe. Probably the first
European to reach Nupe was Friedrich Hornemann (see p. 165), who died in
this country about 1800. Nupe came completely under Fula influence during
the middle of the nineteenth century, and grew increasingly hostile to Euro-
peans. At last the emir of this country attempted to prevent the Royal Niger
Chartered Company from navigating the river above the Benue confluence.
In the warfare which ensued (1897) Nupe was completely conquered by an
expedition of six hundred Hausa soldiers, under the directions of Sir George
Goldie.

breakfast with a little honey or salt. The Nupe people have a pudding made of millet flour and boiled in the lye of wood ashes (which gives it a red colour); this is always eaten with fat or stewed meat, fish, or fowl. They always stew or grill their meat—it is purchased from them (if in large quantities) half-grilled and smoked to preserve it until it is required for eating. Boiled beans (*waki*), made up in papers of a pound or a half-pound each, and wrapped in leaves, are sold in the Nupe markets. Small balls of boiled rice, mixed with rice flour, are mixed with water, and serve as meat and drink. Sometimes these rice-balls are eaten with honey and pepper. Another article of food in Nupe consisted of bean flowers pounded and pressed into balls, which were then fried in fat. The intoxicating drinks of Nupe were palm wine, called roa-būm, buza (beer made from grain), and rum or "aguadent" (*aguardente*, the Portuguese word for ardent spirits), very much adulterated and mixed with pepper.

At daylight the whole household arose — the women began to clean the house, the men to wash from head to foot; the women and children then wash themselves in water, in which the leaf of a bush has been boiled, called *bambania*—when this is done breakfast of *koko* is served out, everyone having their separate dish, the women and children eating together. After breakfast the women and children would rub themselves with the pounded red-wood and a little grease, which lightened the darkness of the black skin. "A streak or patch of the red powder is put on some place where it will show to the best advantage.   The eyelids are blacked with kohl.   The mistress and the better-looking females stain their teeth, and the inside of the lips, of a yellow colour with *gora* (the flour of the tobacco plant) and the bark of a root—the outer part of the lips, hair, and eyebrows are stained with *shuni*, or prepared indigo."

Then the women who attended the market would prepare their wares for sale and depart for the marketplace.   The elderly women would clean and spin cotton at home and cook the victuals; the younger females were generally sent round the town selling small rice balls, fried beans, &c., and bringing a supply of water for the day.   The master of the house generally took a walk to the market, or sat in the shade at the door of his house, hearing the news or discussing the price of natron or other goods.   "The weavers are daily employed at their trade; some slaves are sent to cut wood and bring it to market; others to bring grass for the horses that may belong to the house, or to take to the market to sell; numbers, at the beginning of the rainy season, are employed in clearing the ground for sowing the maize and millet; some are sent on distant journeys to buy and sell for their master or mistress, and very rarely betray their trust."   About noon everyone would return home to partake of a mess of the pudding called *waki*, or boiled beans; and about two or three in the afternoon they returned to their different employments, on which they remained until near

THE BANKS OF THE LOWER NIGER IN THE NUPE COUNTRY

sunset. Then they count their gains to their master
or mistress, who, after receiving the cash of kauri
shells, or precious beads and coral, put it carefully away in their strong room. They would then
eat an evening meal of pudding and a little fat
or stew.

The mistress of the house, when she goes to
rest, has her feet put into a cold poultice of the
pounded henna leaves. The young at nighttime
go out to dance and play (if it is moonlight), while
the old lounge about and converse in the square
of the house, or in the outer *kuzi* (yard) of their
dwellings. Here they remain until the cool of the
night or even the approach of morning.

Returning from his dip southwards into Northern Nupe, Clapperton seems to have persisted
in his attempt to return home through Bornu (by
way of Kano), though from Kano onwards there
are many gaps in his journal, and his proceedings
are not easy to understand. Perhaps he decided
after all to visit the Fula emperor of Sokoto.
In any case he commenced a journey in that direction, having left Richard Lander at Kano in charge
of some Tripoli merchants and of a Hausa servant,
called by the English name of Pascoe.[1] Lander

[1] The Pascoe so often referred to in the narratives of Clapperton and
Lander was a native of the Hausa countries, who had been sold as a slave
and had lived for some time on an English man-of-war, where he was given
this surname. He had proceeded to Benin as an interpreter with the Italian
explorer Belzoni, and had afterwards joined Clapperton. Pascoe was an
extraordinary rogue, alternately robbing his masters and then displaying
remarkable devotion to them in sickness and other difficulties. After going
through incredible adventures with them, or on his own account, he eventually settled down comfortably at Cape Coast Castle on the Gold Coast. In
his old age he did excellent service with Lander on the Lower Niger.

had been so ill with dysentery that he could not accompany his master, who therefore left him behind, thinking that the persons to whom he confided him would be easily able to arrange his homeward journey across the desert at a later date.

On his journey towards Sokoto, Clapperton met the *gadado*, or prime minister, who had travelled towards Hausaland to find the white explorer. Together they joined the Emperor of Sokoto in his war camp on the outskirts of the Guber country, where he was attempting to subdue the people of Kunia — negroes who had revolted against the Fula rule. "The number of fighting men," writes Clapperton, "brought before this town of Kunia could not be less than fifty or sixty thousand, horse and foot. For the depth of two hundred yards all round the walls of the town was a dense circle of men and horses. The horses kept out of bow-shot, while the infantry went up as they felt courage or inclination, and kept up a straggling fire with about thirty muskets and the shooting of arrows. . . . The Kano forces had forty-one muskets. These fellows, whenever they fired their guns, ran out of bowshot to load. All of them were slaves, not a single Fula carried a gun. The enemy kept up a sure and slow fight, seldom throwing away their arrows until they saw an opportunity of letting fly with effect. Now and then a single horseman would gallop up to the ditch and brandish his spear, the rider taking care to cover himself with his leather shield and return as fast as he went.

. . . At length the men in quilted armour went
up. They certainly cut not a bad figure at a
distance, as their helmets were ornamented with
black and white ostrich feathers, and the sides of
the helmets with pieces of tin, which glittered in
the sun, their long quilted cloaks of gaudy colours
reaching over part of the horses' tails and hanging over the flanks. On the neck the horse's
armour was notched or vandyked, to look like a
mane; on his forehead and over his nose was a
brass or tin plate, as also a semicircular piece on
each side. The rider was armed with a large
spear; and he had to be assisted to mount his
horse, as his quilted cloak was too heavy; it required two men to lift him on; and there were six
of them belonging to each governor, and six to
the sultan. I at first thought the infantry would
take advantage of going under cover of these unwieldy machines; but no, the armoured men went
alone as fast as their poor horses could bear them,
which was but a slow pace. They had one musket
in Kunia, and it did wonderful execution, for it
brought down the van of the quilted men, who fell
from his horse like a sack of corn thrown from a
horse's back at the miller's door; but both horse
and man were brought off by two or three footmen.
The rider had got two balls through his breast;
one went through his body and both sides of the
tobe; the other went through and lodged in the
quilted armour opposite the shoulders. . . .

"The most useful person among us—and as
brave as any—was an old female slave of the

Sultan's, a native of Zanfara, five of whose former governors she said she had nursed. She was of a dark copper colour, and in appearance very like a female Eskimo. This woman was mounted on a long-backed, bright bay horse with a scraggy tail, and a mane as if rats had eaten parts of it. She rode a-straddle; had on a conical straw dish-cover for a hat, to shade her face from the sun, a short dirty white bedgown, a pair of dirty white loose and wide trousers, a pair of Hausa boots, which are wide, and came up over the knee, fastened with a string round the waist. She had also a whip and spurs. At her saddle bow hung about half a dozen gourds filled with water, and a brass basin to drink out of; and with this she supplied the wounded and the thirsty. I certainly was much obliged to her, for she twice gave me a basin of water. The heat and the dust made thirst almost intolerable. Numbers went into the shade as they got tired, and also to drink at the river. . . . The flags of the Fulas are white, and their staff is the branch of a palm. They are not borne by men of honour, but by their slaves. The sultan had six borne before him; each of the governors had two. The Fulas all dress in white tobes and trousers as an emblem of their purity in faith and intentions."

All this campaign ended in nothing; so that we can understand from this description how seventy years later it was easy for six or seven hundred disciplined negro soldiers, with artillery and British officers, to defeat thirty or forty thousand Fula cavalry. Clapperton was allowed to go on to

Sokoto,[1] where he took possession of the same
house that he had inhabited in 1824. From this
place he moved to the town of Magaria, some little
distance to the south, and here he delivered to
Sultan Bello the presents which he had brought for
him from England and the letters from King George
IV. Amongst the presents were portions of the
Bible in Arabic, the Koran, Euclid's elements in
Arabic, and the mathematical works of ancient
Arab writers, together with more modern books in
the Arabic language.

Whilst travelling through the countries watered
by the Sokoto river and near the Fula capital, both
Clapperton and Lander came into contact with the
remarkable Tuareg people of the Desert. This
race[2] belongs altogether to the "white man" type,
much more so than the Fulas. The name "Tuareg" is really an Arab name (*Tawariq*) meaning

[1] Clapperton gives the following pen picture of the country round Sokoto,
near the banks of the Rima or Sokoto river, a district strewn with many
small lakes and pools:—"The borders of these lakes are the resort of
numbers of elephants and other wild beasts. The appearance of the
country at this season, and at the spot where I saw it, was very beautiful;
all the acacia trees were in blossom, some with white flowers, others with
yellow, forming a contrast with the small dusky leaves, like gold and silver
tassels on a coat of dark-green velvet. I observed some fine large fish
leaping in the lake. Some of the troops were bathing; others watering
their horses, bullocks, camels, and asses: the lake as smooth as glass,
and flowing around the roots of the trees. The sun, on its approach to
the trees, throws the shadows of the flowery acacias along the surface of
the water, which is like sheets of burnished gold and silver. The smoking
fires on the lake's banks, the sounding of horns, the beating of their gongs
or drums, the braying of their brass or tin trumpets, the rude huts of grass
or branches of trees rising as if by magic, everywhere the calls on the
names of Mahomed, Abdo, Mustafa, &c., with the neighing of horses
and the braying of asses, gave animation to the beautiful scenery of the
lake and its sloping green and woody banks."

[2] See page 24.

"outlaws". Their own general designation of their race is Tamashek or Imoshagh; but they are nothing else but Berber or Libyan tribes, which for several thousand years have ranged over the Sahara Desert from north-western Egypt through Fezzan to the oasis of Tuat and the Northern Niger and Sokoto river.

Clapperton gives this description of the Tuaregs who inhabit the Sahara between Sokoto and the oasis of Tuat. At this period—1825—he says they consisted of the four tribes of Etassam, Kilgris, Kilawei (Kel-owi), and Timsgeda. Since the commencement of the nineteenth century they usually owed some kind of allegiance to the great Fula Empire over Nigeria, and nearly every year the principal Tuareg chieftain over these four tribes came to Sokoto to pay his homage. This chieftain was apparently elected at a conference of the Tuareg peoples every two or three years. He would retire into private life after his successor was elected. Large numbers of the Tuaregs passed the dry season in Hausaland, arriving there at the end of harvest (in the month of October). They brought with them salt from the Desert, which they exchanged for grain, for blue tobes, and dresses for their women. They also purchased swords from the ironworkers of Hausaland. In their own country they never attempted to sow grain, owing to the prolonged drought, but obtained the greater part of their food supply from the negroes of the Sokoto Empire. Of course, in addition, they lived on the milk and flesh of their flocks and herds, and

on dates which they obtained from the north. The
men were fine-looking fellows, manly and strong,
but extremely dirty in their persons, not even washing before prayers, but instead going through the
form with sand. The poorest amongst them was
armed with a sword and spear, without which he
never went abroad.

Elsewhere Lander writes of the same people:—
"The appearance of the Tuareg salt merchants was
grand and imposing. They entered at full trot,
riding on handsome camels, some of them red and
white, and others black and white.[1] All the party
were dressed exactly alike. They wore black
cotton tobes and trousers, and white caps with
black turbans, which hid every part of the face
but the nose and eyes. In their right hand they
held a long and highly polished spear, whilst the
left was occupied in holding their shields and re-
taining the reins of their camels. The shields were
made of white leather, with a piece of silver in the
centre. As they passed me, their spears glittering
in the sun, and their whole bearing bold and warlike, they had a novel and singular effect which
delighted me. They stopped suddenly before the
residence of the chief, and all of them exclaiming:
'Choir!' each of the camels dropped on its knees,
as if by instinct, whilst their riders dismounted to
pay their respects."

After some weeks' residence, Clapperton fancied
that the Sultan of Sokoto was no longer so warmly

[1] The bodies of the camels were probably painted with white and
coloured clays.

his friend. He gave as his reason for stopping Clapperton from pursuing his journey in the direction of Bornu, the made-up story that the Sheikh of that country had designs against his life; but apparently all these suspicions emanated from Sultan Bello himself. With extraordinary foresight he remarked that if the English met with too great encouragement in the Sudan, they would come into the country, one after another, until they got strong enough to do with it as they had done in regard to India, which land they had already wrested from the hands of the Muhammadans. History shows that Bello was right. But it also shows that both India and Northern Nigeria benefited enormously from the coming of the British, who did not dispossess the people of the country of their rights or their property.

Clapperton, of course, pressed to be allowed to continue his journey; but he was told by the sultan that his best homeward route would be by way of the Upper Niger to Sierra Leone and the sea. Clapperton had been sent out by the British Government to follow the Niger down to the sea from Busa to the Gulf of Guinea; but seems to have forgotten all about that in his intense desire to return to Bornu, and thence once more cross the desert to Tripoli.

We have seen how he left his servant, Richard Lander, behind at Kano, to be forwarded across the Desert as opportunity might arise. This action on Clapperton's part is also rather difficult to explain. He says in his journal that it was due to

Lander being ill with dysentery. But they had both been so ill at intervals since they left Badagri, and so accustomed to lengthy delays, that it seems strangely callous on the part of Clapperton towards a very young Englishman (whom he praises continually for his devotion and courage) to have been so ready to leave him in the very heart of Africa, not over well supplied with stores, and with but a faint chance of regaining his native land.

Very much to Clapperton's surprise, Sultan Bello had sent to Kano to fetch Richard Lander and the rest of the baggage of Clapperton's expedition which had been left at that city. Lander had been much afflicted by the rascality of Pascoe, the ex-slave and interpreter, who had repeatedly attempted to rob him of the best of his goods and then escape. The discussions were now resumed as to the route by which Clapperton should return to Europe. The Fula Sultan was exceedingly jealous and suspicious of the fact that the King of England had entrusted Clapperton with a letter to the Sheikh of Bornu, whom he regarded as his most dangerous enemy and rival. Clapperton made quite an unnecessary fuss about the whole business. He should have remembered that the chief object of his mission was to open up friendly relations with Sokoto by way of the Niger stream, to ascertain where the Niger entered the sea, and what communication there was between the Atlantic and the dominions of Sokoto. If he had been wise, he would have made a virtue of necessity and have abandoned the Bornu presents and letters to Sultan

Bello, who might then possibly have assisted him to carry out the rest of his geographical explorations. In the meantime the sultan was distracted by the news that his eastern territories had been invaded by the Sheikh of Bornu. The prime minister started at the head of all the Fula forces to repulse him. The Bornuese met with a most severe defeat, the power of the Fula was re-established, and Sultan Bello's good humour returned. He once more began to discuss with Clapperton return routes to the sea.

But in the middle of March, Clapperton fell ill with dysentery at Sokoto. It was the Muhammadan fast of Ramadhan, and Lander could get no help in nursing his master, so that at last he was obliged to release the wicked old Pascoe from prison, and the latter—such are the contradictions of negro nature—devoted himself at once with zeal to nursing the sick man.[1] The weather was insufferably hot, the temperature being in the coolest place 107° F. in the morning and 109° F. at three in the afternoon. Every day Lander lifted his sick master from his bed inside the hut to a couch in the shade outside. This terrible illness lasted for twenty days. Clapperton had, of course, no proper medicines, such as we should use for this disease nowadays; neither does it seem to have occurred to his nurses to nourish him with milk only. One of his negro servants made him a decoction of the green bark of the shea-butter tree, and, in spite

[1] Pascoe from this time onwards reformed, and served Lander most faithfully in his Niger explorations.

of Lander's remonstrances, Clapperton drank two basins full of this liquid in less than an hour. Soon after he felt himself to be dying, and gave full directions to Lander how he was to proceed after his death. When he had finished these, he fell into a slumber from which he woke up with perturbation, saying that he had heard with much distinctness the tolling of an English funeral bell. Nevertheless, a revival set in. But two days afterwards he ate some hashed Guinea fowl! A relapse followed, and on the morning of 13 April, 1825, Clapperton died. He was buried by his faithful servant in a small village about five miles south-east of the town of Sokoto.

Sultan Muhammad Bello took by right of the strongest the greater part of Clapperton's goods, leaving Lander in exchange an order on his treasurer for 245,000 kauris.[1] Bello was now anxious that Lander should return to England across the Sahara Desert. The latter, however, preferred the southern route. A compromise was arrived at, and he was allowed to journey to Kano: all roads in Northern Nigeria in those days led to Kano, apparently. On the way Lander travelled with the Fula Sultan of Yakoba, or Bauchi, and from Kano made his way through the Zegzeg countries to the hilly lands of Bauchi, where the pagan negroes went absolutely naked.

"They were soon on the most familiar footing with me, and seem an artless and good-humoured people; but disgusting in their manners, and filthy

[1] About £25.

in their persons; their sheep, goats, and poultry eat and sleep in the same hut with them, and a most intolerable stench is exhaled from all their dwellings. They do not appear to have the least affection for their offspring: a parent will sell his child for the merest trifle in the world, with no more remorse or repugnance than he would a chicken. They invariably wear a large piece of blue glass, in the shape of a semicircle, in their upper and lower lip, and a piece of red wood, about the size of a man's thumb, dangles from their ears. They rub red clay, softened with an oil extracted from the groundnut, over their heads and bodies, which by no means improves their appearance. Yet their features do not resemble in any way those of the negro, but are fine and handsome, and bear great similitude to the European. The Bauchi people make fetishes, like the natives of Yoruba."

At length he reached a place which he calls Dunrora. His route had lain over steep and craggy precipices, some of them being of an awful height.

"On the summit of one of these places the path was barely wide enough for a single beast to pass. The horse that carried the portmanteaux, in which were the journal, papers, watches, &c., struck himself against a piece of rock projecting over the road, and was precipitated a distance of eighty yards, the ropes which were bound round the portmanteaux arresting his further progress. I was horror-struck on observing the poor little animal tumbling head over heels down the frightful declivity, and was much afraid he would be dashed to pieces, the

portmanteaux broken, and their contents destroyed;
but was most happy to see him entangled in some
stunted trees which fortunately grew on the side of
the precipice, some seven hundred yards in depth.
This accident occasioned us two hours' delay; but
the horse was not materially hurt! We had been
travelling about half an hour after leaving this spot,
when we came to a place from which there was an
extensive and beautiful prospect of the surrounding
country, and eight days' journey might plainly be
seen before us. I halted for a moment to gaze upon
the fine and noble scene around me. About half
a day's journey to the east stood a lofty hill, at the
foot of which lay the large city of Yakoba. Muhammad affirmed that there is a river called 'Shar',
or 'Sharry', about half a mile from that place,
which derives its source from the Lake Chad, and
that canoes can go from the lake to the Niger at
any season of the year. The Sharry empties itself
into the Niger at Funda."

The Shari he refers to, of course, was the Benue,
or Chadda, which, though it does not proceed from
Lake Chad, is nevertheless in the height of the
rainy season connected by the swamps and creeks
of Lake Tuburi with the real River Shari.

The " Funda", so much written of by Clapperton
and Lander, and to which Lander now believed he
was bound, was evidently Panda, a place or district
on the Benue, not far from its junction with the
Niger.

But just as the young Cornishman was about to
travel easily down the Benue to the lower Niger,

and perhaps thus outwards to the sea, armed messengers reached him from the King of Zegzeg, or
Zaria, and he was compelled to return northwards,
a hundred and fifty miles, till he reached the city of
Zaria. On this return journey he was frequently
obliged to eat roasted dog, a very favourite dish
of the Bauchi people. On another occasion, the
chief of the village, who entertained him, prepared
a great feast of boiled corn. A large snake was
at the same time stewed with dog flesh in palm oil
and water, and Lander was handed a small bowl
of boiled corn, on which was placed portions of the
cooked snake and dog, while the oily soup in which
both had been stewed was poured over the corn!

When Lander reached Zaria he learned that the
reason why he had been so unceremoniously brought
back from the south was on account of a war having
broken out between the Fula Emperor, Bello, and
the King of "Funda", who on this account might
have murdered the white man. He now learned
that he was to proceed to Badagri over the old road
he had followed with Clapperton through Wawa
and Yoruba.

Reaching Kulfu, where Clapperton and Lander
had had such an hospitable reception in the previous
year, and where the kind woman (the "Widow
Laddie") who had lodged them then, gave Lander
the most hospitable treatment again, he had the
misfortune to lose "Boussa Jack", the horse which
had been presented to Captain Clapperton by
the friendly King of Busa, and which had proved
such a faithful steed to both Clapperton and Lander

on these long and weary journeys.   This horse
deserves a record besides the names of the explorers,
like that wonderful horse of Mungo Park's.

On Lander's return to Wawa, he was received
by the old governor or chief who had been so much
worried by the fat and ambitious widow, Zuma.
This time no mention was made of that lady.   The
chief, however, asked Lander before he left the
place to write him six charms.   Charm No. 1 was
to cause any enemies who thought of making war
on him to lose their memories, and thus forget to
put their intentions into practice.   Charm No. 2 (if
the first one failed) would cause them suddenly to
turn back when they were marching on his town.
Charm No. 3 would see that the arrows discharged
at the Wawa people by their enemies should re-
bound in the faces of those who shot them.   Charm
No. 4 would prevent the guns of the chief of Wawa
from bursting, and charm No. 5 (if No. 4 failed)
would prevent the person who held the bursting gun
from receiving any injury.   The 6th and last charm
was to make the chief of Wawa the happiest and
most successful of men!

As the chief would take no denial, Lander wrote
him out six scraps of old English ballads, which put
him in the best humour in the world.

On reaching the city of Kaiama, Lander went
immediately to King Yarro's residence (remember-
ing his hospitality a year before).   To his surprise
he was received angrily, and was asked how he dared
to come into the town without having previously
sent a messenger to announce him.   "I answered,

I had sent one three or four days before." "That is of no consequence," replied the King, "you should have sent another this morning. Get on horseback directly, return an hour and a half's journey the way you came: on arriving there, send me a messenger, and I will order you a sufficient escort to conduct you into the city in a manner deserving your rank and respectability." Lander was in the act of obeying this mandate when the King bawled after him: "I forgive you this time, Christian, but never be so remiss again."

On his southward journey Lander asked a messenger of the King of Kaiama why he was so much afraid of crossing rivers, pointing out that he himself, Lander, had swum across the largest rivers on his route, not excepting the Niger itself. The man, in great trepidation, however, begged Lander, as he valued his life, not to mention the names of other rivers in the hearing of the one by which they were standing. This was the Mossa (Moshi), and she was a female river, and the wife of the Niger, who, however, loved other rivers as well, and made the Mossa very jealous, causing her constantly to quarrel with her husband, so that when they met they made the devil's own noise with their disputes. If, therefore, Lander was heard speaking slightingly of her as a river easy to cross she would certainly swallow him up.

Without further difficulty Lander reached Badagri on the sea coast, and might have thought that his difficulties and adventures were at an end. But at this place were settled a number of Portuguese

slave-traders (they were probably half-caste Bra-
zilians). These men believed Lander to be a spy
sent by the English Government, and that if he
returned with the information that he had collected,
the English would come and take possession of the
country and cut off any further supply of slaves—
a prophecy fulfilled some thirty-five years later.
Accordingly, Lander was summoned to the chief
fetish hut and told that he must go through the
poison ordeal, to prove his innocence of the
charges brought against him by the Portuguese.
On his way to undergo this critical ceremony,
five or six hundred people gathered about him
armed with hatchets, bows and arrows, and spears.
They waited outside the fetish house till he came
out. On entering, a man presented him with a
bowl in which was about a quart of liquid much
resembling water, saying, "Drink this: if you came
here to do bad it will kill you, but if not, it cannot
hurt you". Without any hesitation Lander swilled
the contents of the bowl, and walked hastily out of
the hut through the armed men to his lodgings.
He there took emetics and plenty of warm water.
This enabled him to eject the whole of the liquid
from his stomach, so that he felt afterwards no ill
effects.

When after five days the King of Badagri and
his chief men found that Lander was perfectly well,
they became extremely kind, and sent him presents
of provisions daily, saying that he was protected
by God, and it was out of the power of man to do
him an injury. He had to remain at Badagri for

two months, and all that time was protected by the
King from the hostility of the Portuguese, who
would certainly have assassinated him if they had
caught him alone and unarmed.   They even prevented him from sending messages to his fellow
countrymen on the Gold Coast.   Part of their fury
and anxiety arose from the fact that in their five
factories at Badagri[1] there were upwards of one
thousand slaves, chained to each other by the neck,
waiting for vessels to take them away to America.
However, at last an English sailing ship, which
had been anchored off Whida, came and fetched
Lander away and took him to Cape Coast Castle;
and from this place he was conveyed to England
in H.M.S. *Esk*.

[1] In 1861 the town and kingdom of Lagos were ceded by its chief to
Great Britain in return for a money payment, and in 1863 Badagri (which is
close to Lagos) was also ceded by its chiefs, and with the former made the
nucleus of the great province of Southern Nigeria.

CHAPTER XII

Richard and John Lander Settle the Niger Problem

RICHARD LANDER was the fourth of six children. He was born at Truro, in Cornwall, in 1804, and was christened Richard Lemon (Lander) merely because a certain Colonel Lemon was elected member of Parliament for Truro on the day on which he was born. His grandfather had been a noted Cornish wrestler living near Land's End, and his mother was a Penrose; so that he was Cornish on both sides. His father was a tradesman in Truro.

When only eleven years old, Lander accompanied an English trader to the West Indies as a page. In that capacity he travelled with his master to the Negro Republic of Haiti and there nearly died of fever, owing his life to the kindness and nursing he had received from some benevolent negro women. After returning to England at the age of fourteen he spent five years in the service of various "noblemen and gentlemen", with one of whom he travelled on the continent of Europe. He then entered the employment of Major Colebrook, a British Commissioner of Enquiry into the State of the Colonies, and with him travelled from one extremity to the

other of Cape Colony.   Apparently he did not
like this master, and quitted his service a year after
entering it, returning alone from Cape Town to
England.   He then became a footman in the establishment of a kinsman of the Duke of Northumber-
land in London.   But on Captain Clapperton's
return to England, Richard Lander offered to enter
his service as confidential servant on the new projected expedition to the Niger, with what results
have been already shown.

After his return alone in 1828 from the last
Clapperton expedition, he apparently married, since
in the terms of his Government engagement allusion
is made to the sums which will be paid to his wife
in England during his absence.   But no allusion
to the fact or the date of his marriage (which on
account of his youth could only have occurred after
his return in 1828) is made in his own books or
journals; and, like Mungo Park, he was restless,
and longed to get back to African exploration.

People in England had grown rather tired of
the Niger problem, except the few who in those
days cared for geography.   Popular interest in
1828 was chiefly centred in Arctic discoveries.
However, the personages connected with the African
Association who were about to found the Royal
Geographical Society, brought pressure to bear on
the Colonial Office (then a department of the War
Office), and Richard Lander, together with his
younger brother, John, were engaged somewhat
grudgingly by the British Government to complete
the exploration of the Niger from Busa to the sea.

On 31 December, 1829, he was informed in a despatch from Downing Street that his offer to proceed to Africa was accepted by the British Government, and that he might be accompanied by his brother, to whom, however, no payment would be made by the British Government. But both the Landers would be transported in one of His Majesty's ships of war to the West Coast of Africa. He would be granted by the Government a supply of such trade goods as were necessary for the journey and a sum of about £50 in cash. He might also draw on the Government in addition for another £75; during his absence an allowance at the rate of £100 a year would be paid to his wife, and he himself on his return would receive a gratuity of £100.

Content with this poor provision, the two brothers started for the West Coast of Africa in January, 1830, Richard Lander barely twenty-five, and his brother about twenty-three. The brothers chose to don for their African exploration a most extraordinary costume, with what aim it is not very clear, as they never attempted to disguise the fact that they were Europeans. But they landed at Badagri from a British warship, and were "flung with violence on the burning sands", as they were obliged to pass in a canoe through the tremendous surf. Yet they were dressed as follows: "On their heads an enormous straw hat larger than an umbrella, while their bodies were clothed in scarlet Muhammadan tobes belted in round the waist; full Turkish trousers and high boots!" Naturally they were followed from the beach to the town of Badagri by a troop of men, women, and children shouting with laughter at their extraordinary appearance.

The King of Badagri, Adule, who had been so friendly to Lander two years before, was now found to be sulky and greedy. He required an enormous present from the two travellers before he gave his consent to their leaving his dominions for the interior. Moreover, like all his headmen and people, his desire for ardent spirits was inexhaustible, and the Landers were detained at Badagri until their stock of rum was nearly exhausted. The chiefs and great personages who visited them filled their mouths with rum and then squirted it into the open mouths of their servile attendants.

Nevertheless there were exceptions among these drunken, bloodthirsty negroes which showed the brighter side of nature. A Hausa malem or Muhammadan priest presented himself at the door of their house one morning, followed by a large and handsome spotted sheep from his native country, whose neck was adorned with little bells which made a pretty jingling noise. The Landers were much prepossessed in this man's favour by the calmness and serenity of his countenance and the modesty of his manners. He was dressed in the Hausa costume—cap, tobe, trousers, and sandals. He wore four large silver rings on his thumb, and his left wrist was ornamented with a solid silver bracelet.

"The chief's eldest son has been with us the greatest part of to-day. The manners of this young man are reserved, but respectful; he is a great admirer of the English, and has obtained a smattering of their language. Although his appearance is extremely boyish, he has already three wives, and is the father of two children. His front teeth are filed to a point after the manner of the Lagos people, but notwithstanding this disadvantage his features bear less marks of ferocity than we have observed in the countenance of any one of his countrymen, while his general deportment is infinitely more pleasing and humble than theirs. When asked whether, if it were in his power to do so, he would injure us two, or any European that might hereafter visit Badagri, he made no reply, but silently approached our seat, and falling on his knees at our feet he pressed me with eagerness to his soft naked bosom and affectionately kissed my hand. I thought that language and expression would not have been half so eloquent as this."

At last they got away on horses given by or purchased from King Adule.

Whilst staying at Badagri the Landers were greatly impressed by the difference between the sober, cleanly, well-dressed Muhammadan negroes (who never touched any form of alcohol) and the half-naked, frowsy, drunken, excessively noisy heathens. They saw here the festivities which follow the close of the Muhammadan month of fasting—the annual fast of Ramadhan.

"They were clad in all their finery, their apparel being as gaudy as it was various. . . . Loose tobes, with caps and turbans, striped and plain, red, blue, and black, were not unpleasingly contrasted with the original native costume of figured cotton thrown loosely over the shoulders, and with the immense rush hats. Manchester cloths, of the most glaring patterns, were conspicuous amongst the crowd; but these were cast in the shade by scarfs of green silk, ornamented with leaves and flowers of gold, and aprons covered with silver spangles. . . . Clumsy muskets and fowling-pieces, as well as Arab pistols, were also handled with delight by the joyful Mussulmans. In number the religionists were about a hundred and fifty. Not long after our arrival they formed themselves into six lines, and having laid aside many of their superfluous ornaments and a portion of their clothing, they put on the most sedate countenances and commenced their devotional exercises in a spirit of seriousness and apparent fervour, worthy a better place and a more amiable creed."

On the way up country, and whilst still in the forest belt near the coast, they arrived at the borders of a deep glen, more wild, romantic, and picturesque than can be conceived, but characteristic of Abeokuta scenery. "It is enclosed and overhung on all sides by trees of amazing height and dimensions, which hide it in deep shadow. Fancy might picture a spot, so silent and solemn as this, as the abode of genii and fairies; everything conducing to render it grand, melancholy, and venerable; and the glen only wants an old dilapidated castle, a rock with a cave in it, or something of the kind to render it the most interesting place in the universe. There was one beautiful sight, however, which we would not omit mentioning for the world; it was that of an incredible number of butterflies fluttering about us like a swarm of bees; they had chosen this, no doubt, as a place of refuge against the fury of the elements. They were variegated by the most brilliant tints and colourings imaginable—the wings of some were of a shining green, edged and sprinkled with gold; others were of sky-blue and silver; others of purple and gold delightfully blending into each other; and the wings of some were like dark silk velvet trimmed and braided with lace."

Farther on in the forest belt of Abeokuta Richard Lander writes:—

"Butterflies were here more numerous than can be imagined. Millions of them fluttered round us and literally hid from our sight everything but their own variegated and beautiful wings."

This is an experience familiar to many African travellers in the forest region. Where the cleared ground is moist the butterflies will settle on it to suck up the moisture, and can then be easily caught between the fingers and thus secured quite undamaged.

Here is another episode very common in West African journeys:—

"We found that a long and dangerous bog or swamp, filled with putrid water and the decaying remains of vegetable substances, intersected our path, and must necessarily be crossed. Boughs of trees had been thrown into the swamp by some good - natured people to assist travellers in the attempt, so that our men, furnishing themselves with long poles, which they used as walking-sticks, with much difficulty and exertion, succeeded in getting over, and fewer accidents occurred to them than could have been supposed possible from the nature of the slough. For my own part I was taken on the back of a large and powerful man of amazing strength. His brawny shoulders supported me without any apparent fatigue on his part; and he carried me through bog and water and over branches of trees no bigger than a man's leg, rendered slippery with mud, in safety to the opposite side. Although he walked as fast and with as much ease as his companions, he did not lay me down for twenty minutes, the swamp being, as nearly as we could guess, a full quarter of a mile in length."

The travellers found it impossible in a country like this to use their horses, and so they travelled in hammocks slung to long poles, which were carried on the shoulders of men. "We were lifted into them with very grateful feelings. It was pleasant after a long day's journey on foot to be carried along so easily on one's back to see parrots and other solemn birds perched on the branches of very tall trees, whilst the trees themselves seemed capering away from us most surprisingly as we were carried swiftly past them."

The people were everywhere most good-
humoured, and testified the wild delight they felt
at the visit of the white men by a clapping of hands
and loud bursts of laughter.

"The chief shook hands with us in great good
humour; and we remarked with pleasure, or fancied
we could, that not only his laugh, but that of his
people, was a more social and civilized kind of
sound than what of late we had been accustomed
to hear. Nevertheless, when I shook hands with
the chief's son, which act is not very diverting in
itself, the bystanders set up so general a roar of
laughter that the town rang with the noise; and
when I ventured further to place my hand on his
head they were yet more amazingly tickled, and
actually

'Shriek'd like mandrakes torn out of the earth'."

The road they followed through Abeokuta passed
through forests "so thick and deep, that the light
of the moon, which had arisen, was unable to
penetrate the gloom, and we were frequently left
in midnight darkness. It would require greater
powers than we possess to give an adequate description of the magnificence, solemnity, and desolate
repose of the awful solitudes through which we
passed this evening. They were enlightened, however, at times, by the appearance of glowworms,
which were so luminous, that one could almost see
to read by their golden splendour; and sometimes
by the moonbeams, which trembled upon the leaves
and branches of the trees. A fragrance also was

exhaled from the forest, more odoriferous than the perfume of violets; and one might almost fancy, when threading his way through scenery which perhaps cannot be surpassed for beauty in any part of the world, that he was approaching those eternal shades where, in ancient times, the souls of good men were supposed to wander. The woods rang with the songs of insects and night birds. . . ."

When they reached Jenna, in Abeokuta, they had an instance of one amongst the many woes of life in Negroland before the establishment of European control. It was the custom at Jenna still—as it is throughout so much of pagan Negro Africa—that when a great man died, his favourite wives should be killed at his funeral, so as to accompany him to the spirit world. The former governor of Jenna, who had been so kind to Clapperton and Lander, had died some months before, but his wives, having no wish to leave this world, hid themselves, and remained concealed till the time of Richard Lander's return to Jenna. Whilst the Landers were staying in the town, one of these wives was discovered, and was offered the alternative of a drink of poison or having her head broken by the club of the fetish priest. She promised to take the poison, and visited the Landers' dwelling (which had once been her home) to spend her last hour in the society of her faithful slaves who addressed her as mother. "Poor creatures! as soon as they learnt her misfortune, they dropped their spinning; the grinding of corn was also relinquished; their sheep, goats, and poultry were suffered to roam at large without restraint; and they abandoned themselves to the most excessive, most poignant grief. . . . Females have been coming all day to condole with the old lady, and to weep with her; so that we have heard and seen nothing but sobbing and crying from morning till the setting of the sun." Notwithstanding the urging of the fetish priest, the poor, old lady kept postponing the dread moment. "Twice she has entered our yard to expire in the arms of her women, and twice has she laid aside the fatal poison, in order to take another walk, and gaze once more on the splendour of the sun and the glory of the heavens, for she cannot bear the idea of losing sight of them for ever. . . . Die she must, and she knows it; nevertheless she will tenaciously cling to life till the very last moment. Meanwhile her grave is preparing, and preparations are making for a wake at her funeral. She is to be buried here in one of her own huts the moment after the spirit has quitted the body, which will be ascertained by striking the ground near which it may be lying at the time, when, if no motion or struggle ensues, the old woman will be considered as dead. The poison used by the natives on this occasion destroys life, it is said, in fifteen minutes."

However, the widow managed by one pretext and another to postpone her taking of the poison so long that the Landers left Jenna without knowing her ultimate fate. It was supposed that by means of giving up the greater part of her property she might bribe the authorities into allowing her to live out the remains of her natural life.

On their road northwards they noticed many people going to the coast, either as slaves or as free men, and women carrying goods for sale. Many of these women carried little wooden figures of children on their heads. They were mothers who, having lost a child, carried these wooden dolls about with them for an indefinite time as a symbol of mourning. Nothing would induce them to part with one of these little affectionate memorials.

In Southern Yoruba, Richard Lander writes in his journal :—

" Beautiful sheep, with tingling bells hung round their necks, are chewing their cud in peace and happiness. . . . Sheep here are regarded with as much partiality, and treated much in the same manner as ladies' lapdogs are in England. Great care is taken to keep them clean and in good condition; they are washed every morning in soap and water; and so greatly are they attached to their masters or mistresses, that they are constantly at their heels, following them indoors and out, from town to town, and in all their peregrinations."

John Lander was seriously ill with malarial fever after passing through the forest belt of Abeokuta, and reaching the comparative comfort of Yorubaland. In the course of a few minutes his body was overspread with a burning heat, and he suffered under another attack of fever, more violent than any of the former. Richard Lander resorted to the most powerful remedies he could think of at the time. He bled him, and applied a strong blister to the region of the stomach, where the disorder seemed

to be seated. It was swollen and oppressed with
pain, and he felt as if some huge substance lay
upon his chest. His mouth being dry and clogged,
and his thirst burning and unquenchable, he drank
so much water that his body became greatly swollen.
He afterwards described to his brother the horrible
phantoms that disturbed him whilst in this state,
and, by contrast, the delicious emotion that ran
through his whole frame when the dreadful visions
passed away. Tears gushed from his eyes; a profuse perspiration, which had been so long checked,
gave him immediate relief, and he recovered. But
during the whole journey he was frequently subject
to these attacks, and nine years afterwards, though
still a young man, died from their effects. Here are
characteristic incidents and descriptions written in the
Landers' journal as they passed through Yoruba:—

"We are daily accosted on the road with such
salutations as these: 'I hope you go well on the
path'; 'Success to the king's work'; 'God bless
you, white men'; 'A blessing on your return', &c.
Grown-up people in Yoruba dress somewhat
neatly, if not gracefully: the men wear a cap, tobe,
and trousers, mostly blue, and the women wear
a large loose cotton cloth, which is thrown over
the left shoulder, and comes down mantling below
the knee: the right arm and feet alone are bare."

The markets in Yoruba were often held at night,
and the marketplaces were well lit up by the many
lamps used by the merchants. These were lamps
of oil or fat, and of Moorish design: that is to say,
very like the lamps used by the Romans. In the

forest countries of Africa, south of the Sudan, lamps
are almost entirely unknown, and artificial light is
obtained from torches or bundles of reeds.

Here is a picture of the parklands of Africa which
lie between the Forest and the Steppe. "The
scenery" (write the brothers Lander of Western
Yoruba) "became infinitely pleasing, blocks of
granite are scattered over the surface, but in between them the soil is richer and deeper; patches
of verdure and cultivated land are more frequent,
the latter being neatly fenced. Fine handsome
trees with their spreading branches and thick foliage
embellish the country in every direction. . . . One
would be inclined to suppose that these trees had
been carefully planted by the hand of man, for they
grew at equal distances from each other, and none
seemed to interfere with the order, beauty, and
regularity of its neighbour. The soil between them
was covered with a soft green turf, which rendered
the whole view remarkably pleasant. It was over
this delightful landscape that we travelled—the
morning was cooled by a refreshing south-east
wind—and we were both on good terms with ourselves, and gratified by everything around us. At
length we came in sight of numerous herds of fine
cattle, attended by little boys, and shortly after we
arrived at a clean and neat Fellata village, whose
inhabitants were employed in feeding calves, and
other occupations connected with an African farm."

But in a Yoruba town their experiences were
not so happy. John Lander writes in his diary:—

" Perhaps of all evils that can afflict a sick person,

noises of any kind are the greatest. In Africa, whether one is ill or well, it is exactly the same, nothing like peace or quiet is anywhere to be found. Independent of the continual fluttering of pigeons, which roost close to our ears, the bleating of sheep and goats, and the barking of numerous half-starved dogs, we are still more seriously annoyed by the incessant clatter of women's tongues, which pursues us everywhere, and which I really believe nothing less than sickness or death on their part can effectually silence. The shrillness of their voices drowns the bleating of the sheep and the yellings of the canine race; and notwithstanding all my brother's exertions, seconded by those of our people, their noise in this town has constantly disturbed me during my illness. A person in England might be inclined to think lightly of the matter; but it is indeed a grievance which can ill be borne by an invalid (in Africa) who has equally as much need of rest and silence as of medicine. Besides these grievances, the shouts of the people outside the yard, and the perpetual squalling of children within it—the buzzing of beetles and drones—the perpetual attacks of mosquitoes and innumerable flies, form a host of irritating evils, to which a sick person is here exposed, and to which he is obliged patiently to submit, until, by a relief from his disorder, he is enabled to stand upon his legs and once more take his own part. But even then noises assail his ears, and he does not enjoy the happiness of perfect silence unless he enters a grove or forest."

.   .   .   .

The Landers thus describe the Fula settlers in Western Yoruba, who move about usually from pasturage to pasturage with their flocks and herds. They were not much lighter in skin colour than the negroes, but had much longer hair. This the women plait with astonishing ingenuity, and dress it so that their heads exactly resemble a dragoon's helmet.[1] The men tie the long side plaits of their hair under the chin.

Richard Lander writes as emphatically as other early explorers of West Africa on the modesty, charm, and "European"-like character of Fula women:—

"A company of women and girls from the Fellata village of Akba, impelled by a curiosity so natural to their sex, came likewise to see us in the afternoon; but *their* society, instead of being disagreeable, as the company of all our other visitors proved to be, was hailed by us with pleasure. For these females were so modest and so retiring, and evince so much native delicacy in their whole behaviour, that they excited in us the highest respect. Their personal attractions are no less winning. They have fine, sparkling, jet-black eyes, with eyelashes that are dark and glossy. Their features are agreeable, although their complexions are tawny. Their general form is elegant, their hands small and delicate; and the peculiar cleanliness of their persons, and neatness of dress added to these,

---

[1] It is remarkable that this style of hairdressing, even at the present day, prevails almost everywhere amongst the Fula women from Sokoto to Sierra Leone.

rendered their society altogether as desirable as
that of their neighbours was disagreeable."

Like all the earlier explorers of Africa down
to the middle of the last century, the Landers took
practically no European provisions with them,
merely medicines, cordials, and a supply of rum.
They found that the people of Yoruba were not
very delicate in the choice of their food, and were
often disgusted at the diet offered to them, for their
Yoruba hosts ate frogs, monkeys, dogs, cats, rats,
mice, locusts, white ants, and caterpillars. Perhaps
a dog was considered the most delicious form of
meat. The large caterpillars were stewed and
eaten with yams and palm oil. The locusts were
fried in butter.

The Yoruba (this word is also pronounced Yarba
and Yariba) people of eighty years ago were very
well disposed towards Europeans. The most
powerful among the Yoruba chiefs was Mansola,
the "King" of Western Yoruba, who resided at
Katunga—a place now known as Oyo. Mansola
received the travellers dressed in a tobe of green
and crimson silk and velvet. He was a very merry
person who, for a mere nothing, would laugh long
and heartily for a quarter of an hour, his roars of
laughter being closely imitated by his wives and
courtiers. His courtiers and attendants indeed
were very servile. When they approached their
prince they prostrated themselves on the ground
and rubbed their heads two separate times, finally
lying with their faces in the dust near the place
where the chief was seated. They also kissed the

ground on which he was sitting fervently, and placed each cheek alternately on it. Then, and not till then, with their heads, faces, lips, and breasts stained with the damp, red soil, they were allowed to seat themselves near the monarch and join in the conversation. But others wishing a further sign of their loyalty would roll themselves on the ground. As they were very fat they seemed to the Landers like immense turtles floundering in the sea. Many of these creatures were bald-headed old men, whose wool had been literally rubbed off by repeatedly rolling their heads on the ground whenever the prince happened to make his appearance.

As there were robbers and masterless men on the road to the north in the borderlands between Yoruba and Borgu, Mansola gave the Landers an escort of his soldiery. Their appearance, though warlike and romantic, was also highly amusing. "They were clad in the fashion of the East, and sought their way between the trees on our right and left; but sometimes they fell in behind us, and then again dashed suddenly by with astonishing swiftness, looking as wild as the scenery through which their chargers bounded. The effect was rendered more imposing by the reflection of the moonbeams from their polished spears and the pieces of silver which are affixed to their caps, while the luminous fireflies appeared in the air like rising and falling particles of flame.

"The leader of our escort was a strange-looking, powerful fellow, and might very well serve the writer of a romance as the hero of his tale, in the character of keeper of an enchanted castle, when fierce, scowling looks, terrific frowns, and a peculiarly wild expression of countenance are intended to be described; for the man's stature was gigantic; his eyes large, keen, piercing, and ever in motion; his broad nose squatted over both cheeks; his lips, immensely large, exposed a fine set of teeth; the beard was black, thick, and grizzly, and, covering all the lower part of his face, reached to his bosom. The famous Blue Beard was nothing to him; and, in gazing on his features, one would almost be inclined to believe that all the most iniquitous and depraved passions of human nature were centred in his heart. Yet with so unlovely and forbidding an appearance, the man is in reality as innocent and docile as a lamb. He wore on his head a small rush hat, in shape like a common earthenware pan inverted, or like the hats which are worn by the lower class of Chinese. His breast was enveloped in a coarse piece of blue cloth; from his left shoulder hung a large quiver of arrows; and in his right hand he held a bow, which he brandished like a lance; a short pair of trousers covered his thighs, and fantastically-made leathern boots encased his feet and legs. His skin was of jetty blackness; his forehead high; but his tremendous beard, which was slightly tinged with grey, contributed perhaps more than anything else to impart that wildness and fierceness to his looks which at first inspired us with a kind of dread of our leader."

In order to obtain his goodwill and friendly influence in their descent of the Niger, the Landers journeyed north to visit the Sultan of Yauri in the city of that name. Yauri they describe as being of "prodigious extent, surrounded by high walls of clay about twenty-five miles in circuit, with eight huge entrance-gates which were well fortified after the manner of the country. The Yauri people manufactured gunpowder, very neat saddles, thick cotton cloths, and other articles of clothing; and grew indigo, tobacco, onions, wheat, sorghum, millet, and vast quantities of rice. The better sort of women in Yauri town wore their hair plaited elaborately and dyed a very dark *blue* with indigo. Their lips were stained yellow and blue, which 'gave them a very odd appearance'; and their eyelids were blackened with powdered antimony."

After long delays, the consent and rather grudging co-operation of the Sultan of Yauri, the kings of Busa and Wawa, were obtained by the Landers in their project of descending the Niger in canoes to its outlet into the sea. These potentates, though often kind and hospitable, were not above wringing all they could in the way of trade goods and presents from the poorly-provided Cornishmen. They would sell them canoes and exact the price in advance, and then either not deliver the article or pass on the order to someone else, who failed to execute it. However, on September 20, 1830, the explorers left Busa in two small leaky canoes, and reached in a short time the large and fertile island of Patashi, forty miles down stream from Busa. Hence, in two other borrowed canoes (lent by the chief of Patashi) they proceeded to a place called Leyaba or Liva, where they were to make the acquaintance of an important potentate styled in Hausa "Sariki-n-rua", or King of the River.

"Between nine and ten a.m. we heard a number of men singing and keeping time to the motion of many paddles, but we could see no one. However, in a very few minutes a canoe, . . . propelled by above twenty very fine young men, whose voices we had been listening to just before, drew nearer. We were not only surprised at its extraordinary length and uncommon neatness, but likewise at the unusual display of pomp and show which we observed in her. In the centre a mat awning was erected, which was variously decorated, and on the front of it hung a large piece of scarlet cloth ornamented with bits of gold lace stitched on different parts of it. In the bow of the canoe were three or four little boys, of equal size, who were clad with neatness and propriety; and in the stern sat a number of comely-looking musicians, consisting of several drummers and a trumpeter, whilst the young men who had the management of the boat were not inferior to their companions either in decency of apparel or respectability of appearance. They all looked, in fact, extremely well.

"As soon as this canoe arrived at the landing-place, the 'Water King' came out from beneath the awning, and, followed by the musicians and a suite of attendants, walked to the hut, wherein all public matters are transacted. . . . When the usual compliments had passed on both sides, he informed us, with much solemnity, of his rank and title; he then alluded to the cause of his coming, which, he said, was to do us honour. . . . This being done, he presented us with a pot of excellent honey and two thousand kauris in money, besides a large quantity of kola nuts, which are cultivated in the country, and which are held in such great esteem, that the opulent and powerful alone have the means of procuring them. . . ."

The "King of the Dark Water" was a fine-looking man of considerable age; his skin was black as coal; his features coarse but benevolent, and his stature commanding. He was dressed in a full burnus, or Arab cloak, of blue cloth, underneath which was a variegated tobe made of figured satin, cotton cloth, and crimson damask silk, all patched together; he likewise wore a cap of red cloth, Hausa trousers, and sandals of coloured leather. Two pretty little boys, about ten years of age and of equal size, and who acted in capacity of pages, followed him into the hut. Their clothing was neat and becoming, and their persons nicely clean; each of them was furnished with an ornamented cow's tail; and they stood one on his right hand and the other on his left to brush away flies and other insects from his person, and supply him with kola nuts and tobacco. The king was also accompanied by six of his wives—fine handsome jet-black girls, dressed in neat country caps edged with red silk. Native cloths, made of cotton and silk, were fastened round their waists, beneath which they wore a sort of short frock. Their fingers and toe-nails were stained with henna, their wrists

were ornamented with neat silver bracelets, and
their necks with coral necklaces.

But though, under the guidance of this personage, the Landers reached an island, forty miles
lower down, opposite Rabba (Rabba itself they
feared to visit, because their supplies of presents
were very meagre), the much-vaunted "King of
the River" not only supplied them with no new
canoes, but even tried to snatch from them the
canoes in which they had travelled from Patashi!
To their deep regret, they were reduced to com-
mitting the seemingly shabby act of going off with
these two borrowed canoes.

For many miles they met with no more risks in
travel than those incidental to the furious weather
of the end of the rainy season, and the troubles
of hippopotami, hidden rocks, snags, and shoals.
Here is an excellent description of such experiences
in the journal kept by the two brothers.

"The day had been excessively warm, and the
sun set in beauty and grandeur, shooting forth rays
tinged with the most radiant hues, which extended
to the zenith. Nevertheless, the appearance of the
firmament, all glorious as it was, betokened a coming storm; the wind whistled wildly through the
tall rushes, and darkness soon covered the earth
like a veil. This rendered us more anxious than
ever to land—no matter where—and procure some
shelter for the night, if not in the village, at least
under a tree. Accordingly, rallying the drooping
spirits of our men, we set them the example of
vigorous paddling, and our canoe darted silently

and swiftly down the current. We were enabled
to steer her rightly by the vividness of the lightning, which flashed across the water continually,
and by this means also we could distinguish any
danger before us and avoid the numerous small
islands with which the river is interspersed, and
which otherwise might have embarrassed us very
seriously. But though we could perceive almost
close to us several lamps burning in comfortable-
looking huts, and could plainly distinguish the
voices of their occupants; and though we exerted
all our strength to get at them, we were foiled in
every attempt, by reason of the sloughs and fens,
and we were at last obliged to abandon them in
despair. Some of these lights, after leading us a
long way, eluded our search and vanished from our
sight like an *ignis fatuus*, and others danced about
we knew not how nor where. But what was more
vexatious than all, after we had got into an inlet,
and toiled and tugged for a full half-hour against
the current, which in this little channel was uncommonly rapid, to approach a village from which
we thought it flowed, both village and lights seemed
to sink into the earth, the sound of the people's
voices ceased of a sudden, and when we fancied
we were actually close to the spot we strained our
eyes in vain to see a single hut—all was gloomy,
dismal, cheerless, and solitary. It seemed the
work of enchantment; everything was as visionary
as 'sceptres grasped in sleep'.

"We had paddled along the banks a distance
of not less than thirty miles, every inch of which

we had attentively examined, but not a bit of dry land could anywhere be discovered which was firm enough to bear our weight. Therefore we resigned ourselves to circumstances, and all of us having been refreshed with a little cold rice and honey, and water from the stream, we permitted the canoe to drift down with the current, for our men were too much fatigued with the labours of the day to work any longer. But here a fresh evil arose, which we were unprepared to meet. An incredible number of hippopotami arose very near us, and came plashing, snorting, and plunging all round the canoe and placed us in imminent danger. Thinking to frighten them off we fired a shot or two at them, but the noise only called up from the water and out of the fens about as many more of their unwieldy companions, and we were more closely beset than before. Our people, who had never in all their lives been exposed in a canoe to such huge and formidable beasts, trembled with fear and apprehension, and absolutely wept aloud; and their terror was not a little increased by the dreadful peals of thunder which rattled over their heads, and by the awful darkness which prevailed, broken at intervals by flashes of lightning, whose powerful glare was truly awful. Our people tell us that these formidable animals frequently upset canoes in the river, when everyone in them is sure to perish. These came so close to us that we could reach them with the butt end of a gun. When I fired at the first, which I must have hit, every one of them came to the surface of the water and pursued us so fast over to the north bank that it was with the greatest difficulty imaginable we could keep before them. Having fired a second time, the report of my gun was followed by a loud roaring noise, and we seemed to increase our distance from them."

Below the confluence of the Niger with the Benue (an important geographical feature duly noted by the Landers) they landed somewhat imprudently at a market town called Bokwa, in the Igara country. The timid people of Igara were not so used as the semi-civilized Muhammadans of Nupe, Busa, and Yauri to the comings and goings of strange human types, and mistook the white men and their followers for some new type of pirate-conquerors like the Fulas. They advanced on the tired white men, and their black followers prepared for a desperate fight. Only the calm bravery of the Landers[1] saved the situation, together with the kindly intervention of a Hausa *malem* or learned Muhammadan, whose behaviour towards them was worthy of the best evidences of Christianity. The people of Bokwa ended by becoming the enthusiastic friends and helpers of the white explorers. So did the chief and people

[1] "Just as the chief was about to pull the fatal cord a man that was nearest him rushed forward and stayed his arm. At that instant we stood before him, and immediately held forth our hands; all of them trembled like aspen leaves; the chief looked up full in our faces, kneeling on the ground—light seemed to flash from his dark rolling eyes—his body was convulsed all over, as though he were enduring the utmost torture, and with a timorous, yet undefinable, expression of countenance, in which all the passions of our nature were strangely blended, he drooped his head, eagerly grasped our proffered hands, and burst into tears. This was a sign of friendship—harmony followed, and war and bloodshed were thought of no. more."

of Damuggu, a place near the modern Asaba or
Onicha.   Here, indeed, they obtained safer and
better canoes for the continuance of their journey.
But as they neared the commencement of the
Niger Delta the Landers met with grave disaster.
They ran suddenly into a great concourse of Ibo
and Ijō[1] canoes, meeting at the Kirri markets just
below Abo.

"At seven a.m. we saw a small river enter
the Niger from the eastward, the banks of which,
as well as those of the Niger, were elevated and
fertile.   Shortly afterwards we observed a branch
of the river (the important Warri branch which
enters the sea as the Forcados River) running
off to the westward, about the same size as that
from the eastward.   On the right bank of this
river, close also to the bank of the Niger, we
observed a large market, which I was informed
is Kirree (Kirri), and that the river, flowing to
the westward past it, runs to Benin.   A great
number of canoes were lying near the bank.   They
appeared to be very large, and had flags flying
on long bamboo canes.   We took no notice of
them but passed on, and in a short time afterwards we saw about fifty canoes before us coming
up the river.   They were very large and full of
men, and the appearance of them at a distance
was pleasing.   Each had three long bamboo canes
with flags flying from them, one fixed at each end

[1] The Ibo tribes inhabit mainly the districts to the east of the main
Niger, above the confluence; the Ijōs are a very isolated group in affinities.
They are the people of Opobo, Bonny, Brass, and thence eastward to the
Forcados River.

of the canoe, and the other in the middle. As
we approached each other I observed the British
Union flag in several, while other flags, which were
white, had figures on them of a man's leg, chairs,
tables, decanters, glasses, and all kinds of such
devices. The people in them, who were very numerous, were dressed in European clothing, with the
exception of trousers.

"I felt quite overjoyed by the sight of these
people, more particularly so when I saw our flag
and European apparel among them, and congratu-
lated myself that they were from the sea coast.
But all my fond anticipations vanished in a moment
as the first canoe met us. A great stout fellow,
of a most forbidding countenance, beckoned me
to come to him, but seeing him and all his people
so well armed, I was not much inclined to trust
myself among them and paid no attention to him.
The next moment I heard the sound of a drum,
and in an instant several men mounted a platform
and levelled their muskets at us. There was
nothing to be done now but to obey; as for running away, it was out of the question, our square-
built loaded canoe was incapable of it, and to fight
with fifty war canoes, for such we found them,
containing each above forty people, most of whom
were as well armed as ourselves, would have been
throwing away my own and my canoemen's lives
very foolishly. In addition to the muskets, each
canoe had a long gun in its bow that would carry
a shot of four or six pounds, besides being provided
with a good stock of swords and boarding-pikes.

"By this time our canoes were side by side, and with astonishing rapidity our luggage found its way into those of our opponents. This mode of proceeding I did not relish at all; so as my gun was loaded with two balls and four slugs, I took deliberate aim at the leader, and he would have paid for his temerity with his life in one moment more had not three of his people sprung on me and forced the gun from my hands. My jacket and shoes were as quickly plundered from me, and observing some other fellows at the same time taking away Pascoe's wife, I lost all command over myself and was determined to sell my life as dearly as I could. I encouraged my men to arm themselves with their paddles and defend themselves to the last. I instantly seized hold of Pascoe's wife, and with the assistance of another of my men dragged her from the fellow's grasp; Pascoe at the same time levelled a blow at his head with one of our ironwood paddles that sent him reeling backwards, and we saw him no more.

"Our canoe having been so completely relieved of her cargo, which had consisted only of our luggage, we had plenty of room in her for battle, and being each of us provided with a paddle, we determined, as we had got clear of our adversary, to cut down the first fellow who should dare to board us. This was not attempted; and as none of the other canoes had offered to interfere, I was in hopes of finding some friends among them; but at all events was determined to follow the people who had plundered us to the market, where they seemed to be going. We accordingly pulled after them as fast as we could."

Then followed a visit to the Ibo king, whose name, Obi, was probably only the title of "Medicine-man", a root from which the term "Obia" —witchcraft, sorcery—is derived.

"The dress of the king of the Ibo country somewhat resembles that which is worn *on state occasions* by the monarch of Yoruba. Its appearance was altogether *brilliant*; and from the vast profusion of coral ornaments with which he was decorated, Obi might not inappropriately be styled 'the Coral King'; such an idea at all events entered our minds as we contemplated the monarch sitting on his throne of clay. His head was graced with a cap, shaped like a sugar loaf, and covered thickly with strings of coral and pieces of broken looking-glass so as to hide the materials of which it was made; his neck, or rather throat, was encircled with several strings of the same kind of bead, which were fastened so tightly, as in some degree to affect his respiration and to give his throat and cheeks an inflated appearance. In opposition to these were four or five others hanging round his neck and reaching almost to his knees. He wore a short Spanish surtout of red cloth, which fitted close to his person, being much too small. It was ornamented with gold epaulettes, and the front of it was overspread with gold lace; but this, like the cap, was entirely concealed, unless on a close examination, owing to the vast quantity of coral which was fastened to it in

strings. Thirteen or fourteen bracelets (for we had
the curiosity to count them) decorated each wrist,
and to give them full effect, a few inches of the
sleeves of the coat had been cut off purposely. The
beads were fastened to the wrist with old copper
buttons, which formed an odd contrast to them.
The king's trousers, composed of the same material
as his coat, stuck as closely to the skin as that,
and were similarly embroidered, but they reached
no further than the middle of his legs, the lower
part of it being ornamented like the wrists, and
with precisely the same number of strings of beads;
besides which, a string of little brass bells encircled
each leg above the ankles, but the feet were naked.
Thus splendidly clothed, Obi, smiling at his own
magnificence, vain of the admiration which was
paid him by his attendants, and flattered without
doubt by the presence of white men (who, he
imagined, were struck with amazement at the
splendour of his appearance), shook his feet for
the bells to tinkle, sat down with the utmost self-
complacency, and looked around him."

The "palaver" with the Ibo king was attended
by "King Boy", the son of an Ijō chief—"King"
Forday, who lived near the mouth of the Brass
River, one of the mouths of the Niger. King Boy
agreed to ransom the Landers and their people for
the value of twenty slaves (in gunpowder and trade
goods), and also to convey them safely on board
an English vessel at the mouth of the Niger. For
this last service he was to receive in addition the
value of another fifteen slaves.

King Boy carried out his contract faithfully; but you can imagine the horror of Richard Lander when he reached the deck of an English sailing vessel—the *Thomas*—and found it commanded by an ignorant, foul-mouthed ruffian (Lake), to whom the revelation of the Niger problem was as indifferent as it might be to an African savage, and who refused absolutely to honour Lander's bill for the trade goods to be paid to King Boy.

The last-named was almost mad with fury at being cheated, especially as, by a ruse of the captain's, he himself was detained on board the ship until the ship's mate, John Lander, and the rest of the men of the expedition had come on board; after which the captain weighed anchor and put out to sea. The *Thomas* very nearly got wrecked on the bar of the Nun or principal mouth of the Niger—for it is interesting to note that Richard Lander was not taken by the Ijō canoes to the Brass outlet, but to the central and head-stream of the Niger at Akassa; but having lurched free of the breakers into the open sea, the *Thomas* crossed over to Fernando Pô without further incident. Here the Landers were in safety, for at Fernando Pô in those days there was an Admiralty establishment (for suppressing the slave trade) and a government superintendent.

After some two months' delay[1] a passage was found for them in a ship proceeding to Brazil, and

---

[1] Whilst waiting at Fernando Pô the Landers actually witnessed from shore the capture of the *Thomas* by a pirate ship; and in all probability the uncivil Captain Lake met with a tragic end.

from South America another ship conveyed them to England in June, 1831.

Their arrival with news of their wonderful exploit, and the certain knowledge that there were no insuperable natural difficulties in the way of vessels entering the Niger from the open sea and penetrating far into most productive regions of the African continent aroused great enthusiasm at Liverpool and Glasgow. A remarkable man came forward—Macgregor Laird—who resolved to apply to the Niger the solution of the newly-invented steamboat. He built two paddle-wheel steamers of light draught, and with Richard Lander and others started on a great expedition to open up the Niger to legitimate British trade. The adventures of the *Quorra* and the *Al-burkah* cannot be related here, but they effected great additions to our knowledge of the Lower Niger. Richard Lander had the great satisfaction of paying off with interest his debt to King Boy; but unfortunately this great explorer died after his third trip up the Niger—he was attacked by some savages about 84 miles from the Nun mouth, received severe wounds in his attempts to defend the people with him, and died of those wounds shortly afterwards at Fernando Pô. His brother, John Lander, died in 1839 in Cornwall, never having quite recovered from the effects of severe attacks of malarial fever on his Niger exploration.

It is said that the grave of Richard Lander at the cemetery of Puerto Santa Isabel is unmarked by any sign or memorial. This, if true, is a disgrace to Great Britain, for to Richard Lander, ex-page-boy, valet, and footman, we owe more than to any of the other early pioneers in West Africa, the existence of an empire over the eastern Niger and its great affluent the Benue, which at the present day comprises an area of 333,660 square miles.